WOMEN AT THE READY

THE REMARKABLE STORY OF THE WOMEN'S VOLUNTARY SERVICES ON THE HOME FRONT

PATRICIA AND ROBERT MALCOLMSON

LITTLE, BROWN

First published in Great Britain in 2013 by Little, Brown

Copyright © Patricia Malcolmson and Robert Malcolmson 2013

The moral right of the authors has been asserted.

Mass Observation material reproduced with permission of
Curtis Brown Group Ltd, London on behalf of The Trustees of the Mass
Observation Archive. Copyright © The Trustees of the Mass Observation Archive.

A CIP catalogue record for this book
is available from the British Library.

ISBN 978-1-4087-0410-3

Typeset in Bembo by M Rules
Printed and bound in Great Britain by
Clays Ltd, St Ives plc

Papers used by Little, Brown are from well-managed forests
and other responsible sources.

MIX
Paper from
responsible sources
FSC® C104740

Little, Brown
An imprint of
Little, Brown Book Group
100 Victoria Embankment
London EC4Y 0DY

An Hachette UK Company
www.hachette.co.uk

www.littlebrown.co.uk

The greatest disservice a woman can do, at the moment, is to consider herself useless.

Lady Reading, 1939

We must all help to win this war on the Home Front – as well as those serving – and overcome the difficulties in doing so.

Mildred Elwes, WVS Village Representative
Weston, Lincolnshire, 1941

CONTENTS

LIST OF ILLUSTRATIONS

Lady Reading, Chairman of the WVS (WRVS Archive & Heritage Collection)

Uniformed members in Mablethorpe (The Second World War Experience Centre)

WVS members escorting evacuees in 1939 (IWM000717)

A Christmas party for evacuees in Wisbech (Courtesy of the Lilian Ream Collection)

A mobile canteen outside a bombed-out London hotel (WRVS Archive & Heritage Collection)

WVS members serving tea to demolition crews (WRVS Archive & Heritage Collection)

A produce stall in Wisbech (Courtesy of the Lilian Ream Collection)

WVS members practising emergency cooking in Gainsborough (WRVS Archive & Heritage Collection)

Collecting salvage with the help of local children (WRVS Archive & Heritage Collection)

Processing salvaged material (WRVS Archive & Heritage Collection)

Salvaged aluminium for making aeroplanes (WRVS Archive & Heritage Collection)

A soldier selects a book from a WVS mobile library (WRVS Archive & Heritage Collection)

WVS members garnishing camouflage netting (WRVS Archive & Heritage Collection)

A work party knitting (WRVS Archive & Heritage Collection)

A WVS clothing exchange (WRVS Archive & Heritage Collection)

A boy is fitted for new boots (WRVS Archive & Heritage Collection)

A social centre in Rickmansworth (WRVS Archive & Heritage Collection)

Re-homed residents of Sutton receive donations from Nottingham (Courtesy of the *Croydon Times/Croydon Advertiser*)

INTRODUCTION

A CALL TO ARMS

The Women's Voluntary Services was the largest women's organisation in British history and, for a few years, perhaps the most important. It was created in 1938, in expectation of another major European war, and from fear as to what such a war might mean for the safety and security of Britain's civilian population. The central threat was the prospect of enemy air raids on the homeland – a threat that had vastly increased since the Great War – and the principal response to this danger was the establishment of Air Raid Precautions (ARP). As the Home Secretary, Sir Samuel Hoare, put it in a letter of 4 May 1938, the local authorities would be in need of 'large numbers of women ... for first aid, ambulance drivers, for clerical work and in connection with communications, and also for Wardens'. This letter was addressed to Stella Isaacs, the Marchioness of Reading (1894–1971), whom the government had selected to head the about-to-be founded WVS. Her late husband, thirty-four years her senior, had been Viceroy of

1

India. She had significant leadership experience in the voluntary sector, especially through the Personal Service League, and enjoyed a solid reputation for getting things done.

It was the government's intention to foster initiative and constructive activity among ordinary citizens, so that 'all responsible persons shall gradually learn what to do for themselves and for others in the event of air raids, and I know that women, particularly those with families of their own, are concerned about this'. The preparations would be 'for saving loss of life and reducing suffering and maintaining the ordinary life of the community if war should regrettably come upon us'. 'In the tradition of this country we are trying to do this by voluntary methods', Hoare observed in a letter of 20 May 1938; and he conceived of this women's movement of volunteers as an expression 'of what a free people can organise for themselves', for he thought that the 'order and discipline that come from the responsibility of a free people is . . . much more enduring than any discipline enforced from outside'.[1]

The WVS was set up, then, to ensure that women were prepared to deal with air attacks, should they occur, and that they would be properly organised for self-protection and the protection of their fellow citizens prior to any hostile action. The WVS was not a charity. Rather, it was a state service to be staffed by volunteers. The formation of the WVS was publicly announced in mid-June 1938 and headquarters were established at 41 Tothill Street, Westminster, in London. During the following fourteen months the WVS created an administrative framework based on the twelve regions for civil defence, ten in England and one each in Wales and Scotland (it was also active in Northern Ireland). Each Region had its own Administrator, sometimes a titled woman and invariably socially well-connected, and under her were County Organisers, then

Borough and Rural District Organisers, and finally village or neighbourhood representatives; all but the last were demanding positions, requiring full-time or near full-time commitments.

Senior WVS members and notably the service's chairman, the energetic and highly competent Lady Reading, toured the country to spread the WVS's key messages and gather recruits. The WVS membership of around fifty thousand in early 1939 quadrupled by mid-May, and by the late summer of 1939 it had enrolled around a third of a million members and set up over one thousand Centres – and was still growing. The commitments of WVS members varied enormously: while some women were prepared to volunteer for fairly long hours, most, because of family responsibilities or age or health, could only be part-timers, and this was all that was expected of them. The WVS appealed to women to give what time they could to do whatever jobs they thought they would be comfortable with. There would, so Lady Reading promised, be some useful job for every woman, regardless of her family commitments or (say) her shyness or inexperience or her limited mobility. This flexibility and sensitivity to the diversity of women's temperaments and circumstances was one reason for the success of its recruitment campaign.

These first months of activity were rooted in a few basic principles. The WVS was not mandated to take initiatives of its own. Rather, it existed to assist the local authorities with regard to civil defence and to do whatever tasks these authorities asked it to do. (Requests were later to come from many other authorities.) Whatever influence the WVS might exercise would be a consequence of authority being delegated to it by other bodies with established powers. Emergencies were anticipated, most of them associated with enemy action, and it was expected that the WVS would be a key player in helping others to deal with them. It was seen as important that, in

3

the event of air attacks, suffering be alleviated, loss of life be minimised and the ordinary life of the community continue as far as possible.

Such work would help to sustain morale. Lady Reading saw the WVS as an antidote to panic and defeatism and a means of instilling confidence, and she felt that these goals could best be achieved by stressing efficiency and disciplined organisation, and sometimes specialised training such as First Aid or learn-ing how to drive motor vehicles, without mimicking the culture of militarisation. The essential message to women was clear: their homes and homeland were likely to be threatened, should it turn out that war was inescapable, and women should do what they could as individuals to confront this danger, sen-sibly and confidently and with appropriate tools – and in company with others, for there was bound to be strength in numbers. Many of Lady Reading's promotional efforts during the year or so prior to the outbreak of war were designed to combat lethargy and timidity and to proclaim that women could act prudently and effectively both in their own defence and the defence of the nation. From 1 September 1939 they were called upon not only to prepare but to act as well.

While this could be said to be a book about the wartime WVS, it is really about the WVS *in* wartime society. We must say something about organisational and institutional history, but we are mainly concerned with social history and the wartime experiences of WVS members and some of the hun-dreds of thousands of people who had contacts with them. The richest of the WVS sources show their writers as keen observers and often thoughtful interpreters of lives close at hand, and of people needing to be understood. These reports show us the WVS at work, and through them we also see something of the texture of everyday life. The WVS was in some respects a top-down organisation, but it had a broad base and at the local level it tapped into the experiences of huge numbers of people, whose individual circumstances were often vividly described.

Our goal as historians is not only to tell the story of a remarkable organisation, but also to allow its records to reveal something about the character of lives lived in wartime Britain, especially of those to whom harsh things had happened and were happening. These were people who were obliged to cope as best they could with what they could not avoid, though, as we shall see, they usually did not have to cope entirely on their own.

There is no doubt that the Women's Voluntary Services was a hugely important movement for large numbers of people. 'How proud I felt to be a member of such a magnificent and self-effacing organisation': these were the words of the WVS Centre Organiser in Blackwell North, Derbyshire in February 1953, well after the war's end, when the WVS was helping the victims of the massive floods at that time,* and was a widespread sentiment. Justified pride, of course, should be rooted in accomplishments. The following chapters are intended to portray the wide range of deeds done by the WVS and responses to challenges, and to assess its impact during these tumultuous years of Britain's social history.

A NOTE ON SOURCES

The most important collection of sources by far is the WRVS Archive & Heritage Collection in Devizes, Wiltshire. (The 'R' for Royal was added in 1966.) This outstanding collection, which was awarded UK Memory of the World Status by UNESCO in

*See Appendix C.

2010 and is very capably managed by its archivist, Matthew McMurray, is the foundation for this book.

The single most important category of WVS document from the war is what was known as a Narrative Report. These Reports were expected to be composed monthly by WVS Centre Organisers around the country, some two thousand of them; and they were intended to record the various WVS activities in that area for the preceding month. Tens of thousands of Narrative Reports have survived, but while certain boroughs and rural districts are well documented, others (Leeds, for example, and parts of London) are hardly documented at all. In some places these reports were at some time systematically destroyed: for the most part only those concerning evacuation have survived for Scotland, for example. While most reports are only one or two pages, some typed and others handwritten, a minority are detailed and expansive, written with verve; some include substantial descriptions only when activities out of the ordinary occurred; others still are routinely brief and unrevealing, sometimes even cursory. Naturally, we draw most heavily on the reports that are particularly conscientious in providing detail and commentary. Occasionally there are attachments to the reports, such as a newspaper clipping or a special account of some subject or other. Together, these Reports, with their appended information, comprise vital testimony concerning the work of the WVS and its links with wartime society.

In the WRVS Archive & Heritage Collection, the Narrative Reports are clearly sorted by county and year, and within each box the files are arranged monthly and often separated by borough or district. It is easy to locate the Report from a given place for a particular month (assuming, of course, that it was in fact submitted and has survived). Whenever we write in this book that, for example, 'According to a report from Luton in

June 1943', or 'It was said that in Bristol in April 1941', or 'There were problems in Liverpool in December 1940', or 'The WVS in Tunbridge Wells in August 1943 took on new duties', we are invariably quoting a passage or drawing on evidence from the relevant Narrative Report of the date stated, and no other reference is provided. Occasionally a Narrative Report is undated but has been filed with others that are dated; in these cases we use language such as 'in late 1939 in north Lincolnshire', 'from the beginning of 1942 in Nottingham', and the like. The author of any report is normally the Centre Organiser or her deputy. Unless otherwise indicated, the WVS statistics we cite, mainly concerning membership, are drawn from Box 229 in the WRVS Archive.

The major printed source for understanding the wartime WVS is its monthly *Bulletin*; a complete collection is held in the WRVS Archive. The *Bulletin*, which was usually eight pages in length, often has the feel of a publication of record, with its messages from Lady Reading, letters of thanks, statistics, notices of public events, accounts of operational successes and worthwhile initiatives, honours given, the names of donors from abroad and the like, as well as regular advice on food preparation. One of its key purposes, unsurprisingly, was to sustain morale and commitment among its members, so it had to be persistently upbeat, confident and resolute. Its value is mainly to be found in its revelations of views from the top, its national perspective and its explanations of policies and reports of successful activities, though a particular action or event is often not explicitly attached to a named place, especially if bombing was involved. Still, the official, often fact-driven and nationwide material in the *Bulletin* is a useful complement to the localism of the Narrative Reports.

We also cite or quote from the diaries of five women who were active in the WVS, all of which are found in other archives. A brief account of each diarist and her diary is produced below. All our quotations and citations from these diaries are specifically dated and thus can be readily located by anyone who wishes to check the original.

Dorothy Dixon* (born 1906) was a shop assistant in a working-class district of Dewsbury, West Yorkshire. She seems to have joined the WVS in later 1942. Her diary starts in July 1941 and is held in the Mass Observation Archive at the University of Sussex (no. 5331). We plan to publish soon an edited version of her diary under her real name.

Nella Last (born 1889) lived in Barrow-in-Furness, Lancashire (now Cumbria). She joined the WVS in 1939, shortly before the war started. Her husband was a joiner and she was the mother of two adult sons, one of whom was in the army. Her massive diary, which starts in late August 1939, is held in the Mass Observation Archive at the University of Sussex (no. 5353). Selections from her wartime writing are available in Richard Broad and Suzie Fleming (eds), *Nella Last's War* (1981; London: Profile Books, 2006) and our (eds), *The Diaries of Nella Last: Writing in War and Peace* (London: Profile, 2012), Part One.

Helen Lloyd (born 1899) came from a well-off family and lived in Albury, near Guildford in Surrey. She joined the WVS soon after its inception and throughout the war was the Centre Organiser for the Guildford Rural District – and also the author of the Narrative Reports from this district to WVS Headquarters. Her diary, which starts in April 1940, is held at the Surrey History Centre in Woking, under references 8261 and 8916. Almost all of

*A pseudonym.

her diary for 1940–1 has been published in our (eds), *Warriors at Home 1940–1942: Three Surrey Diarists* (Surrey Record Society, 2012).

Phyllis Walther (born 1904) wrote her diary for Mass Observation (no. 5454). Early in the war she self-evacuated, along with her young son, from London to her parents' home in Blandford Forum, Dorset, where she had grown up and where her father was managing director of the Hall and Woodhouse brewery. Her husband remained in London for most of the war. She was already a member of the WVS when she started her diary in May 1941. It has been published in its entirety, edited by us, as *Dorset in Wartime: The Diary of Phyllis Walther 1941–1942* (Dorset Record Society, 2009).

Doreen Wright (born 1907) wrote her private diary in the form of letters to her husband, who was serving in the RAF and went missing in action on 22 May 1940. Her diary is now deposited in the Warwickshire Record Office, and an admirable edition of it has been published by the Leek Wootton History Group as *Doreen's Diary: She Could Not Have Loved More – The Wartime Diary of Doreen Wright* (2012). Doreen Wright was a member of the WVS for about six months in 1940.

The other sources that we have used are all acknowledged in the endnotes. This material falls into three main categories. First, the Cumbria Archives in Kendal has an exceptionally complete collection of sources (including Narrative Reports) for that borough and the county of Westmorland, and most of our references to Westmorland are from documents in this rich collection (WDSO 92/1-2). While this county and city together had fewer than three thousand members in 1944, they were certainly active, and their Organiser was exceptionally thorough in recording their activities. Second, there are sources in the WRVS Archive that are not Narrative Reports. They may be special accounts, usually typewritten, of one matter or another (such as raids, canteens or clothing schemes), or speeches, or perhaps printed ephemera, or pamphlets, or correspondence, or newspaper clippings. When we cite or quote from one of these, a specific box or file number is given in a note. Third, we have also used sources from other repositories, such as county record offices and the Imperial War Museum, and we have often drawn on accounts of WVS work from local newspapers, most of which are held in the newspaper library of the British Library at Colindale. On all these occasions suitable references are given in the endnotes. From time to time we make a general statement that is supported by scattered archival evidence, from Devizes and elsewhere, and in these instances we do not usually provide specific references.

In quoting from contemporary sources, we have silently corrected obvious errors, often revised punctuation in the interest of clarity, and sometimes standardised such usages as dates, monetary values and acronyms. The wartime WVS was and still is often referred to as 'Service' rather than (as is correct) 'Services', but we have usually retained the singular usage when it was employed by a contemporary observer or participant. And since members of the WVS commonly spoke of their organisation as 'WVS' rather than 'the WVS', quotations in this book that lack a definite article where a modern reader would expect to find one are in fact accurate.

CHAPTER 1

EVACUEES 1939–40

In late summer 1939 almost all Britons knew they were living through a crisis. Many felt they were on the cusp of a catastrophe. As the clouds of war darkened many branches of the WVS were preparing for the worst. Among the challenges was the protection of the country's most vulnerable citizens – its infants, pre-school children, pregnant and nursing mothers, schoolchildren, the elderly and people with disabilities – as the threat of the bombing of cities became more likely. These people were, once war was imminent or declared, to be moved by the government away from the big cities in which they lived. The plan, which was at this time voluntary, was to relocate most of them, over the course of a few days, to hundreds of hamlets, villages and small towns – 'reception areas' – where, it was hoped, they would be out of harm's way.

The evacuation of early September 1939 was a massive and unprecedented undertaking, involving thousands of officials and many others assisting them. The Home Office saw the

WVS as a major player in helping to organise and carry out these evacuations, and local authorities in reception areas were encouraged to look to it for help; most did so since they knew they could not manage on their own. Members of the WVS in some of the counties nearest to London were well aware that they were likely to receive large numbers of evacuees, and they had strong incentives to plan ahead. Within days of the declaration of war their preparations were put to the test. (Private evacuations, involving individuals choosing to move or send loved ones to safer locations, were an entirely different story and rarely concerned the WVS directly.)

Huntingdonshire, a thinly populated rural county, was close enough to London yet far enough away from obvious major industrial and military targets to make it an ideal reception area. The county's WVS members were briefed on the government's evacuation scheme, which envisaged that schoolchildren would be evacuated with their classmates and pre-school children evacuated mainly with their mothers. WVS volunteers attended lectures that dealt with the expected requirements of evacuees. In cooperation with the British Red Cross, working parties were set up throughout the county to handle all sorts of clothing needs and to organise the knitting of such comforts as sweaters, scarves, mittens, caps and socks. On the brink of the war, some eighty local WVS committees were functioning in Huntingdonshire, many of them prepared to take whatever civil defence measures might be needed. All this testifies to considerable commitment, foresight and thoughtful organisation. Huntingdonshire's WVS was not, though, responsible for formal billeting arrangements; this was very different from Surrey and some other counties, where the WVS took a leading role in dealing with billeting issues.[1]

Huntingdonshire played from strength in a number of ways

and especially, it seems, in the quality of its leadership. The Lord-Lieutenant of the county, the Earl of Sandwich, chaired the National Service Committee and his wife was the president of the county's WVS as well as being active in its work. Major support for the efforts of the WVS in 1939 came from the County Council, 'whose Clerk has been, from the first, the organisation's best friend' – here, as in other counties, the effectiveness of the WVS was closely linked to the competence and zeal of the local government.

More than ten thousand evacuees were expected from London,[2] and in January 1942 the WVS County Organiser for Huntingdonshire reflected on what had been done in preparation for this. In February 1939, she thought, 'evacuation was nothing but a remote contingency. Few of us were able to conjure up the dread possibilities which must follow on an outbreak of war and any who urged concrete preparations were apt to be labelled "alarmist". Fortunately for this County, our [WVS] Regional Administrator, the Clerk to the County Council and others were more far-seeing and so September 1939 found us not wholly unprepared.'[3]

The first evacuations to Huntingdonshire began on Friday, 1 September 1939. Around six thousand evacuees arrived from all parts of the capital: some four hundred from Islington, Holloway and other areas of North London ended up in and around Ramsey, while hundreds more arrived in Warboys, Tolbrook, Pidley, Offord, Ellington, Kimbolton and other villages. By 4 September, the morning after war was officially declared, the WVS began providing meals at the Corn Exchange in Huntingdon and on the following day 128 mothers and children were reported to be eating there. Palliasses were ready to be stuffed with straw, some emergency clothing was in stock and facilities were soon in place for those with special needs, such as the sick, young children – there was a 'short-stay home for toddlers' – and women who were pregnant or had just given birth. Empty houses were found 'for mothers or children who could not be billeted in the ordinary way' and, according to a write-up from mid-October 1939, 'buyers have combed out second-hand shops for miles in search of furniture, or have laid in stocks of new goods before these disappeared from the market'. A social centre for evacuated mothers and children was quickly up and running in Huntingdon, and there and in the neighbouring town of St Ives bathing and laundry facilities were made available for the newcomers.[4] There was a lot for the reception area to think about and act upon. The central WVS office in Huntingdon was kept busy trying to meet a wide range of demands, 'from bedsteads, bedding, and layettes for mothers, to darts boards for nurses marooned in country loneliness at some improvised institution'. A social worker was hired to support young single women, including nurses, evacuated teachers, hostel staff and teenage schoolgirls away from home, and to arrange suitable recreations. Communal feeding centres for evacuees were opened in both Huntingdon and St Ives; such centres (and they cropped up in many other places) usually provided hot mid-day dinners and thereby avoided forcing 'foster mothers' and others accommodating strangers to take on additional cooking burdens themselves.

On the whole, welcomes were said to be warm and overt mishaps thought to be minor, though no doubt much distress during these few weeks was unreported. One child fainted, but appeared to thrive under the attention of the ambulance crew, and one five-year-old boy was temporarily lost. Most small children were efficiently processed through the reception tent where they were registered, sometimes medically examined and given food – a bag of rations to take to their billets, which included a tin of corned beef, tins of sweetened and unsweetened milk, two packages of biscuits and even a quarter-pound of chocolate. Some children arrived not only without a parent, but with few words of English. Many of the English-speaking children, such as those evacuated to St Neots, were said (initially at least) to have been happy in their new surroundings – some played on the green – and acting as if they were on holiday. By Friday 8 September a Docklands Settlement Nursery School from Canning Town in London's depressed East End had been relocated to unaccustomed splendour at Hinchingbrooke Castle, the home of the Earl and Countess of Sandwich, just outside Huntingdon. Seventy-two youngsters between two and five years of age were expected but not all had yet arrived because they were with their parents hop-picking in Kent, the Cockneys' traditional late-summer break from smoky London.

If Huntingdon's initial reception of refugees and evacuees went relatively smoothly, as it apparently did, this was a result of some factors that went beyond solid planning, excellent logistics and abundant local support. One was an unusually enlightened anticipation of the emotional needs of youngsters suddenly wrenched from their parents and plumped down in a strange new environment. In early 1939 the WVS sponsored a series of meetings at several centres in the county, at which local foster mothers could discuss the difficulties that displaced children might encounter. They concluded that evacuated children were likely to need psychological support, and this led to a request to WVS headquarters for a woman psychologist to be assigned to Huntingdon – the county was, perhaps, unusual in requesting support from someone with such qualifications. Miss A. T. Alcock, a child psychologist who had worked at the Tavistock Clinic in London, was a well-known child guidance officer and offered her services to escort children to Huntingdon, but no funds were available. Her WVS supporters cabled friends in America for assistance and, as a result of their enthusiastic response, her expenses were paid for three months, along with a salary rather smaller than what she usually commanded. Writing about this programme, an unnamed author remarked that 'a great many of these nervous children are very disturbed about their parents, who have remained in London. Miss Alcock knows them and she is the link with them. There are children who must have other treatment than that can be given by the ordinary health visitor, or by the general practitioner.'[5] By February 1940 142 children in Huntingdonshire (almost all of them evacuees) had been referred for counselling by teachers, doctors and billeting officers because of 'maladjustment'.[6] These measures of practical psychological interventions were thought to have significantly eased the anxieties of children who were struggling to adjust. The possible emotional difficulties associated with evacuation, both for children and adults, were also anticipated in Cambridge in 1939 by those charged with planning for the reception of evacuees.[7]

Almost all evacuated children and their mothers were bound to be anxious and upset, but those from radically different social backgrounds had even more to cope with. Jewish women from London's East End were part of a distinct culture, which was inward-looking and intensely gregarious within their own communities. Evacuation must have been terribly disorienting for them, and Huntingdon tried to help by providing a residence specifically for Jewish women and children. East Lodge in Leighton was refitted for their use, and each family had its own bedroom. There was a communal dining room, a room set aside for the sick and a playroom that the children loved — it was said that with the help of donated toys supplied by the WVS the children 'can hardly be kept out of it'. The Ministry of Health provided beds and new mattresses for all, while local efforts produced chairs and tables but too few chests or cupboards for storage. Without the latter, the writer of the reports said in January 1941, it was 'difficult to encourage higher standards of tidiness among the evacuees'.[8]

East Lodge looked drab and was far from cheering, but what was worse was the isolation. Women who were accustomed to a companionable if sometimes fractious cheek-by-jowl life were lodged in a re-purposed farmhouse two miles from the nearest bus stop and ten miles from Huntingdon, itself a fairly small town. To counteract this isolation a little, the WVS arranged lectures to which local villagers were also invited and also a weekly visit to Huntingdon. The library lent some welcome books but the new residents felt the 'urgent need of a wireless'. An evacuated London County Council teacher came over twice weekly to offer advice. The weekly visits to Huntingdon were greatly appreciated by the mothers who could, as a result, eat cheaply at the WVS canteen and gossip there with other evacuees. At the end of the year Lady Sandwich funded a Christmas tree, presents and a party – not perhaps, to later eyes, entirely culturally appropriate, but a welcome distraction no doubt. (A Communal Feeding Centre in St Ives carefully provided Kosher meals.[9])

These were months of major upheaval in people's lives. Tensions, fatigue, worry, frayed nerves, suspicions, misunderstandings, the prejudices of social class: all these were, to a degree, inevitable. To be suddenly accommodated in a hostel – an uncommon experience for almost anyone – was bound to be a strain. For a woman with a pre-school child to be billeted in a stranger's home was sure to be a hit and miss experience, with many misses inescapable. Personal habits and accustomed ways of doing things were difficult if not impossible to maintain when women no longer controlled their own houses. Sharing a kitchen was unlikely to induce social harmony. A

17

strange residence might make for problems sleeping. For those who expected privacy to be observed and respected, there were certain to be irritations. It was the rule in late 1939 and 1940 for people to be thrown into the company, like it or not, of strangers, some of whom were bound to displease. Evacuation was certain to require many efforts to make the best of an unwelcome situation.

One is surprised, not by failures and missteps in these weeks and months of national crisis, but by the successes and flexibility of approach. There is much evidence of conscientious efforts to adapt. For example, after more than a year's experience the East Lodge hostel's manager/warden concluded her report in January 1941: 'So we are really settling down, with some ups and downs, chafing a little under the strain of our partial isolation and at times getting quite angry at each other. But I think on both sides, evacuees and warden alike, there exists an ample tolerance for each other's shortcomings and a growing spirit of comradeship.'[10] At least a few households were actually invigorated by the presence of evacuees. In Worcester in July 1940 a Mass Observer* reported on a visit to a WVS sewing meeting where she heard a widow of about sixty say that 'she had been very lucky in getting a nice family to share her house. There is one little girl. They all get on very well and she is not now so lonely. The mother was making a blackberry and apple pudding this morning, and was most particular that she should go back to have it with them.'[11]

Surrey was also a county active and generally well organised in planning for evacuees, though there were major variations among the fifteen local councils. In a number of districts the

*Mass Observers were volunteer investigators and reporters for the social research organisation Mass Observation, which was founded in 1937.

WVS joined forces with other, more established women's organisations, notably the Women's Institute and the Girl Guides. Some local authorities planned to rely heavily on volunteer workers, others only to a limited extent. In three areas, it was said, 'the Clerks to the Council handed over very large responsibilities to the WVS'; one of these was Woking, where they were asked to take charge 'of the children after their dispersal at railhead to the schools to be used as clearing stations during their probable three days' stay there. The WVS was arranging for canteens at railheads; provision of equipment and bedding in the schools; care of children in the clearing stations in conjunction with the school-teachers; cooking and canteens at the clearing stations; transport and guides to billets from the schools. In addition the Women's Institutes were prepared to open three crèches for children under five.' In Haslemere the WVS was tasked with organising the accommodation of six hundred children in uninhabited houses, and in the Guildford Rural District the WVS 'were asked to undertake the entire responsibility of the evacuated children during their probably two days' stay in schools and public buildings. The WVS was prepared to deal with feeding, sanitation and equipment in these clearing stations. In addition the WVS found 253 people willing to take in and care for babies under five.' In each village in this district the billeting officers were expecting to call on WVS representatives for help if necessary. Some councils showed considerable foresight in their planning to receive evacuees, others, such as in Walton and Weybridge, not nearly enough.[12]

Tens of thousands of evacuees were to be received in Surrey: at the beginning of the first weekend of September 1939, more than three thousand mothers and children were evacuated from London to Dorking with an efficiency that the local press said 'had gone wonderfully well under the circumstances' and with a 'smoothness that was thrilling'; an eyewitness likened it to 'the wheels of a well-oiled machine'. Soon enough, though, these wheels began to wobble. On a Saturday afternoon in September a trainload of mothers and children arrived for whom billeting arrangements were inadequate. The next day, with the arrival of two more trainloads, tensions escalated. Mothers with young children – two, three, or even four of them – understandably did not want to be separated from their children, but billets for more than two individuals were hard to find, even when billeting was, on occasion, made compulsory. Such failures were not for want of trying. 'Working under Mrs Lindsay's leadership,' the newspaper reported, 'members of the Women's Voluntary Services did their noble work magnificently', working long hours and frequently with little food and scarcely any sleep.[13]

Successes, then, were mixed with failures. While many parts of Surrey were well prepared for evacuees, inevitably there was some slippage between the supply of and the demand for suitable accommodation. The surveys of available billets in some places were probably incomplete and thus space was underutilised; some parishes received fewer children than they had prepared for, others more. Helen Lloyd, the head of the WVS in the Guildford Rural District, reported in November 1939 that the total number of people evacuated to her area fell short of what had been expected but that some villages received more than their planned quota because of the desire to keep school classes together. As in Dorking, it was evacuated mothers who proved to be the most 'irksome' to house, 'many of whom were quite unsuited for private billets. A large proportion of the poorer mothers have returned to London, being unable to afford the expense of keeping up two homes. The remainder are now happily settled.' Each village had a billeting committee made up of three WVS members, the billeting officer, the local head teacher and the London head teacher, as well as the health visitor or district nurse. Two representatives from the WVS Centre would attend all meetings and acted as a liaison between the committee and the District Council. The system worked reasonably well: 'A very considerate attitude has been shown by the Billeting Officers and if difficult circumstances have arisen the householders have been relieved of their evacuees. In consequence the spirit in which the District has adopted the Evacuation Scheme has been excellent.'[14]

The WVS, the Home Office and the local authorities were trying their best to anticipate, at a time of national emergency, the needs of the nation's youngest members. At the outbreak of war some 765,000 children had been evacuated in school groups, plus 426,000 mothers and their (usually) pre-school children.[15] These were big numbers, and without the WVS the welfare implications would have been grim for no other organisation had enough people to do all the jobs that manifestly needed to be done. As it was, there was a great deal to think about: education, contagious diseases and other illnesses (impetigo was a common problem), sanitation and hygiene, recreation, companionship, emotional breakdown, the tensions resulting from children being separated from their parents. Houses were – or were expected to be – visited regularly to check on the evacuees' welfare, and the WVS did some of this inspecting. After-school games were organised for children; a few nursery schools were started for pre-school children; and maternity hostels were established.

Of course there were blunders. Communications among those in charge were not always up to the mark, and Helen Lloyd was especially critical of the efforts of the London County Council: 'The neglect by the LCC of all matters concerning the health of the school-children after their evacuation is a cause of constant complaint amongst the London school teachers'. She also claimed that 'the LCC has maintained a consistently negative attitude when asked for help or advice in difficult cases, especially in regard to the treatment of mental defectives and blind persons of difficult temperament unsuitable for private billets'. She was particularly concerned that the London children's medical records had not come with them. 'This ignorance about the children's medical history continuously hampers the care of their health. A child loses his spectacles, but he cannot obtain another pair without a visit to the oculist as the prescription is on his medical card; talk is heard of children receiving sun ray and other treatment, but the reason for this is not known, while even past tubercular cases have not been notified.'

There was almost no end of practical issues of welfare to manage. Adequate footwear for children would prove to be a chronic headache: by November 1939 Helen Lloyd had already noted that 'the provision of boots for children whose parents cannot or will not pay is still an insoluble problem'. By contrast, in Rickmansworth, Hertfordshire, the WVS was already running a boot-repairing service, and it also collected furniture and blankets for evacuees.[16]

Finding a bed for the night was one thing; finding ways to spend the day while far from home was quite another, especially for adults. While hostels for evacuees tended to be all-inclusive or nearly so, the mothers and children billeted in private houses needed other facilities, for they could not be expected to spend almost all their time under the roofs of their hosts, some of whose houses were small or at least not well suited for putting up permanent guests. (Large houses had often been earmarked for public purposes, such as hospitals, nurseries and hostels for children with special needs, or they had been commandeered by the military.) The evacuees needed places to go to, unless they were to tramp the streets – this was obviously undesirable – and thus the importance of clubrooms and other recreational centres, where evacuees could chat and knit and have a cup of tea in the company of others in similar circumstances.

The WVS was active in setting up such facilities in later 1939. In Dorking a social centre was open to all evacuated mothers and their children every weekday for most of the day-light hours;[17] it was said in December that a meeting room for evacuees in Littlehampton, West Sussex, where friends met and teachers could speak with the parents of their students, was developing 'more and more into a play centre for these children and the young schoolchildren'; social centres for evacuees in different parts of Portslade, East Sussex were provided with magazines, toys, a gramophone and records; and such clubs and recreation rooms were opened in at least four towns in Bedfordshire. In Bedford the centre was in the Corn Exchange and included a canteen, nursery, playroom and clothing depot; in Leighton Buzzard the centre for evacuees was in the tem-perance hall, where the WVS dealt so effectively with billeting complaints that the *official* appeals tribunal did not have to meet.[18] At Fairford, Gloucestershire, there was 'a club where mothers can spend the whole day, with a children's playroom, bathroom and facilities for laundry work'.[19] Other local author-ities took steps to make baths and showers more readily available to the visitors. This was of no little importance since many of the private houses in which evacuees were billeted had mani-festly inadequate bathroom facilities.

These social facilities were also aimed to ease the pressures on householders who were billeting evacuees, and to protect them from having further guests forced upon them in the treasured hours of the weekends. In Leighton Buzzard the WVS opened a centre to receive the relatives of evacuees on Sundays. 'The idea', it was said in October 1939, 'is to relieve the house-holders to some extent. Instead of having to have numerous relatives in their homes on Sundays we are endeavouring to get them to come to this centre with their evacuated children, etc. Refreshments are provided.' Similar provisions were being offered in Hailsham, East Sussex by the following month, in parts of Surrey and at Rickmansworth, Hertfordshire, which was not far from central London and where slightly more than 1400 evacuees remained in October 1939. In regions more remote from London, such as parts of Wiltshire, the WVS sometimes met the Sunday excursion trains that brought in evacuees' visiting relatives, and arrange for their local transport. In Dorking a Toc H hut – Toc H was geared mainly to pro-viding club-like facilities for members of the Forces – was open on Sunday afternoons 'for evacuees and their friends'.[20] One village near Guildford 'opened a monthly Sunday canteen in an endeavour to limit the parents' visits to once a month'. (In the villages around Guildford many of the social activities were actually organised by the Women's Institutes and the Girl Guides, whose help was duly acknowledged by the WVS.)[21]

Some of these practical initiatives were also an acknowl-edgement of the social disconnectedness that evacuees, marooned to some degree among strangers, were prone to feel. While the sexual implications of women being separated from their husbands were hardly ever mentioned explicitly, the *WVS Bulletin* for December 1939 included one sentence indi-cating that the issue was not completely ignored: 'There is news from Kent of a "honeymoon house" where fathers from the city and evacuated mothers can meet at the weekends.'

Schooling was another vital need, though the lion's share of this work was usually done by teachers and education author-ities. Still, the WVS was active in giving support to these educators, including the assistance of volunteer 'helpers'. The results were mixed. According to Helen Lloyd in the Guildford Rural District, 'In some villages the teachers and helpers have been excellent in every way but in others the teachers have refused to do anything but teach and the helpers have given little or no help. The helpers in several case were not wisely chosen, some being the wives of school teachers and others the mothers of large families.' She thought that 'some of the difficulties would have been avoided if the instructions issued by the LCC to the teachers had corresponded with those given to the receiving authorities. It was an unpleasant revelation to the teachers to learn that the official helpers were intended primarily to help the householders rather than the schools and that they should be under the instructions of the local authorities.' Another 'urgent problem' she wanted to mention

is the payment of bus fares for children billeted in scattered villages. There are several infant schools evacuated to the District, and the children under five require assistance in bad weather in getting to school, while even the older children find the walking of perhaps three or four miles a day a hardship. No help is received from the educational authorities unless the children have to travel over two miles by bus. At present the children's fares are being paid by the foster parents or the school teachers out of their own pockets.[22]

Here was one of many issues on which rules, as officially proclaimed, needed to be bent or broken in order to minimise hardship.

While Huntingdonshire's employment of a child psychologist was rare, the importance of keeping evacuated children as happy and secure as possible was widely recognised. It was common for WVS visitors to oversee the well-being of billeted children. 'The weekly welfare visiting scheme continues to work very well,' Bath reported in June 1940, 'and is a help to billeters as well as a safeguard for the children.' Almost all localities with evacuated children in 1939 put a lot of energy into laying on traditional Christmas celebrations, including seasonal treats, decorated trees, a Santa Claus, parties that featured a conjuror, pantomimes, the distribution of toys and the like; and there are numerous accounts from late 1939 that take pains to describe what was planned throughout a particular district to do the right thing by these children at Christmas. One senses from these reports that local people, supported by the WVS, were working hard to treat evacuated children as their own. Sometimes questions did arise as to who would foot the bill for these festivities and whether billeted children might be a nuisance over the holiday – but not, apparently, in the Guildford Rural District, where 'the official suggestion that householders may wish to be relieved of the evacuees at Christmas has been received in most places with considerable indignation'.[23]

In November 1939 the WVS in Cromer and the Erpingham Rural District of Norfolk was 'arranging a rota of WVS members to take the children out for walks at weekends, playing with them in the winter evenings between tea and dinner, and otherwise look after their welfare'; and just after Christmas one of the cinemas in Cromer put on two free performances for all the children in the area, both permanent residents and evacuees. 'WVS helpers attended and superintended the seating. It was a very snowy day, so a bus was chartered to convey the smaller evacuee children back to their billets after each performance.'[24] Play centres were set up in some parishes; toys, new or second-hand and some of them hand-made, were given to the children; and some branches organised out-of-school sports and games or learning activities. Near Huntingdon a neglected plot of land had been donated by the County Council for cultivation by the

WVS, partly to supply produce that could be used in canteens, and it was thought to have potential appeal to children as well. 'The scheme would also combine possibilities for giving evacuated children instruction in gardening, and it is hoped that other places in the County will adopt it.'[25]

No doubt each reception area did things somewhat differently, and with varying degrees of success. The WVS in Worcester summed up its work in a report written in February 1940, a half-year after evacuation began. It recalled how its members 'were at once asked to assist the local education authority by making 900 palliasse covers to be filled with straw to supplement the mattresses already available. Owing to the magnificent response to this call, it was possible by relays of work parties at the Guildhall to complete the work in time for the children's arrival. The Director of Education also asked for help in collecting blankets, beds and bedding, and the WVS were glad to be able to collect 147 of such articles, either as gifts or loans, within 24 hours.' While the need for such services had diminished by February, 'there are many still nobly receiving evacuees in their own homes, and giving them a happy and healthy new life'. Saturday clubs had been set up for some of the children and it was said that 'the venture is still running very happily, although now so many Birmingham children have returned home there are more of our children in the clubs than there are evacuees'. Early in their stay in Worcester the evacuees had been taken on outings to the countryside, where they picked blackberries and 'climbed to the top of the Beacon. Some of the children had never seen the country; most had never been in a motor car; and one small boy said he "had seen apples in the shop, but never seen them growing on a tree".' The WVS supplied these Birmingham children with clothes as needed and at Christmas collected toys for the 391 children who did not return home for Christmas.

Many WVS activities were responses to local facts on the
ground and to needs identified as a result of practical experience. Thus one finds certain communities in reception areas
doing things that might well have been done nowhere or
almost nowhere else. On 31 January 1940 it was reported from
Aldeburgh, Suffolk, that 'Two voluntary helpers from
Dagenham, professional tailoresses, have moved here from
Framlingham where they have been working. Have come for
a month to start a workroom and instruct local workers to
carry on making children's clothing for evacuees and
Aldeburgh children and surplus for county evacuees.' Parcels
of clothes and material arrived in Deal, Kent, in December, a
gift from the Imperial Order of the Daughters of the Empire
in Canada, and the WVS arranged for members of the Girl
Guides to make underwear from this material for later distribution. (Inadequate underclothing became even more of a
problem in later years.) Then there were the distinctive needs
of individuals who might require greater-than-usual support.
In Horsham, West Sussex, in November 1939 a WVS member
accompanied an expectant mother on a hospital visit to
Brighton 'as the woman was too nervous to travel by train
alone', and in April 1940, according to the Centre Organiser
in East Central Essex (Chelmsford), 'WVS helpers have assisted
the Borough Billeting Officer in transporting an evacuee child
to the hospital several times a week for special treatment, and
we have been asked to find helpers to take this child out in her
invalid chair'. Humanitarian acts of this kind were obviously
important, and had the WVS not existed they might not have
happened, or they would have happened more randomly.

While the tone of the WVS reports on evacuations in late
1939 and early 1940 was generally upbeat, even self-
congratulatory, stressful realities did not go unnoticed. 'The

difficult time for billets is now beginning', wrote the WVS Centre Organiser in Ely on 30 November 1939. 'Ely is a small place of 7 to 8,000 people. No big industry, and so the major part of us are middle to old aged, and we find the *continual* strain of children very wearing to nerves and bodily strength. Also the 8s 6d* does not leave anything to wear and tear of furniture – and we have over 900 children and teachers.' She foresaw 'a trying time' at Christmas, as 'Householders want to "visit Mother" or "have children home". In either case the evacuee is a marplot.' A retrospective account of work in Region 7 of the WVS, essentially the counties around Bristol and south-west of it, which was apparently composed in 1944, recalled some of the strains associated with evacuation in 1939:

> evacuees poured into the Region in no sort of order [and] in conditions of cleanliness, sobriety and discipline which upset the cleanly homes and God-fearing duty-doing lives of the people of the South West. The services given by WVS in cleaning heads [of lice], clothing children, organising socials, giving parties, forming clubs, lending furniture, providing blankets, and administering soothing syrup to outraged householders should be emblazoned in letters of gold on everlasting tablets.[26]

In the countryside around Barrow-in-Furness, fifty-year-old Nella Last, already an active worker at her local WVS Centre and one of the great diarists of the mid-twentieth century, 'noticed a lot of sacrifice on people's part since they had evacuated children' – she was writing on Sunday, 15 October 1939, so only a few weeks after evacuations had taken place:

*A householder was paid 8s 6d per child for child maintenance when more than one was billeted in the household; 10s 6d was allowed for the first child.

When two children of different families were lodged in a cottage, Sunday often brought as many as eight or ten grown-ups 'out for the day' to see them. They rarely brought food, and asked for a 'cup of tea' which meant at the very least biscuits as well and on Monday the villagers were left with a dirty house to clean – on wash day – and their pantry depleted. There were exceptions but in the main it was the thoughtlessness of the visitors, coupled with the fact they could always call at the pub before they left, that rankled!

Such small but galling annoyances and inconveniences must have been commonplace. There were, as well, complaints from reception areas that visits by mothers to their evacuated children were often disruptive rather than reassuring and undermined the children's inclination to settle in their new surroundings.

The arrival of perhaps dozens of children in small communities was frequently unsettling. Some villages in the 1930s were known to be suspicious of outsiders; and strange young lads from the rough parts of a city, some with accents disagreeable to local ears and looking and perhaps acting like ruffians, were liable to get a frosty welcome. In Wylye and Nadder Valleys, a rural area west of Salisbury, a village hall was at first used to house 'fourteen difficult boys – WVS arranging it all', according to the Centre Organiser in January 1940. When the village hall proved unsuitable other accommodation was sought by the WVS, and a house in Bishopstone was requisitioned by the clerk of the Rural District Council. 'There are now 26 difficult boys safely housed under the care of officials from Portsmouth and the cottages are relieved of a burden that had become really too much for their limited resources.'

What was considered 'difficult' about these particular boys was not specified, but there is no doubt that one of the most pervasive problems, and a nightmare for some households with evacuees, was bed-wetting. This was a very common problem, which was often remarked on; the WVS and other bodies published pamphlets with advice on how to deal with it. One can readily sympathise with the unhappiness of all parties, the afflicted children, many of whom had rarely if ever before travelled outside their own neighbourhoods, and the inconvenienced adults. One should also recall that, since many homes in the 1930s had only primitive laundry facilities, soiled bed sheets (not to mention mattresses) were a significant additional burden for evacuee-accommodating homemakers, many of whom were already over-stretched. There must have been many scenes of adult anger and children's tears when urine-soaked bed linen was discovered. The psychologist Miss A. T. Alcock, Child Guidance Officer in Huntingdonshire, thought there was clearly a connection between enuresis and anxiety that was rooted, at least in part, in a child's separation from its mother. By contrast, a medical observer and investigator in Brighton concluded that bed-wetting was a social habit rooted in parental negligence and indifference and a 'low social standard', and that evacuees with this problem had mostly brought it with them from poor parts of London. 'In dealing with these evacuees', he claimed, 'the fact that they seem to be quite comfortable and happy even though they are lying in sopping beds has been very noticeable. Equally noticeable has been the absence of any sense of shame in a large proportion of them.'[27] (His was a portrait strongly conceived of in terms of respectability, or rather the alleged lack of it among the poor.) A different perspective is revealed in a much later recollection by a man who had been unhappily evacuated to Herefordshire at the age of seven: observing that bed-wetters tended to get sent home, he duly offended – or at least this is how he remembered what had happened. 'I managed to be sent home by Christmas. It was rather uncomfortable but it worked.'[28]

Helen Lloyd, the assiduous WVS Centre Organiser in the Guildford Rural District, saw bed-wetting as no small matter. 'Enuresis has been my care and problem since the beginning of the war', she wrote in a notebook dating from around 1940 that described her work with evacuees (it is not certain that these words were composed before German bombing, but they probably were).

> It has caused quarrels, discussions and ill-temper; it has wrecked the peace of mind of nearly every household in the country – in fact it has caused more harm to England than anything yet accomplished by the enemy. It is only within the last few days that I have learnt the medical name for this complaint. Enuresis in plain English is bed-wetting! It's queer, isn't it, that this unpleasing childish habit which is associated in my mind with dimly remembered incidents of nursery days should have shaken Government departments to their depths?

All sorts of experts were offering opinions:

> Everyone has a different solution to the problem. There is the No Drinking School, the Over Drinking School, and the Fear of Darkness School that pins its faith to a night light in the bedroom. There is the Cure by Psychology and the Cure by Suggestion, and I have even heard of a Local Authority that has called in a Spiritualist to its aid. On one thing all these pundits are agreed – the complaint must be taken naturally and on no account should the children be corrected.

The WVS in Littlehampton reported in December 1939 that non-punitive techniques – 'a system of cheerfulness and firmness, plus rewards' – were being used with success, while Nella Last noted on 4 November 1939 that evacuated children in a village north of Barrow-in-Furness were 'dosed with herb tea to cure bed wetting, and turned out to run wild over sands and woods, and in most cases the treatment worked!' Helen Lloyd's own view – and her two-page account does have a slight air of deliberate hyperbole – was that 'all that is needed is a legion of old-fashioned nannies who love the children dearly but who stand no nonsense from their charges'.

Dedicated facilities were provided in some places for troubled evacuees. A hostel near Guildford had been opened with special responsibility for the care of these children.[29] Dunstable reported in April 1940 that it had a 'hostel for unruly children and enuretics', which then housed six boys and one girl. Occasionally one reads of change for the better. A report from the Erpingham Rural District and Cromer Urban District in Norfolk at the end of 1939 stated that 'bed-wetting is almost a thing of the past, and we have satisfactory reports of increased cleanliness'.[30] A residential home for 'difficult' children (around half suffered from enuresis, half from other emotional disorders) in Godmanchester, Huntingdonshire took in twenty children and worked hard to integrate them into the community and help them adjust to their new surroundings.[31] It was claimed that many of the children made significant progress and that 'the whole atmosphere of the Home is extraordinarily happy, the children becoming more and more engaged in constructive activities in the house and garden'.[32] In February 1940 the WVS in Ely had a 'lodge for bed-wetters and children whose hosts are ill, with an average of 10–12 inmates. It is a *very* happy home and children do not wish to leave. A fire escape has been put in and chess is played down to five years old.'

Of course, it is impossible to judge claims about the 'happiness' of the evacuees in particular facilities, for individual experiences must have been varied enormously. But it is clear that in many places the WVS was trying hard to buffer children from the serious disruptions to their lives that war was forcing on them. And the WVS on this and other issues concerning evacuation was hardly ever acting alone: it was almost always partnered with at least one other agency, sometimes another voluntary organisation, and almost always an arm of the local council. In some counties, such as Huntingdonshire and Surrey, the WVS played a leading role, in others it was much less visible – and might even have felt under-valued by condescending local authorities.

It is hardly surprising that some country communities felt inundated and struggled to adapt to the presence of dozens, perhaps hundreds, of visitors in their midst – and, they might well wonder, visitors for how long? In some places, where the very poor were billeted on those who were only a little better off, everyday life must have been very strained. In November, in the Hailsham district of East Sussex, it was observed that the evacuees billeted in one village, Ninfield, 'seem to be very poverty-stricken' and were expected to benefit from assistance coming from others in the county – clothing for the children and 'a layette for two evacuated expectant mothers' were specifically mentioned – 'particularly as the village has no very well-to-do residents'. Individual freedoms and habits of privacy were taking something of a beating. There were no precedents for mass billeting. Trial and error were bound to loom large, and the approaches to evacuation were in some places less successful, or faced more resistance, than in others.[33] We do not really know how frequent disputes were – most would have been disclosed only in conversations that were never documented – but we do know that members of the WVS were frequently involved in efforts to resolve them, to broaden choices and to calm dissension. Certainly a great deal of diplomacy was required, as WVS leaders discovered in the course of confronting practical problems and addressing individual grievances in their own localities.

The need for tact was already recognised prior to actual evacuation. In Surrey in 1939 some of the local WVS leaders were advising that when 'children were to be billeted in private houses, a full explanation must be given to the householders as to whether or not the children would receive Government rations. Summary written orders to the householders compelling them to take in children without explanation or instruction is not sufficient.'[34] Appeals that were couched in the language of explanation and sympathetic understanding were more likely to succeed than coercive demands. Later, when tensions arose between householders and their evacuees, it was acknowledged that showing sensitivity to both sides was of the first importance. It was said that in Huntingdonshire, while a change of billet was sometimes desirable,

> often it is possible by advice and sympathy to overcome these difficulties sufficiently to enable the child to remain happily in the same billet. Not infrequently it is found that householders and children are in desperate antagonism because neither feels that their point of view has been considered. If, on the other hand, both have a sense that their troubles are being treated with sympathy, and if they have an opportunity of unburdening their souls to some outside person, it is surprising how often these difficulties disappear.[35]

The mediators in these circumstances were often members of the WVS.

There were sure to be a few bad apples on both sides, though 'badness' could hardly be objectively established. The great majority of evacuees were probably reasonably cooperative and orderly. The WVS Centre Organiser for Cromer and the nearby Norfolk villages spoke well of her child evacuees, many of whom came from Dagenham, whom she did not consider an 'undesirable presence' in the countryside, and she emphasised the warm relations between them and their 'foster parents'. There were regrets all round, she claimed – she took the trouble to make this point in a letter to *The Times* – when the children had to leave Norfolk in early June 1940 (by that time coastal regions had been classified as restricted defence areas and were considered unsafe for children).[36] Similar positive feelings were reported at the end of 1939 from rural – more than the urban – districts in Caernarvonshire: 'The children adapt themselves very quickly to country life, and enjoy it, and all the residents in the villages seem to take a pride and genuine interest in all the children billeted in the village.'[37] There are many other reports from late 1939 and the first half of 1940 of the strong bonds formed between evacuees and their foster parents, not to mention the children's improved health and nutrition, which was unsurprising given the often dismal conditions in the inner cities. What we hear little of is how these children felt. Evacuation was bound to be hit-and-miss for children, but the WVS must at least have helped to soften the blows of a harsh and disruptive reality.

Naturally some evacuees, given the huge numbers of them in 1939–40, were bound to be headaches for their hosts. And of course irritating and over-demanding or truculent people got noticed and were probably more likely to be written about than the compliant sorts. WVS reports occasionally included details on difficult people, and their tone of displeasure was usually unconcealed. In November 1939 it was reported that, while the women's hostel in Ely was very useful, 'One inmate nearly set it alight the other day, in consequence of which she is said to propose to return to London. It is not proposed to put any insuperable difficulties in her way, as she is not a *persona grata* and her room is wanted for someone else.' In Little Langford, Wiltshire (Wylye and Nadder Valleys), the WVS Centre Organiser noted in January 1940 that 'after some difficult cases (very dirty and ill-behaved mothers and young children) had returned to their homes and the joys of city slum life, a very nice London mother with three children are happy and well at a pleasant farm house'.

Evacuees and those trying to help them sometimes had very different perspectives on the crisis at hand. An account from around early 1940 found in a mainly WVS scrapbook from Dorking testifies to one volunteer's frustration – 'Episode' was the title of her page. She cited three evacuees, one of whom 'was peculiarly aggressive, wanting everything she couldn't have, and being upheld by her husband who threatened us with dire penalties. Luckily she went back quite soon.' As for the other two,

Leonard [her surname] was brought in from the rural [district] plus tons of luggage, followed later by Gurney, who had decided that Yeovil was too far from 'home sweet home'. Each arrived with small child in tow and were loaned a small house where they promptly proceeded to cause as much trouble as possible, finishing up by setting light to a door. They were then offered other accommodation but the call of the wild was once again their undoing and back home they went to everyone's relief.[38]

Such evacuees were clearly regarded as fish out of water by those well-bred ladies who had been called on to act both as their protectors and hostesses.

While the thinking of the evacuees was rarely thoughtfully recorded, a few WVS observers – and most of the leaders were women of privilege – did display some sympathetic insight into the attitudes of the unprivileged. Two or three little boys evacuated to Cromer 'were found to be stealing from the shops. These children come from a very poor district where pilfering appears to be a recognised temptation.' According to the Centre Organiser who wrote this report for March/April 1940, 'the worst offender, who had stolen articles he could not possibly have wanted, confessed to me after a somewhat lengthy cross examination that he "did it for the fun". He then with increasing delight explained the whole procedure of this particular form of stealing, which evidently provided an outlet for the spirit of skill and adventure.' There must as well have been a lot of worry and soul-searching and some heart-breaking incidents for those working-class parents who, with mixed feelings and no little guilt, had permitted their children to be sent away and housed with strangers. On Sunday, 31 January 1940 some parents arrived by train in Bath to visit their evacuated children, but upon arriving there 'the weather was too bad for some of them to travel on to see the children' – one can imagine their disappointment – and about fifty parents were offered temporary sustenance by the WVS in an 'emergency canteen'. This was presumably a day of much despondency.

Despite official counsel, many evacuees soon returned home. As early as the fourth week of October it was said that only thirty-seven evacuees remained in Doddington, Cambridgeshire of the 146 who had originally been sent there; earlier in the month about three-quarters of the 554 mothers and young children who had been evacuated from London to the Wisbech Rural District had already left.[39] Only 36 per cent of the schoolchildren evacuated to Staffordshire remained there in February 1940;

less than a third of the children from Newcastle and South Shields evacuated to Westmorland were still there at the beginning of April.[40] In Scotland the return to their homes by evacuees was probably even more pronounced than in England.[41] Some 1,300,000 children and adults – almost all of the latter women, including the teachers – had been evacuated in September 1939; at least 60 per cent of them were back at home by the following January, and more still by the spring of 1940, when there were probably at most about 350,000 child evacuees left in all receiving areas. (Private evacuations and self-evacuations were in addition to these official evacuations, and had been somewhat more numerous.)[42] Nella Last wrote on 4 November 1939 of the many evacuated women who had already returned home – and she sympathised with their decision: 'I could never have stayed in country and let my husband come home from work to a cold house and know he had to make his own meals.'

From the evacuees' perspective or that of the parents of evacuated children, why not return home? Why not reunite the family? Women were, as Mrs Last suggested, sometimes concerned about their husbands still at home and struggling to function as homemakers, a role with many time-consuming responsibilities that hard-working labouring men had never been expected to perform. Why continue to endure the pain of separation? What was the risk? No bombs had been dropped on civilians. Since the alarming predictions of destruction from the air had not been fulfilled, the whole point of evacuation was being called into question. As Nella Last noted on 19 December 1939:

I was talking to a clergyman from Dalton, a small town five miles out of Barrow, and he says that most of the *hundreds* of evacuated children are going or have already gone back to Salford and Manchester. They are 'gone for Xmas' but as he said old ties and associates would pull for them staying at home and he deplored the strength of a Government who could carry out such a stupendous scheme and the weakness that could not sustain it. If this 'going home for Xmas' is general it will mean the complete breakdown of the whole evacuation scheme.

About a month later she was told that of the approximately forty evacuated children in Greenodd, north-east of Ulverston, who had gone away before Christmas, only six had come back. WVS Narrative Reports from Staffordshire in March/April 1940 indicated that in many reception areas at least 80 per cent of the child evacuees had returned home. Evacuated mothers were even more likely to be gone by then.

By early 1940 all the vexations and disruptions of evacuation seemed to many people, especially the families immediately concerned, to be unnecessary and unwarranted. It was commonplace to speak of the 'phoney war'. Most people were more concerned with the brutally cold winter. Whatever sense of urgency there had been in September 1939 was fading fast or had even, for some people, largely gone. The children were missed at home, sometimes for very practical reasons since the older ones might well have performed useful tasks such as child-minding or earned a little money in a casual trade. Moreover, what mother would want her children to be raised by strangers, whatever these strangers' merits or material means, unless this was truly essential? By the early spring of 1940 members of the WVS were finding a much diminished demand for their services, at least with respect to evacuees. It was commonly felt that time and energy had been wasted.

But then came big changes. From May 1940, even perhaps from the previous month when Norway was invaded, war

40

ceased to feel in any way phoney. Threats that had long been proclaimed by the experts began to seem very real indeed and a feeling of emergency returned as the war came much closer to home. The Netherlands and Belgium fell to Germany's military might. One Prime Minister, Neville Chamberlain, was forced from office and his successor, Winston Churchill, spoke eloquently of the perils on the nation's doorstep. France seemed to be on the brink of collapse. At the end of May, with the retreat from Dunkirk underway, Lady Reading sent a letter, a virtual call to arms, to all WVS County Organisers in which she did not minimise the challenges ahead. 'The steadfast pursuance of our work with all the additional calls that may come to us and all the new undertakings we may be asked to perform will strain every nerve and all your strength.' Women were now called upon to do work that was manifestly of national importance: 'I believe that never before in history have a group of individual women in one service been called upon to play so great a part, and upon us and the way we carry through this task which we have shouldered may depend what future generations think of our traditions and beliefs, of the inheritance that has been handed on to us through countless generations.' She went on to use words that she highlighted with literal underlining: '<u>It may well be that on the measure of calm shown in your district, on the strength of the background to life you can provide, might depend the local resistance to attack, the local domination of the situation.</u>'[43]

These were undoubtedly stirring words. They were words in the same spirit of those of the new Prime Minister. They called for 'courage and resolution', and they conveyed a robust sense that women had the power to decide and act, often independently and without direction from outside, in the public interest. Leadership was to be exercised by women. Service, at all levels, was to be efficiently and thoughtfully performed.

The following chapters show how and with what effect these newly assigned responsibilities were carried out and what they reveal about British society during the extraordinary upheavals and hardships of the next five years.

CHAPTER 2

MOMENTUM BUILDS 1939–40

Evacuation was not the only concern for the WVS in 1939–40. Other jobs were being taken on by its members, who numbered around six hundred thousand by the end of that winter, almost all of them part-timers – though some were much more noticeably part-time than others. In parts of the country where there were few evacuees or none at all, the organisation was taking root and starting to perform useful service. In this chapter we discuss, first, the work in 1939–40 that did not directly involve evacuees and their welfare, and second, the expanding challenges confronting the WVS between May and early September 1940 as the nation came to stand alone against ferocious enemy attack.

The WVS existed to support civil defence, but aside from the huge task of helping to carry out the government's evacuation plans, few could have seen all that might actually need doing if war was declared. The future looked both murky and grim.

One exception to this thinking was J. B. Kelly, the far-seeing and decisive Clerk to Huntingdonshire County Council. On 15 July 1939 he wrote a letter to the honorary secretary of the WVS in his county, outlining his sense of the future:

> If the country were at war there would be shortage in fuel, food stuffs would be rationed, and labour would be scarce, and it seems to me clear that in relation to our added pop-ulation [from evacuees] there would be, by communal arrangements, manifest economy under all heads, for, instead of a large number of people providing for their own needs, labour and material would be pooled. Furthermore I believe that the relief this would give to the householder would do much to ease the inevitable discomforts of domestic congestion.

Kelly foresaw, quite accurately, the sorts of hardships and emer-gencies that would push towards a diminution of individual freedom and a strengthening of communal practices. Many households would lose a degree of their independence and look for and benefit from social support from outside. He anticipated other changes that would bear on millions of households – and would also require innovative public responses. 'It is certain that large numbers of women will, by reason of the shortage of men, have work to do in addition to running their houses, and if they could be relieved of one or more of the day-time meals their minds would be eased and there would be less danger of over-work.'[1]

Aside from assisting with evacuation, the other concrete commitments of the WVS during the first months of war were largely undramatic, though not insignificant, and they certainly show how elastic the concept of 'civil defence' was proving to be. There were working parties that took old garments, washed them, cut them up and sewed and altered them for renewed use, sometimes by evacuees who lacked appropriate clothes. Blackout curtains might be sewn for those who were unable to do this for themselves. Then there was wool, a staple of WVS activities. In the first few months of 1940 knitting (along with making hospital supplies) was probably the activity that engaged the largest number of volunteers across the country; it was, after all, a skill that large numbers of women already had and thus did not need to be trained for. Knitting groups were set up almost everywhere, mainly to make what were usually referred to as 'comforts'.

The beneficiaries of all this manual dexterity included members of the Forces, sailors and merchant seamen. Nella Last frequently mentioned goods given to the men on minesweepers and trawlers who were exposed to harsh weather, and in April 1940 volunteers in Barrow-in-Furness were packing comforts for the men who were about to depart on the new aircraft carrier, HMS *Illustrious*. 'A lot of the men who are coming into town to join her are from tropical service and to each the WVS and Mayoress together are giving a helmet, scarf, mitts and pullover', Mrs Last wrote on 20 April 1940. In May 1940 in Cromer, Norfolk and the surrounding countryside an 'SOS was received from Miss Gray [administrator of Region 4] for a large amount of knitted garments for the Air Force – to be completed in three weeks. Our village representatives were immediately circularised and applications for wool poured in without delay. As a result two packing cases were sent to Cambridge containing 213 garments.' Mending and knitting socks for men in uniform was also a routine activity: in Bath in January 1940 the WVS had received 'a free issue of oiled wool from the Admiralty' to make sea-boot stockings, which 'must be made very accurately according to the official patterns, and every pair is measured and passed by WVS examiners before being forwarded'.

Women's handwork found other useful outlets. Thousands – probably tens of thousands – of women throughout the country were working for the Central Hospital Supply Service, which had existed for decades. These volunteers were making and/or labelling such items as bandages, swabs, gauze, operating gowns, surgical cloths, pillow cases, bed jackets, pyjamas, nightdresses, bed socks, slippers, dressings, instrument bags and covers for hot water bottles. Some of this work was undoubtedly tedious. On 20 June 1940 Nella Last wrote in her diary of how at the Barrow WVS Centre that day,

> four of us stood by two trestle tables laid end ways and while one folded, measured and cut many tails, another clipped in strips ready for the next one to tear full length and the fourth to lay in two short and five long and tie in bundles of five. Talk about Ford's motor works and working on a "belt" – we were like clockwork. I was unlucky for I was tearing all morning but as Miss Ledgerwood had a bad head and she would have been next to do it I just stuck to it. At lunch time I broke a cup – such a rare thing – and it was because my fingers had gone clumsy with gripping flannelette for a good hold when tearing it.

In Leicester during the summer the WVS was 'busy making a new pattern of anaesthetic mask, which will be more economical than the old pattern. We have had 200 of one kind and the same amount of another, and a good worker makes four in an hour. However, it is all very interesting and the workers enjoy the variety of work.' All this labour testifies to the limitations of mass manufacturing in the 1930s: much production was still by handwork, and these hands usually belonged to women.

Many women also invested lots of time in making and

mending blankets. A usual practice was to knit woollen squares, often from remnants, which would later be sewn together to make blankets. In early 1940 in Dewsbury, Yorkshire the WVS received a parcel of blanket ends from an anonymous mill owner, which they made up into twenty-one large blankets and 'arranged for dispatch of same together with large parcel of clothing to Finnish Relief Fund' – Finland was then at war with Russian invaders. In January 1940 fifty blankets were sent by the Leicester WVS 'to men of the Anti-Aircraft units who were in great need of them', as that winter was exceptionally cold. In Hailsham, East Sussex in December 1939 some two thousand blankets were packed in mothballs by WVS workers, with 'people from other villages kindly coming in to help'. Some of the work on garments and blankets – knitting in particular – was done at home, and some in the company of other women in rooms that had been hired cheaply or borrowed. When Nella Last looked in on the sewing room at the WVS Centre in Barrow on 14 December 1939 she saw that 'there was a cheerful hum as if they were all talking together'. Working together and in solidarity with others was commonly one of the appealing features of volunteering with the WVS. Newspapers sometimes published pictures of between a dozen and two dozen of these women in working groups, all with busy hands, and almost all in hats and carefully attired.

Various other activities were well under way by the first third of 1940. A lot of organisational work was undertaken in anticipation of air raids, which would come sooner or later. In many places women were being trained for first aid posts – in fact, basic First Aid training was required for many jobs – and others were taken on to be ambulance drivers and assistants and members of clerical staffs. Baby gas masks and children's respirators were distributed and members of the WVS often helped to ensure that they fitted properly and that care-givers knew how to use them. Some members were recruiting blood donors and staffing blood transfusion centres. Ambulance drivers were commonly drawn from the WVS and would continue to be so throughout the war. In late 1939 the Centre Organiser in Coventry reported that she 'was surprised to have three applications from women desirous of becoming mortuary attendants! As we may require these later I had no hesitation in enrolling them.'

The list of jobs can be readily enlarged. Collections were made of second-hand clothes – new clothing was getting expensive (at least for the poor) and harder to obtain – for with so many people on the move and already uprooted or expected to be uprooted there was sure to be an increased demand for garments, notably ones suitable for the season. Volunteers were needed to sort and pack the clothes and arrange for their storage at depots. In some places the WVS concerned itself with the welfare of Land Girls or members of the ATS (Auxiliary Territorial Service). Magazines and books were collected for men in uniform, some of whom were soldiers posted in places with limited access to libraries or newspapers, others sailors expecting to be at sea for some time. There were numerous reports of WVS members distributing anti-gossip posters or anti-waste posters, and plans were initiated in the spring of 1940 to send parcels to POWs. Recruiting and enrolling these hundreds of thousands of women in 1939–40 was a job in itself: the WVS Centre in Oxford opened on 10 June 1940 and had enrolled around 357 women by the end of the month.

WVS Centres were also active in fund-raising, and some of this money was used to buy the materials needed for their work, such as wool and cotton. Raffles, rummage sales, whist drives, garden parties, concerts, flag days, dances and teas were standard money-making fare and would continue to be prominent for the rest of the war. Weekly dances were put on by the WVS in Branston, Staffordshire, with 'the double purpose of raising funds and giving enjoyment to the young people in the parish'.[2] In Fakenham, Norfolk, according to the Narrative Report for July 1940, 'it is amazing how the villagers continue by sales, entertainments or other means to raise money to keep the wool funds going' for their working parties, though in June some of the women had been distracted as they were 'very busy in pea picking'. The WVS in Thatcham, Berkshire reported in 1941 that 'On Fridays there is a "shop" day at Headquarters, when gifts, ranging from ancient fur coats, wireless sets, and machines to strings of beads and children's toys are on sale, the proceeds of which go to cover our many small expenses and pay our evacuee children's birthday gifts',[3] while in Wisbech, Cambridgeshire, the WVS had taken a more inventive approach in September 1940, raising eleven pounds and eight shillings by auctioning a red setter dog.[4]

Other WVS appeals for money during the war were in support of a 'War Weapons Week', 'Salute the Soldier Week' or similar patriotic fund-raiser, or for the Red Cross or some other good cause, rather than its own activities. ARP grants from the Home Office helped to cover WVS expenditures with regard to civil defence, and its work with evacuees was partly government-funded, usually by the Ministry of Health. As distinct from other and more longstanding voluntary bodies, the WVS had no financial independence and did not solicit funds for itself.

Since one of the commitments of the WVS was to turn down no job, many 'emergencies', large and small, landed in its lap. During the early months of the war most military action was on the seas, and on 21 November 1939 Nella Last in Barrow, a prominent port, wrote of getting 'a real thrill today at [the WVS] Centre for the Port Missionary came to us for help' – two hundred seamen, 'utterly done', the victims of U-boats, had been 'dumped on him':

> He went round begging for mattresses, clothes, blankets, etc. and someone told him to come to us. Best of being a voluntary service there is no red tape and we hastily packed 50 good cloth blankets and emptied the cupboard of all men's clothes that we had intended for Gas Contamination Dept. It made our work seem worthwhile to see it go off with Port Missionary – something 'personal'.

This was the kind of sudden call upon their services that became commonplace for the wartime WVS. In Bath, 'Special emergency transport was supplied on Monday night, January 29th [1940], when severe weather made it essential for 100 sick soldiers to be removed from a marquee which was being used as a temporary hospital', and the WVS moved the patients to billets. In Brighton, the WVS had to contend with severe weather at the end of January and was at pains to keep open the three canteens it was running. 'In most cases the helpers had to struggle through heavy snow on foot from their homes. The ARP authorities cooperated with us on two days, as our drivers could not get chains at once, and lent us a van and a driver to take the food out.' One canteen 'was completely cut off from the outside world' and the WVS members took pride in their success in keeping it going 'quite independently of all other help for two days'. In early 1940, at the request of the Ministry of Labour, the WVS in Hereford undertook to find billets at short notice for three thousand munition workers.[5] Canteen workers in Wales sometimes met shipwrecked men on the coast arriving at night in open boats.[6] In Essex in the summer of 1940, with Germans occupying the other side of the Channel, wattle hurdles were being made 'for defence purposes'.[7]

Other services were occasionally rendered. Leicester's WVS was asked to supply 'volunteers to act as casualties for the regional ARP exercise' on the first Sunday in May 1940. In the same month it was reported that in Coventry 'a trained hairdresser offered her services for WVS work. She is now touring the reception areas around Coventry giving hairdressing services to evacuees.'[8] In some areas the WVS sponsored a scheme whereby poorly accommodated soldiers were provided with hot baths in private houses. A close working relationship was established with the Army Welfare Officer in Leicestershire 'and in one place a member of the WVS has been made Assistant Welfare Officer. Yellow tickets are displayed in windows where teas and hot baths can be provided for soldiers.'[9] For a few weeks in the summer of 1940 WVS members served as escorts for overseas evacuated children to their ports of embarkation; this was not unlike their accompanying of trainloads of evacuees in early September 1939. In some cities there was already an acknowledged need to provide hospitality for members of the services: in August 1940, plans were taking shape in Hull to welcome women of the WAAF (Women's Auxiliary Air Force) when they were on forty-eight-hour leaves. Many members of the Forces were unable to get home on short leaves and thus appreciated the pleasant surroundings, including bathing facilities, that might be offered to them in private houses. Nor were sporting pleasures ignored: 'At South Shields two football teams of the balloon barrage have been fitted up with boots and stockings.'[10]

Some of the jobs to be done were routine. Many volunteers did clerical jobs or sewed on badges or went to work in local food offices to help with ration books – food rationing had started in early 1940. In Leicester, thirty members worked for a fortnight in June helping to prepare new ration books. Other volunteers were employed in nursery schools to assist the trained nurses, others still worked part-time as telephone operators, usually for ARP, one of the fire services or for a health-care facility. Thousands of women trained to be auxiliary nurses.

Savings groups were getting started from around March 1940 and women were encouraged to purchase, and to get others to buy, War Certificates, activities that were to persist for years. Nella Last persuaded her sister-in-law to become secretary of the WVS savings club in Barrow. The WVS usually took pains to foster good relations with other welfare organisations, such as the YMCA and the Red Cross. In Ely in May 1940 the WVS lent the Citizens' Advice Bureau an office in their building, to be open two days a week, and a year later in Rugeley, Staffordshire the WVS was lending space to the Advice Bureau and its volunteers were helping to staff it.[11]

Transport of many kinds was a prominent aspect of WVS work from the start: driving patients to and from hospitals, fetching and delivering supplies and goods, moving children or families of evacuees from one place to another, driving VIPs on tours of inspection,* even sometimes driving for the Forces (the WVS provided drivers for the Admiralty in Liverpool). These were in part efforts to address the gaps and deficiencies in public transport services that were arising in wartime, and the driving – the blackout was one critical novelty – often required skills beyond peacetime norms. In the Soke of Peterborough a

---

*In October 1940 in Camberwell, South London, the WVS drove sanitary inspectors around to inspect houses that had been commandeered to accommodate the homeless after air raids.

fairly elaborate training scheme was in place by March 1940. The tests of the WVS trainees included 'Driving in the dark, driving in convoy, driving a lorry – in a yard, in the street, in the yard in the dark, and in the street in the dark – [and] with trailers. Special attention is given to smoothness and cornering. An examination in map reading is held and also the trainers go to the Corporation workshops and work with mechanics.'[12] Quite a few members of the WVS were sufficiently affluent to own a car, and these women served as drivers for both civil and military authorities, while those without their own cars might volunteer to drive some sort of utility van, and a few women may specifically have got their licences in order to drive for the WVS. Driving was, however, usually a class-limited skill. A few weeks before the outbreak of war it was reported from Rowley Regis, Staffordshire that there was an 'urgent need of ambulance drivers and attendants, but little response as this is a working-class district'.[13]

Carrying messages could be considered a branch of transport, and this service was sometimes provided by cyclists, many of them teenagers or young women. In November 1939 the WVS in Bexhill-on-Sea, East Sussex was 'running a regular service of girl messengers. This, we find, saves much time in receiving replies to messages and also saves postage.'

Canteens were being set up to meet the needs of non-evacuees, both civilian and uniformed. Some were intended to serve soldiers and other uniformed personnel stationed in isolated places, such as searchlight posts. Mobile facilities, which were required to serve the itinerant wartime population, were becoming more evident during the spring and summer of 1940. Many of these specialised vans had been presented as gifts to the WVS, some from Americans, Canadians and Australians, as well as other parts of the Empire. The simplest canteens were trailers to be pulled by a car (which would require enough horsepower to do the job); others were standard motorised vehicles, perhaps vans converted to serve refreshments and sundries, mainly cigarettes. By the middle of 1940 the WVS was running at least seven hundred canteens.[14] Food preparation, of course, was a staple of women's traditional duties. In the Coventry region in late 1939, 'at the request of the Commanding Officers in several Army camps established here we supplied canteen workers to help cook the Xmas dinner. We did this willingly although we missed our own dinner, but it was worth it. WVS got a tremendous reception by the boys afterwards.'[15]

Reports from the WVS typically stressed the appreciation and satisfaction of those served, but not always. Writing from Guildford in August 1940, the Centre Organiser was candid about what she saw as the surly behaviour of one particular squad of ARP workers in the WVS canteens. These men, she claimed,

> grumble without ceasing and, although they get all meals free when on duty, appear to think nothing good enough and are not in the least grateful for all the time Miss Nye puts in on running it. They even threatened the Food Controller that they would resign if their sugar ration was not increased beyond the amount allowed by the Government. We are now using saccharine but they have not yet spotted it – only they have said that the tea tastes strange! ... These men do not seem to understand that if things are rationed it is not possible to get more than the amount allowed. I was so exasperated at one moment that I threatened that WVS would wash its hands of this canteen and they could run it themselves or go without, but of course there was an outcry and I let Miss Nye carry on, but I think, in the end, we shall have to give it up.

The woman running another canteen, for St John Ambulance personnel, was said to have 'anything but an easy or pleasant job', for those she was serving 'pay 1s per day for four meals and expect the Ritz'; they were at times sending sausages back to the cook as not up to their standards, and it was suspected that some were stealing food and other supplies from the larder. As a result, 'It is becoming exceedingly difficult to keep the voluntary workers at their job at this canteen.'

Around the end of the first quarter of 1940 the war still seemed quite remote to many people. The WVS County Organiser in Staffordshire reminded members in early March of the need to show 'staying power by refusing to become bored or indifferent during the present time of waiting'.[16] But from early May 1940 the realities of war became much more intense and WVS Centres that had not previously been especially energetic suddenly became focused on disciplined activity. The June 1940 report from Swansea testifies to this rapid change of mood as the Centre Organiser threw herself into revitalising the work of the WVS on a variety of fronts and forging cooperative relations with the local authorities. Meanwhile, in nearby Bridgend, where nightly alerts of potential raids were the norm, 'A rota has been worked out, and the women go on duty [at the report centre] one night in five. Everyone has got to her post in the quickest possible time, and it is thrilling the way all of them turn out so quickly – not a sign of fear or nerves.' The writer went on to report on her members' transport duties: 'The ambulance and car drivers have been called out every night this week, sometimes twice. My transport officer has arranged a rota so that the same women are not on duty two nights running, though some of them insist on coming, and getting some sleep in during the day. They are all full of pluck and ready for anything – a fine example to us all.' Here is evidence of the pride and confidence that were building in what was still in many regions a fledgling organisation. The WVS was having little trouble recruiting new members.

While some social needs had levelled off or even declined during the first months of 1940 – by April most evacuees had returned home – the demands for help from the WVS escalated as German forces invaded and quickly over-ran much of Western Europe. First there was the arrival of refugees from newly invaded and soon-to-be conquered nations. In Fakenham in May 1940 volunteers were making shirts for Norwegians who had recently fled their country, while in Rotherham 'a request for clothes for Dutch and Belgian refugees resulted in such a good response that we not only sent a lorry full to Leeds Refugee Headquarters but have stored large quantities at the Public Assistance Board Centre in readiness to replenish wardrobes of people rendered homeless after air raids' (which, despite not having occurred thus far, were still expected). At this time, it was later recalled, crowds of refugees arrived at a port in Dorset, and 'the WVS were actively engaged in helping with the reception of those miserable people who had fled from a merciless foe in such haste that none of the necessities of life had been brought with them. The Regional Organiser with the staff of the WVS Centre concerned received boat-load after boat-load.'[17] These people were desperately in need of help: they usually arrived in Britain with few belongings and nowhere to stay, and perhaps with little knowledge of English. In London the WVS often staffed reception centres for these refugees. In Dewsbury in May 1940 the WVS 'canvassed the town on behalf of the Billeting Officer for homes for Belgian and Dutch refugees' and 'made arrangements for helpers to be at the depot day and night on the arrival of the refugees'. Then, in July, another 140

Belgians arrived in the town from South Wales and had to be accommodated.

Wherever refugees were received – in the early summer they included Channel Islanders (four hundred arrived in Bradford in June) and Gibraltarians, bringing the total throughout the nation to a little over seventy thousand people – billets usually had to be found and clothing handed out, as well as the basic necessities supplied for any babies. Sometimes, translators were made available. These were features of the social work that was becoming central to the WVS's raison d'être, as tens of thousands of people were displaced from their normal abodes and manifestly in need of care. Often volunteers met refugees at train stations and took them under their wings, affording them the basic necessities of life in the course of their journeys to who knew where (many of their destinations had to be determined hastily). It was reported in June that one WVS organiser 'stole 1500 bananas from a damaged cargo of fruit under the blind eye of the Excise, to help to provision the refugees'.[18]

As one might expect, not all of these encounters with strangers were problem-free. At a WVS meeting in Dewsbury in May 1944, when there was talk of the prospect of another blitz bringing in new refugees from the south, two middle-aged sisters 'told of when we were at Wakefield in 1940 and had the Channel Island folk plumped on us. How dirty and lazy they were and how the men got drunk and rowed to get into the women who were separated from them. This led to talk of sexual matters in our own district.'[19] (As the war dragged on, many observers became convinced that sexual licentiousness was rampant.)

At the request of the police in late May and early June 1940, the WVS agreed to escort the female 'enemy aliens' – mainly Germans – who had been rounded up for internment on the first stage of their journey to the Isle of Man. This was not a

pleasing assignment for some in the WVS, since most of these
'aliens' posed no threat to security and many were highly anti-
Nazi. However, whatever their personal views, WVS
members – and hundreds were suddenly called upon – were at
least able to give some degree of attentive care and consider-
ateness to the women and children being imprisoned.[20] WVS
Headquarters in Kent reported in July that twenty of its members had escorted 240 of these aliens living in the south-east to
Liverpool, a trip that might have been distinctly disagreeable
but, thanks to police thoughtfulness, was not:

> We should like to record our very grateful thanks to the
> Chief Constable for *insisting* that the Railway Company
> should provide a corridor train for the purpose. It had been
> their intention merely to provide the old fashioned separate
> compartments. As the journey was non-stop from 12 noon
> to 9.30 pm our gratitude can be imagined![21]

It should be remembered that toilet facilities at this time, in
trains and other public venues, were often inadequate or even
absent altogether, a problem that was sure to concern women
more than men.

The evacuation from Dunkirk was another major event in
which the WVS saw action, once these exhausted troops were
delivered home. There was a stark emergency to be dealt with.
In the course of only a week or so, around a third of a million
servicemen, both British and Allied, arrived on British soil, and
everyone agreed that whatever could be done to give them
relief should be done. At Biggleswade, Bedfordshire in early
June 1940, 'Our WVS Canteen was kept *exceedingly* busy when
nearly 2000 troops arrived (straight from France) in our little
town. We fed over 650 soldiers *entirely free* for two days and sold

halfpenny cups of tea at the Canteen afterwards.' There was a similar flurry of activity in Bedford where WVS members 'at half an hour's notice opened a canteen at the station and the Corn Exchange, working night and day to feed relays of men returned from France. Many letters of thanks have been received from Commanding Officers.' In Bournemouth the WVS was 'worked off its feet' in June in dealing with French troops and the British Expeditionary Force; about 350 were fed at a canteen at the town hall and some of the French troops were billeted in various schools. 'Clothing and food was collected for the men and they were entertained by members in their homes.' The WVS in Kent met dozens of trains coming through Tonbridge and Ramsgate, and gave the exhausted soldiers an enthusiastic welcome.[22] WVS members were even called upon to refresh troops arriving suddenly in relatively remote Barrow-in-Furness.

Dunkirk was a key moment in the war – not a victory, obviously, but certainly a merciful and morale-boosting escape from catastrophe – and it was experienced in Britain with intense excitement, not least by those WVS workers who came into direct contact with the men who had just landed on British shores. Tens of thousands of these men passed through the train station at Guildford in Surrey, and WVS members who helped there gave vivid accounts of what they witnessed and the work they did, notably Helen Lloyd of nearby Albury, who composed a six-page essay on 'How the BEF passed through Guildford station' and also wrote at length about these experiences in her diary.

It was, said Miss Lloyd, 'by chance that the WVS heard that the BEF troop trains were stopping at Guildford station. Weary soldiers had been seen on the platform searching for water, some even drinking from fire buckets' – testimony, no doubt, to the muddle when proper plans were not in place. 'After a struggle with the authorities, permission was given, late on Thursday evening [30 May], for the WVS to be admitted to the platform.' She went on to describe what was done during the next few days and the scenes at the station: how 'canteens sprang up in haphazard fashion, some manned by organisations, others by private individuals'; how buns, sandwiches, hot sausages, sliced oranges, chocolate and cigarettes were served up in a sort of frenzy as thousands of men poured through the station; how wash basins were set up and newspapers handed out – there was 'an eager demand for them' – and postcards provided, in both English and French, so that the men could tell loved ones of their safety. There were 'huge urns full of hot tea and steaming coffee, the latter provided specially for the French, and at intervals down the platform were placed milk churns filled with lemonade which was kept cool by blocks of ice'. Despite the chaos and a certain amount of jockeying among volunteers to be most evidently helpful, this was a week when just about everybody was pulling together. There was an outpouring of public support, both financial and emotional; 'the supplies could not have been kept going without the enthusiastic support of the Guildford tradesmen who were willing to be knocked up at all hours of the night and who gave goods often at a discount of 60 per cent.' Helen Lloyd concluded by observing that 'it was an inspiring and deeply moving experience and those who were present counted it a high privilege to have been there'.[23]

These were days when there was a need for some organisation to take charge, give directions and combat confusion. This is what the WVS did in many places, and it was not the end of their aid for men in uniform. A few weeks after the flurry of post-Dunkirk activities in Guildford, its WVS organiser reported that a scheme was taking shape 'whereby we shall keep a list of lodgings, free or otherwise, for the wives and relations of wounded [servicemen] on the danger list. These people are, if necessary, to be met at the station and taken to the Hospital or billets. If we can get petrol – which is more than doubtful – by car, if not by bus or on foot.'[24] There were injured soldiers at Warren Road Hospital near Guildford and the members of the Rural District Council's WVS were tasked with supplying them with such items as ashtrays, handkerchiefs, drinking beakers and books and games.

The very real threat of invasion in the summer of 1940 triggered a second wave of evacuation, this one focused on the vulnerable coastal regions of the south and east. Children who had previously been considered safe – those living, for example, in Essex, Sussex and Norfolk – were now clearly in harm's way and would have to be moved to points inland, usually without their parents. This meant that the WVS was again called upon to manage issues of the sort that its members had confronted in the early months of the war. Between early June and early August 1940 more than two hundred thousand school-age children were evacuated by the Ministry of Health. Helen Lloyd reported that in July there were two fresh waves of evacuation to the Guildford Rural District, '200 children from Portsmouth and 800 children re-evacuated from Brighton and Shoreham. The WVS made arrangements for their medical inspection, feeding and billeting.'

As in 1939, the welfare of the evacuated or re-evacuated children was the dominant concern, which meant, among other things, trying to ease the pain of separation from their parents. 'What will happen to sensitive children who are thrust into homes where they are not wanted?' asked Nella Last on 9 July 1940. 'Children so need happiness and kindness far more than good clothes or lots of toys.' No doubt there was a great diversity of outcomes for these children, depending on their own sensitivity and adaptability; the companionship of friends and siblings, or lack of it; the appeal of the countryside – many city-bred children were drawn to the freedom and openness of rural life; and the character of their foster parents, which ranged from admirable to awful. The WVS did their best for these children: in July in Hemel Hempstead, Hertfordshire it had sixty-five welfare visitors to keep track of how the children were doing.

The WVS worked hard to try to satisfy the needs of these evacuees. Many of the challenges that had been confronted in autumn 1939 re-emerged in the middle of 1940, and recent experience helped in handling this second wave of evacuees. The events in Whaley Bridge, Derbyshire in early June 1940 must have been fairly typical. On 2 June 287 children and twenty-nine adults (teachers and helpers) arrived from Southend, Essex. They were received and given refreshments indoors, and the 'WVS had arranged for a fleet of private cars and after tea and medical examination they were all billeted in private billets with the exception of thirty children who went to a holiday home, which was manned for the first 48 hours by members of the WVS. Since then two members have been up each morning to help with the housework.' At the request of the Council, the WVS was visiting each child and accepting overall responsibility for their welfare, and plans were afoot to open a play centre on Monday evenings. There was a similar flurry of activity in Stafford. On 3 June some 1800 children and their teachers arrived from Ramsgate. WVS members helped to carry their luggage from the station to the market hall, where refreshments were laid on; several volunteers acted as billeting officers; and more than a dozen members turned out with their cars to provide transport.

Since some children arrived ill, they required special care. In June 1940 the Leek Rural District in Staffordshire received 620 children from coastal areas, nineteen of whom were accommodated in a sick bay which was 'kept open for three weeks and manned night and day chiefly by WVS helpers. A day and night nurse was also on duty.' During the weeks after the children's arrival in these inland areas other needs were likely to arise and demand attention, notably adequate clothing and footwear. Evacuated children, even if well kitted out for the journey, were allowed to travel with only minimal luggage, and some children from poor families were sent off ill-clad and ill-shod. In July 1940 it was said that in the Peak District, where over two thousand children had been evacuated from the coastal regions of East Anglia, 'There is a certain amount of difficulty in obtaining clothing and shoes for the children from the parents. This is not very serious at present, but will probably become more acute when warmer clothes are required.' Indeed, there would soon be a need for 'adequate clothing and strong shoes for the wetter and colder weather' of Derbyshire's higher ground.

The critical months of the late spring and summer of 1940 also saw the acceleration of a campaign that had been initiated earlier that year and would become a central aspect of WVS work for the rest of the war: the collection of salvage. This was primarily a job for local authorities, who controlled most of the equipment for refuse collection, and they varied considerably in their zeal for the cause. Some started early to promote the reclamation of waste, while others lagged behind. Initially, the WVS was mainly involved in raising the consciousness of housewives – getting them 'salvage-minded' – concerning the merits of not throwing out items to which they had previously attached little value but which in wartime could usefully be recycled and in some cases reduce the need for imports, such as wood pulp. The emphasis at first was often on collecting paper goods, sometimes house-to-house; bones, which could be used to make glue, explosives, soap, fertiliser and animal feed; and kitchen waste for pig swill. (Pig-keeping was actively encouraged as one aspect of national self-sufficiency. Also, Denmark, the traditional source of bacon, was occupied in April 1940.) In the Camberley district of Surrey in mid-1940 the WVS had an arrangement with a company in Reading to collect and supply it with waste paper 'from our eight depots when it is sorted', the sorting and initial collecting having been done by WVS volunteers.[25] The WVS was actively involved in Guildford's salvage week in May 1940 as it was in the campaigns in many other places, both urban and rural.[26]

It often took considerable time and effort before people would accede to appeals for regular recycling. People, mainly housewives, had to be induced to do things differently in terms of household management. They had to be taught how to separate refuse, told what could and could not be salvaged and where to place dustbins to facilitate collection, and given explanations as to why all these small acts and changes to their routine were important to the nation. In Hull the Public Cleansing Department prepared a leaflet that offered detailed advice on these matters, and the WVS probably distributed it.[27] The report of the WVS from Chelmsford, Essex in July 1940, which noted the collection of waste for pig food, gives some sense as to how change came slowly and lots of persuasion was needed: 'Some difficulty was experienced in getting pig keepers to provide receptacles and also to find householders willing to have these in their gardens, but this situation is improving, and we now have twelve bins and supply two pig-keepers, and hope to increase the amount of pig food obtainable. In addition to this, many of our workers have made private arrangements with pig and poultry keepers.' In the following month seventy bins for food waste were set up in various parts of the town and three pig-keepers were being regularly supplied, but the local authorities were said to be still deficient as collectors.

During the summer of 1940 collecting aluminium was a very big deal – prompted by the call from the Ministry of Aircraft Production for the redirection of this vital material from home use – that is, kitchen ware and other utensils – to the manufacture of propellers and other vital equipment for the RAF. Here was a way that housewives could make sacrifices for the sake of national survival, and the response was impressive. 'With tremendous enthusiasm the women of Hunts have answered the call,' noted the *Hunts Post* in mid-July, 'and a small mountain of aluminium at the County Supply Depot in Huntingdon is the result. Everywhere women have been going round their districts with small handcarts, asking for any pots, pans or other aluminium articles that can be spared.'[28] Tons of items were gathered up; there are photos from these weeks of truckloads of everyday aluminium goods en route to factories. By July, collecting salvage was efficiently organised in approximately forty villages around Fakenham, and it was reported by the Centre Organiser that 'There has been a wonderful response to the aluminium appeal from the whole district. The villages have produced, I think, getting on for a ton, and there has been a good response in Fakenham, where an aluminium week was held.' In Hull, it was reported in August that some eleven tons of aluminium had been collected and arrangements made with private firms to ship them out of the city, mainly to Chesterfield. Most metals, of course, had military value of some sort, and helping to collect them became a significant WVS commitment; it was only later that iron railings were torn down and committed to the war effort, a task that usually required the muscle power of men.

In the months prior to September 1940 the WVS expanded what was to become an important part of its work for the rest of the war – the Housewives' Service. This was very much a grassroots venture, which emerged in Ilford, Essex and Barnes, Middlesex in late 1938.[29] It was based in the intimacies of neighbourly relations and face-to-face contacts in the residential streets where women, particularly those with young children, spent most of their time. (In a few places the original unofficial name for this initiative was the 'Neighbours' League' or 'Neighbours' Group'.) The Housewives' Service – which from 1942 was known as the Housewives' Section – was designed to help communities be well prepared to deal with some of the consequences of a bombing raid and to minimise the fear, confusion and uncertainty that were anticipated when bombs fell and fires raged. The service was to function in support of the air raid wardens, supplementing ARP work and focusing more on conditions inside or near the home rather than in the street. Members of the Housewives' Service were generally women who were not mobile because they had dependents at home, and who had or felt they had limited time to devote to volunteering yet wanted to do something for the war effort. This was a way for housewives to have public responsibilities on the street where they lived and to be better able in a crisis to help themselves and their neighbours.

Women in the Housewives' Service received instructions on how to act in an emergency. It was advised that they should always have a torch at the ready, know how to guide others to shelters and be able to take in anyone, such as a child, caught in the street at the time of an air raid. They were to ensure that buckets of water were placed outside in case a warning sounded; and if the noise during a raid distressed them they were advised to have cotton wool handy to put in their ears. They might also be expected to know something about emergency cooking, and they were asked as well to be informed about some of the details of their neighbours' lives: which residences housed infirm and elderly people who might be unable to seek shelter on their own and would thus need special assistance; which houses were unoccupied; which families had guests who might need rescuing and which had children or other relatives who were temporarily living elsewhere, possibly as evacuees (and thus were not an immediate concern); and which houses were occupied by large families – it was felt that a mother with a large family was likely to feel less anxious when the air raid sirens sounded if she was confident that a neighbour would come by to help her out. Some of the Housewives' work, then, was much like that of census-takers. The point of having this street-by-street bank of information was, in part, to ensure that when rescuers arrived at the scene of a raid they could be given accurate information as to who, if anybody, was likely to have been in each house and might need to be rescued, and which residents were or were not accounted for. It was also anticipated in some places that members of the Housewives' Service would help to clean up after a raid and provide such neighbourly services as comforting distressed children and their mothers and others with weak nerves; listening to the victims' stories, perhaps of close escapes from death; and facilitating the transport of people whose houses had been damaged or destroyed, along with their surviving personal property, to Rest Centres and other safe places.

It is uncertain as to exactly how widespread the Housewives' Services was by the end of the first year of the war, and thus how well rooted the innovation was when bombing began. It is, however, certain that the numbers registered in the Housewives' Service at least quintupled between June 1940 and the end of August, when it reached around 27,500 members (about 3.6 per cent of the total WVS membership), and the numbers, which were probably underestimates, grew dramatically with the onset of the Blitz. The government saw the

Housewives' Service as a very good thing, a potential steadying influence and a morale-booster during a moment of crisis, and it had sanctioned the issue of an official sign – black letters on a blue background – to be placed in the window of each trained WVS woman's house. She might also identify her standing in the community by wearing a WVS armband.

The Housewives' Service underlined the key purpose of involving and energising many 'ordinary' women, especially working-class and lower-middle-class women, in planning for their own protection. As the *WVS Bulletin* for August 1940 pointed out, 'The Ministry of Information is taking a keen interest in this service because it induces women who would never have joined any other organisation to form groups, and by thus pooling their courage and sharing their difficulties to strengthen the morale of the whole community.' Here, in short, was a means of promoting solidarities and self-confidence through practical knowledge and mutual commitments that almost all women could readily appreciate and, if necessary, act upon. Some women were reported to have felt 'exhilarated' by the fact that they were able to contribute directly to the war effort.[30]

Several generalisations can be offered about the history of the WVS in 1939–40. First, its membership expanded significantly, as did the list of tasks it took on. By late 1941 around a million women were enrolled; that summer Lady Reading estimated that one in every thirteen women in the country was a WVS member.[31] What started as an organisation geared to assisting ARP added more and more responsibilities to its mandate, for the bias of the WVS was to do (or at least try to do) whatever was asked of it by established authorities. Second, while the initial requests for help came mainly or entirely from civil authorities, most of them local but some national, requests soon came from the military as well. WVS members were increasingly asked to provide such services as canteens at remote or temporary work sites, or at the train stations through which many troops were accustomed to pass. Had these not been made available, the morale of the Forces would almost certainly have suffered. Third, the work of the WVS during this period was characterised by flexibility and adaptability, an absence of bureaucracy and a capacity to innovate and improvise as circumstances changed and new demands arose. Local branches enjoyed significant independence, and while this could be a liability if the local organiser lacked competence (and some who initially held these positions were undoubtedly not up to the job), it was more likely to mean that the WVS members who were called upon to act knew the local situation well: they knew or were themselves people of influence; they were familiar with the topography of town and country and how to get about; they had at hand details on the material resources and personnel available; and they were aware of any special constraints that should be kept in mind. Consequently, the WVS could respond in a timely manner, and often at short notice, when calls were made upon its time. And these calls became more and more frequent as the 'women in green' – the WVS uniform was greyish-green – proved their value to others and demonstrated their efficiency in all sorts of circumstances.

By September 1940, the WVS had a history of a little over two years. In some localities it was nicely up and running and well organised; in others it had little or no presence, though Lady Reading was very active in moving around the country making speeches, probably on average two a week, and opening new branches. Districts with energetic and assiduous organisers turned the WVS into a major actor. In others, with weaker leadership, the WVS made much less impact. Some members – the 'stalwarts' – were dedicated and reliable, others rather lackadaisical (surely to be expected in any voluntary organisation), self-regarding or picky in the work they were prepared to do. Lady Reading herself always discouraged such snobbery and endorsed a classless outlook, even though in practice upper-class women held almost all the leadership positions. Of course the specific nature of the jobs being done varied significantly depending on location (city or country), the relative wealth of the community, the ages of the members (in some places few were under forty), their capabilities, and whether or not they had dependents. The drive, imagination and open-mindedness of the local authorities were also central to the success of the volunteers' work.

There were casualties from German bombing before the Blitz. Air raids, though initially targeted by the enemy on military and military-related facilities, inevitably disrupted everyday life. It was said in August 1940 that the WVS canteens in Romford, Essex were being used more and more frequently by ARP workers, rescue parties, fire-fighters and demolition squads, not to mention anti-aircraft and observation posts. The Blood Transfusion Service in Bedford was started on 28 August, after a week's campaign for donors, and this was fortuitous timing since all the blood drawn on the 28th was used the very next day when a factory in Luton was bombed.[32] Raids drove hundreds of people from their homes in late August and the beginning of September: the raid on Portsmouth at the end of August left large numbers homeless and in need of shelter, food and clothing. The American Red Cross was a major supplier of clothes for distribution by the WVS, and the Service also helped with the crucial re-housing effort. Meanwhile, there were temporary disruptions to the various activities that had been getting off the ground in

Portsmouth in previous weeks. The salvage campaign, for example, was stalled because the city's refuse carts 'were working overtime to clear away broken glass, rubble, etc.' Swansea endured a bad raid on the night of 1–2 September – thirty-three people were killed and property damage was extensive – and the WVS was kept busy at a number of church halls aiding the many people made homeless, while in Hull there was 'a rather serious raid' on the night of 24–5 August. Six Rest Centres were called into action to care for the homeless in the city, the municipal kitchens laid on food for them and some 177 families had to be re-housed. During this week a barrage balloon also broke loose in Hull, 'the cable damaging a number of houses', whose occupants were duly looked after; and another Rest Centre 'had to be opened to give temporary shelter to the occupants of houses near which suspected time-bombs had fallen'. These were relatively small previews of the future.

With the terror bombing of, first, London, starting on 7 September 1940, the anticipated crisis that the WVS had been created to meet quickly became a terrifying reality. The Blitz marked a dramatic escalation in destruction: almost as many people were killed in London alone on 7 September as in all of the country during the month of August. It had been widely predicted in the 1930s that the bomber would always get through. This proved to be mostly true, although the resultant deaths, while certainly substantial, turned out to be many fewer – by a factor of about fifteen – than had once been feared. But if fatalities from bombing had been vastly over-estimated, the problems and extent of homelessness had been underestimated. It would soon be learned that only three or four bombs could easily damage more than one hundred houses. The following two chapters describe some of the work of the WVS between September 1940 and the middle of 1941.

They report the experiences of some of those volunteers who were engaged in the chaotic, dangerous battlegrounds in and near their own localities, as well as the experiences of those in relatively safe districts who were committed to helping families in flight from the bombing. War was now striking brutally and indiscriminately at home and family, and the WVS was very much at the centre of this drama.

CHAPTER 3

'A SUPREME BATTLE FOR THE WORLD'S FREEDOM' 1940–1*

One of the most violent of years for British civilians began on 7 September 1940. London's East End was heavily bombed that day, making perils that had thus far been imagined but barely experienced become frighteningly real. London would suffer dozens more attacks in the period up to the second week of May 1941, and other cities were soon to join the capital as the targets of mass German raids. The months of the Blitz left at least 43,500 people – almost all of them civilians – dead, and 71,000 seriously injured; hundreds of thousands of people were made homeless, and the nation's housing stock was severely damaged.[1]

In these eight months, from September 1940 to May 1941, the Home Front became the focus of Britain's war. As domestic warriors (and many of them thought of themselves

*This phrase was spoken by J. B. Priestley in his widely listened-to talk on the BBC on 15 September 1940 (*Postscripts* [1940], p. 73).

this way), the women of the WVS were inevitably pressed into service. They played a major role in helping to cope with the crises as hand, usually in association with the Civil Defence authorities and the various arms of local government. They were commonly on the spot when property was still aflame and while rescue efforts were underway. They were frequently the first or nearly the first workers to give aid to people bombed out of their homes. This chapter recounts the work of the WVS at various bomb sites, where fire, collapsed buildings, damaged houses, serious injuries and death were the norm.

Esme Glyn, a senior member of the WVS, was playing tennis on that fateful September afternoon. It was a day, she wrote, when 'the sun, the flowers and the carefree mood of the visitors seemed to push the war into the background'.[2] As sirens sounded the silver of RAF defenders was seen in the sky and anti-aircraft guns opened up. 'Tennis clothes and bathing shorts were laid aside for uniforms and civilian clothes, transport was pooled and the trek home started.' Approaching the Mall, Glyn saw that 'huge mountains of smoke draped the skies behind the Houses of Parliament, it seemed as if the whole of east and south-east London was ablaze'. She made straight for her organisation's Tothill Street headquarters for 'our hour had come; after fifteen months of preparation WVS machinery was at last to be tested in London'. Reminded by a 'nimble colleague' to do so, she called her group coordinating officer to ascertain the amount of damage in her area, Group 1. Upon learning that the area, comprising Westminster, Chelsea, Hammersmith, Fulham, and Kensington, was little damaged, she set out for Group 5 (Southwark, Lambeth, Wandsworth, Battersea and Camberwell) where fires were spreading and many houses had been destroyed.

Before leaving, she and her colleague had 'climbed to the

roof of a Westminster building and saw in front of us three gigantic fires that lit London from east to south. It was one of the saddest and most majestic sights I have ever seen. I never knew until then how much I loved London and how anxious I was to soothe her suffering. As we crossed Waterloo Bridge the heat of the fires seemed to hit us in face, the barrage balloons turned from silvery-grey to flaming scarlet and burst before the heat.'

When they reached a Rest Centre* in Southwark it was already full of men, women and children bombed out of a tenement house, including exhausted mothers, youngsters apparently unperturbed playing noisily and a tearful prospective bride distraught at the loss of her trousseau. The London County Council supervisor seemed to have the situation well in hand but welcomed the offer of a WVS mobile canteen and extra volunteers to help with breakfast the next day.

The next stop, a Rest Centre in Peckham, was very different. A caretaker was just opening a school and welcomed Esme Glyn and her colleague as helpers, directing them to turn on the gas and get out blankets for homeless people who, having being bombed out of another Rest Centre near by, were expected shortly. Along with a few other volunteers who arrived shortly after them, they continued to make preparations for the homeless while the Luftwaffe circled overhead, adding more fuel to the fires and then dropping a high-explosive bomb eighty yards behind the Rest Centre – a scare that ended with, as Glyn put it, 'six of us meet[ing] head first under a kindergarten table.' She said that her own 'fears were somewhat allayed by the local women who assured me they had been

---

*Rest Centres, which were usually located in schools, town halls, church and chapel halls and other public spaces, were designed to shelter and give immediate aid to people driven from their homes, and almost everywhere were staffed primarily or in part by the WVS.

through it all afternoon and everything would be alright'. After offering what help they could to these front-line civilians, the WVS women 'packed into the car and set off down the Old Kent Road at breakneck speed with the Luftwaffe roaring above us' to face whatever new challenges would face them.

The next morning, Sunday 8 September, headquarters staff instructed Centre Organisers to stand by but, Esme Glyn later observed, 'our warning was superfluous for many of these faithful women had been up all night assisting the LCC in their gigantic task of accommodating the homeless'. Organisers at East and West Ham were asked, over and above their staggering workload, to 'use their influence to allay alarming rumours that gas had been used by the Germans'. News gradually trickled through from the centres that more mobile canteens, clothes and volunteers were urgently needed. Squads of women collected at headquarters and were dispatched to answer the calls for aid, usually accompanied by quantities of clothing. Their route to the devastated East End was disrupted by detours caused by burst water and gas mains; the trip from Westminster to Stepney reportedly took three hours.

The following day police, firemen, soldiers, local authorities and the WVS all struggled to bring physical necessities and emotional solace to a great city that seemed to be totally at the mercy of the Germans. On 9 September, to the relentless drone of enemy bombers was added for the first time the 'deep and continuous booming of naval guns, accompanied by the sharper rap of mobile anti-aircraft fire'. This was a desperate measure to raise civilian morale – which it did. Many calls were received the following morning from different districts 'and in each one of them was added this confident note: "Had I heard the wonderful new guns that had been sent especially to help London hit back at the Germans?"'

In the following weeks London endured almost nightly raids,

and soon there were attacks on other cities: the major ports – Southampton, Portsmouth, Plymouth, Bristol, Glasgow, Belfast, Hull, Cardiff, Swansea, Liverpool – and great industrial cities such as Coventry, Birmingham, Sheffield and Manchester. Each city experienced bombing in different ways – depending, for example, on whether it was continuous or episodic, on the diligence and degree of preparations of the local authorities, on the possibilities of flight – but in all cities these attacks brought dislocations in ordinary life that the WVS had evolved to respond to and help alleviate. As an account written around the end of September 1940 put it, coping with the destruction was 'a gigantic task', and involved (among other things) moving people from the most heavily bombed districts of London to accommodation in nearby areas thought, at that time, to be safer: Chislehurst in Kent, Brentwood in Essex and even Finchley, in North London, were mentioned.[3] A report from Camberwell in 1941 pointed to the importance of sensitivity in dealing with homeless people: 'One of the first requirements of people who have been bombed is a sympathetic listener. Busy officials have not the time to give this to every case, and experience has shown that when the homeless person has poured out the story of his terrible adventures, he is that much better fitted, psychologically, to deal with the business of making claims.'[4] This was one of many ways in which morale could be bolstered.

Immediate relief was usually given at Rest Centres. In cities thought to be at risk, it is likely that detailed plans were in place or being quickly developed for staffing and equipping them (water, heating facilities, urns, emergency food supplies, blankets, palliasses, soap, clothing and footwear, First Aid) and ensuring that they would do what they were expected to do after a raid. It was said in February 1941 that there were almost 150 of these centres in Leicestershire, all (or almost all) staffed by the WVS. In Luton by May 1941 some 850 women were enrolled with the WVS as helpers at Rest Centres while at Dewsbury in the West Riding of Yorkshire, several Rest Centres were in place when the town was raided on 12 December 1940; one of them was opened and the WVS 'housed and fed about 60 people for one night and the following day'; they later helped to re-house and clothe some of these families. WVS members were usually eager to learn from the experiences of one another, and in February 1941 volunteers from the Dewsbury centres 'visited Sheffield to get first-hand knowledge of the work during raids'.

Cardiff was bombed on 2 January 1941, and the WVS account gives an insight into how operations were managed at the Rest Centres:

> Dwelling houses were extensively damaged and, in addition, a large number of people were evacuated owing to time bombs and unexploded land mines. Altogether about 3700 people were in our Rest Centres, 22 of which were opened. The WVS manned the centres and looked after the people well in spite of many difficulties, one of the chief ones being the failure of the gas, which made cooking in most instances very awkward. After a short time stoves of various kinds were installed and in some case field kitchens were used.

As the writer observed, 'It was the first time we have had such a large number of people on our hands'. Nearby Penarth was bombed the same night and seventy-six people were accommodated in shelters:

> The shelter in the immediate neighbourhood was one of the first buildings to be damaged, and this necessitated the temporary reception of the homeless in a school basement, and their transport to another shelter when possible. Hot

drinks were provided from the stores rescued from the damaged shelter, and further refreshment and blankets were supplied as soon as the people arrived at the other shelter. Breakfast was also obtained for them. It was a bitterly cold night with snow and very icy roads to contend with. Arrangements went smoothly without any mishaps. Mothers with young children were taken to WVS auxiliary shelters in members' homes.

All this testified to a high degree of advanced planning. 'Next day a further rescue shelter was opened to accommodate people evacuated from their houses on account of unexploded bombs.' Meals were provided as needed to all whose houses were, at least temporarily, uninhabitable, and also for twenty workmen who were repairing damaged water mains.

The damage to property was unpredictable: perhaps it was less than anticipated, perhaps worse. Much depended on where the bombs fell, how many failed to explode, how concentrated the bombing was, how well the fires were contained, how quickly repairs were made. Still, dozens of damaged houses were a usual consequence of almost any raid in a built-up area. One WVS report described what happened after an attack on Kirby Muxloe, Leicestershire on 19–20 November 1940: 'Fortunately there were no serious casualties, but nearly 200 people were rendered homeless. Those responsible for the [refugee] scheme immediately made ready and received the people at the golf clubhouse and the schools.' There they were given refreshments and accommodation for the night, 'and the mobile canteen from Loughborough was called on to help with the breakfasts. This was served with the additional help of volunteers from Blaby. Hot dinners were served later and several people spent a second night at the clubhouse, until such time that homes could be found for them the next day.'

Such rapid rendering of short-term aid was a key feature of WVS work in 1940–1. On 23 February 1941, after Swansea was bombed, 780 people were quickly evacuated to Llwchwr in Glamorganshire. 'Only two hours' notice was given, but with the wonderful co-operation of the women everywhere these were housed and fed in three halls in Gorseinon and Lougher and two in Pontardulais. There were tremendous difficulties to overcome owing to the great numbers sent to us.' Many evacuees were given temporary billets, and during the following fortnight some returned to Swansea and others were moved to Morriston, leaving only 20 per cent of the original number in Llwchwr. Unexploded bombs were a common reason for evacuations of just a few days, as the work of bomb-disposal squads was carried out. In Hull, temporary evacuations from dangerous areas were necessary after four raids between 22 February and 1 March 1941 (ninety-two Rest Centres officially existed, of which eighteen were in action during this week). When the city was heavily blitzed in May 1941, at least fourteen thousand homeless people were fed immediately after the raids and before some semblance of normal life was restored (as it always was).

Cities, of course, sustained the most damage from raids, but the rural districts were not immune. Most tried to be properly prepared. In the Sevenoaks Rural District in Kent, where the WVS worked closely with the public-assistance authorities, it was found that the best way of dealing with a high-explosive incident was 'to have a number of the larger houses available to take in a small number of refugees covering the 48 hours during which time the Public Assistance* are responsible for

*Public Assistance Committees in counties and county boroughs were charged with aiding sick, infirm and destitute people, as the Poor Law had done. During the war they were also responsible for Rest Centres, and in some places for helping the homeless.

these bombed-out people'. The Centre Organiser described the detailed plans for such an emergency and went on to report how two recent incidents had been handled. In mid-November 1940 a bomb fell on the village of Leigh,

> which necessitated 130 people being hurriedly moved from their houses in the middle of the night. My village representative there, Mrs Twitchell, did the most excellent work and got the whole 130 [people] housed and accommodated, some in the village hall and some in private houses, with an hour. By 8 o'clock the next morning she had a communal kitchen running in the hall and everyone had a hot breakfast before going off to work. This kitchen was facilitated by the fact that she had the equipment there for a kitchen which she had been running previously for evacuees but which had closed down owing to the reduction in number of evacuated children in this village.

Good meals were served in the hall for the next forty-eight hours, and those people who had taken refuge in private homes 'or in two empty houses which I have commandeered for emergencies' had food taken to them. The Centre Organiser could not 'speak too highly of the efficiency of the work done by Mrs Twitchell and her staff of willing helpers during this time'.

The other emergency in the Sevenoaks district occurred in Shoreham, where four high explosives made

> a large number of people homeless in the middle of the night. Mrs. Lockett, my parish representative, whose house was also serious damaged, did perfectly splendid work but she found that the scheme did not quite work according to plan. There is a very bad shelter in Shoreham which I

understand has about two inches of water on the floor and though Mrs. Lockett opened up the hall and got an excellent fire going and hot drinks and food ready, the people took to the shelter and nothing on earth would persuade them to come out and go into the hall so she carted all the food from the hall, a distance of some three-quarters of a mile, to the shelter and finally at 3 o'clock went home to her own rather dilapidated house. She had just gone to bed at 4 o'clock when one of the wardens arrived to say that the people in the shelter had changed their minds and would now like to go to the hall. By this time, needless to say, there were no hot drinks available and the fire had gone out and everything once again looked rather depressing and desolate. However, she got out of bed, got the fire relit, started all over again, and finally about 5.30 a.m. the people were accommodated in the hall and ready for a fresh supply of hot drinks etc.

There was more to be done, for later that day, when the Centre Organiser visited Shoreham she found that 'Mrs. Lockett was opening a bureau of information for helping people to get new rations, identity cards, assistance with the filling in of forms etc.', for these were matters with which most people had little or no experience and they needed some help in managing the stress, getting back on their feet and resuming a more-or-less normal life.

Canteens were especially valued during the days after a blitz. Fixed canteens, for which the WVS contributed some of the staff, were sometimes attached to Rest Centres and other emergency shelters, or in locations convenient for civil defence and demolition workers, or for troops helping out with the clean-up. Emergency canteens were hastily set up in various parts of London, one of which was under Selfridge's on Oxford Street,[5] but the top priority in the crucial hours and days after raids was to get mobile canteens to places where the needs were greatest. They were a boost to people's spirits and a signal that, at this time of tumult, civilians were not forgotten and would be in certain basic respects looked after.

Mobile canteens, many of them specially designed vans, feature prominently in most accounts of blitzed cities. A Mass Observer who visited Southampton in December 1940, a fortnight after a major raid, was critical of the local authorities and the lethargy of some recovery efforts but reported that 'several mobile canteens were observed and it is now very much easier to get a cup of tea or something hot. The WVS have been doing fine work in this respect.'[6] At the beginning of January 1941 a mobile canteen from London went to Southampton and fed mainly men in the dockyards whose families had been evacuated; some of the food provided was intended to be carried away since many of these men had no one to cook for them.[7] After the severe bombing of Coventry in mid-November 1940, canteens run by the WVS were very active in aiding the victims. It was said that they served fifty thousand meals in the first three days after the raids, and that within a week seventy canteens were distributing food and drink to around twenty thousand people a day. One mobile canteen, sent to Coventry from Oldbury in Worcestershire, begged bones and vegetables to make soup, got gallons of milk from a local dairy and, according to the Centre Organiser, served 'hot drinks all day and through the night, when a doctor from Oldbury came to take us back and bring a new lot of helpers'.[8] On Monday 18 November Leicester's mobile canteen arrived in Coventry with two hundred loaves of bread, one hundred pounds of sugar, sixty-two pounds of tea, milk, margarine, tinned meat, biscuits and cigarettes, 'and carrying two milk churns to be filled with water before entering Coventry. Four helpers and two men went with the mobile. They returned that night, leaving the canteen. On Tuesday, four more helpers went, returning at night.' The next morning the trailer had to be fetched back to Leicester for it, too, had been raided, and the WVS called upon volunteers from Rutland and Loughborough for additional support. 'They brought their vans stocked with food, and when that was finished we replenished them from our stores.'

The first priority for canteens was to respond to urgent needs, wherever they were, which was sometimes outside the locality. Shortly after the severe raid on Portsmouth of 10–11 January 1941, a mobile canteen was sent to the aid of the city by Dorking in Surrey.[9] A new mobile canteen in Bath was dispatched to Bristol after a severe raid on 16 March 1941; a few days later it was sent to aid Plymouth, returning there after further bombing in April. Another canteen, actually a modified furniture van that included a seven-hundred-gallon water tank, had been dispatched from Lincoln to Coventry on Monday 18 November 1940 and served there at a couple of locations. The following day, according to one of the members' report on this five-person mission, 'we were called at 6 and got up in the dark. The only means of light was to hold a torch, well shielded, on our faces, and with very dirty hands try and do our hair etc. I think everyone's appearance was to be congratulated. We then boiled water and restocked in sandwiches which members of WVS cut all day and night in shifts so that it never stopped. We then served tea etc. outside shelters and in the streets as the need arose.' They were forced to take shelter themselves for a while and later served tea to one of the large shelters with several hundred people and afterwards 'to the services about'. The next day, Wednesday, they were up at six and told to go to West Bromwich, which had just been bombed, but had first to go to Birmingham to collect supplies and there 'had a very difficult time . . . as the damage was very bad and the roads were mostly impassable'. Finally, shortly after noon, they arrived at their destination:

the Police asked us to serve the Auxiliary Fire Service who were working still, and I went to the ARP Report Centre to find out how we could help them most. I received a most hospitable welcome and they were delighted to see us as they had been told three canteens were coming through from Coventry and we were the only one who arrived [at West Bromwich]. Here I feel that the driving of George in most difficult and trying circumstances should have special mention.*

She went on to detail the sort of emergency circumstances that would have been observed on dozens if not hundreds of occasions in British cities during the Blitz. 'We were asked to serve the rescue and first aid parties who were still hard [at work] on the wreckage, trying to rescue casualties and any who might still be alive, and we were given a messenger to direct us to the worst area.' Some people had been trapped in cellars up to their necks in water and were found alive – 'one could even walk with help. These rescue men', she learned, 'had been working for 24 hours and went on till dark with no food. After this we fed another rescue party and then went back to the report centre where a very kind man, the Town Surveyor, offered us his empty house for the night', where sheets and blankets were found for all five of the mobile canteen's staff.

*Large vans or lorries were sometimes driven by men, usually when not enough women in a locality were trained to handle heavy vehicles.

A next door neighbour was also very kind and offered to give two baths there at her house to relieve the strain on the electric heaters. Mrs. Frith and I went across and the gunfire started and the sirens went, so we went with a tin hat on and a bath towel over our arm. The water could hardly have been called hot, but anyway we got our clothes off for the first time, and on our return we found ... the other two had produced the most marvellous meal of soup, sardines, and coffee. After washing up we had a quick game of bridge carefully watched by George, and went to bed.

The next day, Thursday, the team was sent to the Rowley Regis area in the Black Country, where bombing damage was substantial and 'there were still many people unaccounted for. We served the rescue [workers] and homeless and other ARP parties and Mrs. Homer, the WVS Centre Organiser, came and told us that if we wanted anything at all we had only to send a message to the office she had started there.' The following day they finally returned to Lincoln, and the author concluded by saying 'how wonderfully the party worked in very difficult and trying conditions' and recommending, based on the week's experience, that certain items be carried on any future call that might be made on the canteen's services. These included a rug to put on top of the urns to keep the tea hotter, 'a refuse bin for old milk tins, tea leaves, etc. with a lid', stools or folding chairs so that members could rest, and two hurricane lamps (the one they took with them had been stolen from the workhouse).[10]

It was a challenge to get enough canteens to cities under attack. A day-by-day record of the responses to the bombing of Coventry in April 1941 shows that mobile canteens – some, but not all of them, run by the WVS – arrived quickly on 9 and 10 April from Wolverhampton, Oldbury, Birmingham, Warwick, Lichfield, Leamington, London, Kidderminster and several other places, with other canteens soon joining them. Logistical arrangements were a source of tension, with disputes as to which canteens to send to which sites, and both gaps and overlaps in service. On 12 April there was an 'awkward hiatus between the London convoy moving out and the arrival of the Manchester convoy', which apparently should have had a WVS member in charge but did not, and it was late getting into service owing to difficulties in heating its water. The same day, the WVS 'was asked to provide domestic help for a labour camp at Stoneleigh Park', where some five hundred men wanted at least a dozen women 'to help prepare food and do housework' (the WVS obliged).[11]

In Bristol, which was bombed several times, the four mobile canteens were said to 'have proved invaluable' during December's raids and 'frequently stayed out throughout the Blitz till daylight, serving the fire and casualty services. There have been many cases of great personal courage and unselfishness among the drivers and attendants.' This emergency service, much of it focused in due course on demolition workers, continued for three weeks; Gloucester and Salisbury had 'rushed their own mobiles here and helped for days'. By May 1941 the WVS canteen service was quite elaborate: fourteen new auxiliary canteens had been opened for First Aid workers; twelve other canteens of various types employed around 450 voluntary and a handful of paid workers; and WVS mobile canteens were 'serving more troops than ever, and we have been feeding dockers for some time' while their own canteens were unusable, having presumably been damaged in raids. Canteen work could be dangerous, as an 'Unofficial Report' on December's blitz in Bristol revealed. 'One of our most valuable drivers was most tragically drowned returning from this work when the mobile canteen got lost in the docks on a dreadful dark winter's night.'[12]

There are intimate accounts of canteen work in the diaries kept by WVS members. On the morning of 4 May 1941 Anne Lee Michell of Wellington, Somerset was sent with several other WVS members to Plymouth, which had just been badly bombed:

> Drove over Dartmoor so lovely in the early morn, frost in the meadows and moors all misty. Such a hard day's work today, never sat down at all. Got out with canteen amid frightful rubbish, ruined homes, soldiers doing demolition very glad of tea – dust so awful. Could never have imagined such scenes – nothing left of whole streets but twisted girders and rubble. People so pathetic, especially the kids ... Hoped to be relieved from Bristol but no one came and had to drive convoy back to Tavistock and come home from there. Got in 9.30 dead tired.[13]

Doreen Wright of Leek Wootton in Warwickshire went with her canteen to aid the victims of nearby raids in late 1940. At half-past two on the morning of 15 November she was telephoned and told that the canteen was needed at half-past six, 'with some breakfast at Lillington and Warmington for bombed out people – [it] was 5 o'clock before I'd got bread and butter cut and all straight for the job'. When she arrived at the bomb site she found a 'stick of bombs right across a housing estate, fortunately no direct hit but 6–10 houses demolished, 40–60 badly damaged, 40 injured people but all cheerful'. However, the next two days were spent with the canteen to Coventry, where she found the destruction 'indescribable'.[14]

Barrow-in-Furness was heavily bombed in mid-April and

early May 1941, and as much of the WVS work that Nella Last had been doing for almost two years, mainly for Hospital Supply, was temporarily suspended she found herself under-occupied. (In fact, the WVS leadership in Barrow seems to have responded poorly to the crisis and Kendal's WVS stepped in to fill some of the void.) Then, at teatime on 15 May, just a few days after the last raid:

as I was going to sit down there was a ring and when I went there was a WVS canteen leader I know slightly. She said 'I've come to ask a favour. I hear you have been upset because you could not find a way to help. I would be thankful if you would take a turn with the mobile canteen. Can you drive?' I said 'No – I've not even driven the car for several years.' She said 'Never mind, you can serve tea and then cut sandwiches for the night trays', so I look as if I have found another job to help someone who needs it. I'm not clear where we will go or who we will feed but that's alright – I'll hear tomorrow.

The following day saw Mrs Last at work with another WVS member on a mobile canteen:

We went round demolition squads and bomb disposal squads, grave diggers and repair gangs, and the cry of 'The Jolly Roger' made me chuckle when they saw our van – it's called that. When I looked at Mrs. Cummins wrestling with an engine that needed attention and when I'd nearly taken a header out of a door whose catch was faulty, I could add only amen to her lurid description of ultimate end of the sonofabitch who was responsible for 'maintenance' but who went out [of town] to sleep each night and had 'absolutely *no* time'!

89

To Mrs Last's disgust, many frightened Barrovians were flee-ing to the outlying countryside each night, or had left entirely, and one of those who had made herself rather scarce was the head of Barrow's WVS, Agnes Burnett. 'I said to Mrs Cummins "Let me get you a rota if you want one. I know of quite a few eager ones – the lower decks of WVS are sound enough. A lot of us waited for a call and there was so much muddle and confusion." And she said savagely "Pity the blasted bomb did not wipe out that inefficient creature of a Burnett and let someone take over who knew their own mind – AND had one to know".' Nella Last, whose disdain for Mrs Burnett had been often recorded in her diary, made a 'feeble effort' (her own words) to defend her, 'a fellow townswoman', against the no-nonsense Mrs Cummins, the wife of a naval officer and an outsider to Barrow.

As at many others places, Barrow's mobile canteen was mainly intended to provide refreshments for civilian clean-up crews. 'The destruction saddened me', Nella Last wrote on 16 May,

> as we went from one group of demolition workers to another and to bomb disposal groups and grave diggers with our welcome hot tea and sandwiches. So many have been brought into town from districts outside town – Cumberland and Westmoreland mostly and many over-age miners – and things are a bit at sixes and sevens yet. Others, coming into town by bus each day and returning to sleep, have no hot drinks but bring food and it's so bit-terly cold. The barrage balloon boys try and wangle tea but we have to be hard hearted for they are well looked after by their own Army and Service vans that *never* give tea to any civilians and our tea has to go round to so many.

The following day, a Saturday, Nella arrived for duty and found that 'no one had thought of a driver for mobile canteen and a mad hunt by phone began'. In due course an official from the ARP showed up and said to Nella,

'Hallo, Mrs Last. I did not know you were on Control' and before I could answer went on about one thing and another and after a few minutes said 'I'll have to pop off. I've a darn fool WVS woman waiting to see me somewhere about!' I frowned and threw my coat back à la Sheriff of Red Gulch and showed my badge and he said 'Good Lord! What are you doing in that bunch of saps!' I said 'Oh, I'm not in the canteen crowd, really. I'm Hospital Supply, really, and only a Jolly Roger *pro tem.*' He said 'Well, take care it *is* only *pro tem* − or they will drive you crazy for they work without system or sense!'

'I suppose', she concluded, 'all towns have the need of "settling in" but, oh dear, there does seem muddle and inefficiency.'

We do not know how accurate this portrait was, though it does have the ring of plausibility, and Nella Last was a shrewd observer. It is not hard to imagine that such a new and untried service might experience teething pains. Still, work did get done. On 21 May, Mrs Last was again summoned to staff the canteen and reported that 'It's cold again and the men were glad of their tea when the Jolly Roger showed up. I'd a fireman again to drive me − another "good help" like last one. Mrs. Cummins had been in such a rush she had not told me how much tea I should make but, to be on the safe side, I made two big urns full and was glad for it meant two cups for all who wanted.' At the end of the shift 'We had a long journey out of our way with the afternoon bread and meat paste for afternoon [working] party to stock the van again and we called in another direction for

91

petrol – and then the siren went' and they made for shelter.
Nella Last continued to serve on Barrow's canteen team, which
later worked mainly at stationary sites, adding it to her WVS
work for Hospital Supply. 'Maybe now if a good canteen service can be formed it will be another worthwhile thing' to do,
she remarked on 26 May, and three days later she was writing
rather optimistically about this commitment:

> I had a canteen meeting to attend tonight and felt happier
> about WVS efforts in that direction when I'd seen the rest
> of the women who go out with Jolly Roger. They are all
> ordinary sensible women like myself, with one exception
> in a rather 'young and silly' girl and three amazon types
> who can drive and who say they will go out in *anything*.
> There seems rather a feeling of resentment with the way
> they have been treated by the men Wardens – a kind of
> 'go-and-do-your-knitting-and-leave-*men's*-work-to-men' –
> which quite naturally they resent when women have been
> so efficient and splendid in other bombed towns. Beside on
> the whole the women of Barrow have been the best about
> air raids. It's a bit sick making to see 'healthy men' rushing
> out of town to sleep every night.

The challenges of feeding people could sometimes not be met
by means of a mobile canteen, notably when people had
nowhere to live or when their damaged houses lacked water
or fuel for cooking, which were common hardships after raids.
Then they would have to resort to communal feeding facilities, which were usually set up by local authorities and often
partly staffed by the WVS;* sometimes the WVS acted to help

*For more detail on communal feeding facilities, see Chapter 5.

these people by means of a hastily constructed emergency kitchen. Since it was soon realised that there would be nutritional needs going well beyond sweet tea and sympathy, the Ministry of Food established the Queen's Messenger Service: mobile catering units with specially equipped vehicles comprising field kitchens, water tanks and food stores, along with a core of WVS staff trained in field cookery. These convoys – sometimes of as many as twelve vehicles – were designed to cook and serve hot, nourishing meals in the days of acute distress immediately following a raid. The teams, which were being deployed across the country from early 1941 and had the capacity to serve hundreds of people, could quickly be dispatched to bombed areas, including distant cities. In 1941 a convoy from the Middlesex/Hertfordshire region was sent to Nottingham, Liverpool and Plymouth.[15] Ultimately, eighteen of these convoys were posted around the country.[16]

On Sunday 4 May 1941, a Queen's Messenger Convoy was summoned from Prestwich, north of Manchester, to aid beleaguered Liverpool, and a vivid and detailed account was later written by a WVS member who was part of the team.[17] The convoy, she said, 'consists of ten vehicles painted in creamy yellow with pale blue squiggles and it is quite an impressive sight to see it going in convoy. There are four canteens, two water wagons each holding 350 gallons, two field kitchens and two food lorries. The Queen gave one of the canteens and the other vehicles have been bought with money given by the American Red Cross.' Forty-five women worked on the Convoy; the drivers were largely or entirely men.

As the writer and her group arrived in Liverpool by bus,

there was a thick mist or haze of smoke and dust over the city and the smell of burning and charred wood grew stronger as we made our way into the city. Many roads were closed either on account of unexploded bombs, or because there was danger from falling buildings or the fire engines blocked the way. It took us nearly an hour to find the place where our colleagues the 'A' team were working. (We were on the 'B' team, and are on call on alternate nights with 'A'.) At last we discovered them, working hard cutting sandwiches, loading the canteens and stoking the boilers so that hot water could be provided and soup made for the canteens to take out to the Civil Defence workers. (The Convoy's first duty is to feed these people and secondly to look after the homeless, but conditions were so disorganised in Liverpool and Bootle that it was impossible to differentiate and you fed all and sundry – babies, cats, dogs – who came to the canteen.)

After chatting for a few minutes, some of the Convoy were left at Rose Hill while others went on to Bootle. The author was one of two workers (plus a driver) on a canteen, which set to work that afternoon 'chiefly feeding the Auxiliary Fire Service, who had come from every part of the country – London, Wisbech, Northampton, etc. – and they had had nothing to eat since they arrived. It was drink that they chiefly wanted, and we had to go back twice to fill up the tea urns.'

The report goes on to describe some of the mayhem on the ground, including a crowd 'clamouring for food' who threatened to overwhelm one of the canteens. The police 'could not keep them back' and needed help from the men at a nearby First Aid post. The Convoy spent a fairly sleepless night in Bootle, which had sustained heavy damage. The following night they were given accommodation in the relative safety of Ormskirk, where they were to spend the next ten or eleven nights sleeping in the town hall. (Comfort at night was highly valued when days were often dangerous or at least dirty: three weeks earlier, when the Convoy was operating in Coventry, 'the vehicles had been taken to Warwick each night and the members had splendid billets at a children's convalescent home'.) 'The days passed very quickly. We used to leave Ormskirk at mid-day, have our meal at Bootle cooked by Army cooks who came early in the first week to help the Ministry of Food, go on duty about 1.00 p.m., and knock off at 9.30 and clean the canteens.' The correspondent thought that 'the cooks have the worst time on the Convoy as they are always near the boilers and get covered with smuts and smoke from the fires. Several times I helped to make sandwiches – we used 750 loaves a day and I don't know how many tins of corned beef.' In concluding her story, she regretted that 'I have probably missed out many amusing and interesting titbits', but 'it was a great experience and I would not have missed it for anything. Each time the Convoy is called out improvements will be made and the teams know what is expected of them and are keen to get on with their job.' Discipline, competence and effectiveness grew with experience.

This and other accounts of the work of canteens underscore a sense that the country was indeed pulling together; that women, many of them socially privileged, were putting themselves at some risk in order to lend a hand to others; that sacrifices were being shared, though of course not equally; that WVS members derived real satisfaction from being of use; and that individuals took some pride in overcoming and controlling their fears and hesitations, and being able to adjust to alarming, painful and sometimes tragic realities, or merely to the sorts of discomforts that had not usually come their way. During the months of the Blitz, as Norman Longmate wrote in 1971, 'respectable middle-aged ladies in WVS uniform could be seen asleep in the street on bomb-damaged doors resting on milk urns. As the girl in charge of the canteen from

Worcester reported, "she had never expected to be cooking stew in the main street of Coventry but she suddenly found herself doing something even more peculiar as she . . . brushed her teeth in the main square".[18]

The importance of mobile canteens and convoys as morale boosters was emphasised by the writer of a report on a very heavy raid on London's docklands in March 1941. The canteen, driven by a man and staffed by the writer and two young girls, 'neither of whom had been out in a raid before', left on its usual 'shelter feeding round':

> Flares hung over the whole of Deptford, and before the round had been going many minutes large fires had started. The canteen did an incredibly slow round, as every shelter was jammed to the door, for, besides our own people, there were hundreds of casuals who had come in from the street. There was, of course, no panic, but there was that feeling of rather grim fortitude which permeates a shelter on such nights. It would have done the givers of the canteens' hearts good if they could have heard the cry of 'here's our mobile' running up and down the crammed benches, and they would also have liked to have seen the two young girls come in radiantly from the crash and din outside, assuring every-one that it sounded much worse than it was.

There was a lot of pride in keeping brave faces, concealing fears and not letting others down. When the canteen reached a shelter under a railway arch in Deptford, where the bombing was particularly intense and fires proliferated, 'we had some trouble in not only getting full trays of hot drinks safely to the people that were needing them, but also in disguising how difficult it had been to get them in, as we were all over dirt and dust and a good deal of flying rubble from smashed houses'.

Later that night the canteen helped to aid injured people – around a dozen were on stretchers. 'Until just before the "all clear" the wounded were with us, as the fires and one thing and another made it impossible for them to get away, and all night ... the canteen succeeded in feeding and serving hot drinks, not only to our wounded but to the grimy, dog-tired stretcher party and the wardens.' Here was the sort of emergency, nobly handled, that was bound to generate solidarities: 'There was a touching tribute to the hard work it [the canteen] had done when the "all clear" went, for exhausted and tired though the men were, they insisted on carrying all the mugs back to the canteen and somehow, though it was incredible how they found the strength or the breath to do it, the men cheered it as it went away.'[19]

Facing danger and death together tended to bring out people's better qualities, and certainly their dispositions to generosity. In August 1940, with the Battle of Britain raging, the monthly report from Hornchurch in Essex noted that 'When we took the [canteen] car into the danger zones the men gave a cheer for the WVS, and again very much appreciated everything that was done for them, poor fellows. They had worked and laboured for many hours and needed refreshment badly.' Reports from the times of raids are suffused with a sense of plans being fulfilled and of people rising to the occasion. The WVS in Penarth, Glamorganshire took pride in their mobile canteen and 'large Thermot Urn', and after a heavy raid there on 4 March 1941 this equipment was said to be 'a God-send':

Hot drinks and sandwiches were served continuously for hours and the [WVS] workers were off again after only a short spell of rest, to provide breakfast for visiting firemen. The heads of services (rescue and demolition, wardens, gas and water services etc.) were greatly relieved to have the problem of food for their extra men solved so promptly and efficiently. The ARP canteen also was kept very busy all night until 5.30 a.m. and we are told that the town feels proud of our women who stayed in this frail bungalow building with not one tin hat between them, preparing the much needed refreshment for those working our of doors (and extinguishing incendiary bombs with a dust-bin lid between times).

The woman in charge of the hostels in Hull was the wife of a senior medical officer, who was killed in the raid on the city on 31 March 1941; it was reported no more than a few days later that she 'has pluckily returned to her post'.

Raids also triggered a demand for clothes. The WVS acted as agents for the distribution of clothing for the homeless, a task made much more rewarding when bales of clothing started to arrive from North America, mostly from the American Red Cross. 'I shall always remember', recalled a leader in the WVS, revisiting her experiences of London's Blitz, 'the pleasure that a pair of dark blue dungarees gave to a small boy who had lost his home; his sad experience seemed eclipsed by the novelty of this gift from America'.[20] In Camberwell, South London in late 1940, 'when the flow of homeless and destitute people was at its height, the WVS Clothing Depots worked from early morning to late at night outfitting families'. During October alone, it was said that 703 people were clothed at the depot, which was open daily, and 4314 garments given out. Further supplies went to Rest Centres and refugees.[21] The following year, in nearby and heavily bombed Lewisham, the WVS's clothing depot was well prepared to meet the needs of 'several hundred people at a moment's notice, so in order to do that quickly we have all the clothes sorted into different categories and labelled. It is therefore not necessary to try on every suit. We just measure a man and then ask him to choose a suit from those of the correct size.'[22]

Welsh experiences also showed the importance of these clothing depots. After the severe raid on Cardiff on 2 January 1941 'a large supply of clothing was taken to the [Rest] Centres by WVS workers with cars, and all necessitous cases supplied with immediate needs, and everything was done to make the people comfortable and happy'. Raids on Swansea in February and March made for many homeless people, and as a result all of March 'has been taken up with the clothing of the distressed people of Swansea'. By contrast, the WVS in Penarth took satisfaction from the fact that, after the 4 March 1941 raid on their town, 'very little help in the way of immediate clothing was needed – most people were up and dressed ready for the raid'.

Help was usually close at hand. Immediately after a repeat bombing of Coventry in April 1941, the following clothes had been received from nearby areas: from Stafford, fifty women's frocks, six skirts, several jerseys, seven men's jackets, twenty-three women's coats and 102 pairs of men's and women's shoes; from Sutton Coldfield, four dozen women's vests and four-and-a-half dozen women's knickers; and from Dudley, fifty women's frocks and sixty pairs of assorted shoes.[23] There was, too, an awareness that the recipients of the goods from clothing depots should not be treated like supplicants, and that even the dispossessed cared about how they looked, as a report from the north-west advised:

However busy the helpers are, their customers are always encouraged to have which they like of the things available. Small vanities, preferences, and weaknesses are sympathetically regarded as signs that a raid victim is feeling fairly normal again, and an old woman who timidly whispers "I suppose you haven't a shimmy, love? I don't feel dressed, like, without" is given the next best thing, a partly worn white shirt, and a note is made that there must be some old-fashioned undergarments in store for next time.

It was said that the women who worked in these clothing centres 'find a particular satisfaction in collecting the bundles of gift clothing that for many raid victims means a fresh start in life'.[24]

In April 1941 Plymouth was heavily attacked for five nights, leaving many people with only the clothes they stood up in – often nightwear or clothing tattered or partly torn away by blasts. 'For three weeks after the last of these raids the Clothing Depot was the centre of an endless stream of white-faced, weary women, many with bandaged heads and limbs, usually dressed in an old coat and dress borrowed from some kindly neighbour, of grimy unshaven men and crying, puzzled children worn out by the awful ordeal which they had been through.' The volunteers interviewed the victims and noted details on their losses and needs, 'all mingled with personal experiences', and

would then dash upstairs to try and find the necessary garments – not to the ordered shelves and sorted clothes that are the now recognised equipment of a depot [this account was written in 1943], but to piles of clothing seized upon by dressers before there was time to sort them, new and second-hand together, in those pre-coupon days, hastily laid trestle tables (and often knocked on to the floor by hurried helpers) – in rooms, the original depot having been blitzed, only taken over by the WVS a few days previously. Then, when the dresser returned to the waiting room and sought out 'her customers' from amongst the crowd, she was lucky if she still had the garments with her when she reached them, as eager hands would clutch them as she passed and exclaim, 'My, that's just the frock I want!', or a rival helper would seize a shirt and say, 'Oh, I've been hunting everywhere for that size!'

Some seven thousand people in Plymouth and Devonport were fitted out from WVS depots after these blitzes.[25]

In 1940–1 Bristol had a lot to contend with. Devastating raids on 25 November 1940 ripped apart large chunks of Bristol, including many of the city's fine buildings, dockyards and industries. There were reports of sinking morale and even defeatism, and conditions in the city in 1940–1 illustrate the range of problems confronted, and tasks undertaken, during those tumultuous months.[26] As usual, the WVS did what it could to help, though the city's Organiser, given the pressures encountered, was unable to submit her report to WVS head-quarters until two months after the first raids; and what she wrote on one page in tiny handwriting reveals a great deal. With an almost audible sigh she begins by saying that 'only Bristol's own evacuees' were dealt with from her office and that hundreds were left homeless by the raids. Eight weeks later most of them were living with relatives or friends or in hostels, or had left the city altogether. However, she thought that thousands in distress had been assisted in some way or other: soup kitchens and Rest Centres had been established all over the city; mobile canteens had daily fed hundreds of troops and demolition and AFS crews as well as civilians. At the time she was writing, in January 1941, the WVS was running twelve stationary canteens, which were feeding over two thousand per day, and 'mobile canteens visit military posts supplying

between 2000 and 3000 troops weekly' – hot dinners were
provided at some, light refreshments at others. Three new
nursery schools had been opened, accommodating around
three hundred children; numerous clothing depots were functioning; many members were using 'their own cars for every
possible purpose' and sometimes at the request of other organisations; a new hospital supply depot had opened, though only
after two others had been destroyed in the raids 'with much
valuable material and stores'; and members continued to be
involved in knitting for the troops, collecting toys and scrap
metal, assembling gas masks, driving ambulances and sustain-
ing the Housewives' Service.[27]

Here, then, was a pretty full range of WVS activities, some
directly a consequence of the raids, others a continuation of
prior work.*

Another narrative, written by the WVS Organiser of the
Clifton district of Bristol, a suburb abutting the famous sus-
pension bridge, records her hectic life during and after the
blitzes of 24–5 November and 2 December 1940. Her efforts
on the occasion of the first attack included visiting elderly and
infirm people in a hospital 'who had been removed to safety on
the backs of Wardens and firemen' and checking on WVS
operations at various hostels and bomb sites. Many homes had
no water: 'One worker said she saw a woman in a queue for
water with a baby in arms and two other children and she went
and got the woman's utensil filled and so enabled her to go
home. There were many deeds of this sort.' At Clifton's clothing depot 'Miss Marden was very busy and did good work. She

---

*WVS interventions were not always appreciated: in Guildford in May 1941, after
bombing left twenty-five houses uninhabitable, it was reported that 'Members of
the Housewives' Service in the only Ward that has it gave help in clearing up
homes in damaged area. Not very welcome owing to Englishwomen's independence and dislike of strangers in the home.'

said the gratitude was touching – the wish "not to be greedy" was most distressing.' On 2 December, 'all hands [were] again on duty helping the firemen with drinks (tea or coffee) as soon as it was clear'. She found one ARP group 'absolutely exhausted for want of food' and arranged for a canteen to visit them; and she reported that 'in the Westbury district women made a chain of their pails of water to help the firemen extinguish a fire'. 'Many deeds of kindness from neighbour to neighbour were rendered and the WVS Housewives Service has done much to break the barrier of unfriendliness and to get the hand of brotherhood extended'. She added a postscript: 'I personally put one incendiary out and burnt my coat!'[28]

Later testimony from Bristol's WVS Organiser, from the spring of 1941, mentions new projects and experiences in a typically wide-ranging file of post-raid activities. The most recent serious raid had been on 12–13 April. Children had been evacuated to Devon and Cornwall, with escorts provided by the WVS – some of the evacuees were fitted with clothes and boots before leaving; a new nursery school was started for the children under three of homeless people; concerts and entertainments were arranged for evacuated and temporarily housed people; and the WVS organised a voluntary telephone service for rescue squads and 'a lost property office to help evacuated people trace their furniture etc.' 'We wrote to the local laundries to send us their unclaimed linen, towels etc.' for the nurseries and hostels 'and the response was splendid – beyond expectation'. (A line written at the bottom of this page – the Narrative Report for March/April – mentions that 'a time-bomb just outside our office for eight days delayed sending in of report!') The following month another initiative is mentioned: 'The first batch of over 100 bombed-out or overstrained mothers and children left last week for a fortnight's rest at Sidmouth. WVS is cooperating with the Health

Authority in arranging for others to follow to various places by the sea or to holiday camps in the country at regular intervals throughout the summer.' Meanwhile, 'the Queen's Messengers for the Region have arrived and are being kept at Weston for service at any time. They are believed to be at Plymouth at this moment.'[29]

Bombing raids tended to be social levellers, in a variety of ways. Certainly they often brought people from different backgrounds face to face with one another and forced into the public eye – or at least the eyes of women of means – the lives and living conditions of labouring and struggling families. On Thursday 15 May 1941, just a few days after one of the most destructive raids on London – and the last really big one for years, though of course no one could know this – Helen Lloyd, the Centre Organiser for the Guildford Rural District, along with two of her equally genteel colleagues, all in full WVS uniform, toured Wapping in east London. They visited a feeding centre, and at midday 'there was a great rush and we were asked to help serve. For an hour we acted as waitresses – it was a rush as the men were only allowed 20 minutes off time for their meal. We were amazed at their politeness. Every man said "Thank you" when he was given his plate, no one was impatient, no one grumbled or tried to cheat over payment. The food was excellent.' The three women were then taken on a walking tour of Wapping by their host, a Father Young – 'the most wonderful person I have come across', thought Miss Lloyd, who was not given to extravagant praise. They looked at the 'pitiful shattered houses and empty docks', the rubble, the 'piles of charred hemp', the 'shuttered shops'; and above all she was impressed by the 'people, charming and kindly and brave. I cannot use the expression "courage" – that to my mind implies grimly sticking to it with forced gaiety. These people were too warmly human, too natural, too kindly for such high sounding phrases. Everyone ragged us, everyone was pleased to see us and eager to talk, especially of Guildford where many people from Wapping had been sent.'

Later in the afternoon the three women toured some night shelters. 'I was surprised at the cleanliness, absence of smell and comparative freshness of the air', although 'we were seeing everything under the worst conditions – no electric current, consequently no fans or light, and no water'. The third shelter they visited, a former wine vault, 'was the deepest and sup-posedly the most safe of the shelters, but there were some grim touches. We walked through a hall in which lavatory buckets stood against the wall, naked of screening, though this room was a huge vault which was used for dances on Saturday night.' A new shelter had just been opened to accommodate 'the habituées' of another shelter that had that morning suffered damage from rising sewage water. There were conversations between the visitors and the locals and 'everyone treated us with a friendly equality' – a familiarity that perhaps would not have been entirely welcomed in peacetime. Arriving home in Albury, Surrey at around midnight, Helen 'felt almost ashamed to have a hot bath and to sink to rest in a silk nightie in a lux-uriously soft bed'. She said it was 'one of the most interesting days I have spent during the war'.

A similar admiration for those outside one's social class was expressed for the work of women during raids in the north-west, many of them working class. In getting from their homes to the Rest Centres, 'some wore enamel basins, some chose colanders when they went through falling shrapnel and worse, their only official uniform a WVS initialled armband, wearing, as rule, their everyday aprons and overalls. During the first days and nights it was the housewives of the industrial districts, in the main, who staffed the Centres, brewing tea and cocoa by candlelight, sometimes with water they had to collect, often on a coal fire they had built themselves.'[30] A crisis put a premium on creative responses – what one observer called 'heroic improvisation' – and these gestures of creativity and courage were observed from all levels of society.

No doubt the WVS workers in raided cities took with them deep impressions of fellow citizens under siege and vivid memories of life on the edge of death. Who would not have been powerfully affected by working at the canteen sent to a mortuary 'to feed the long lines of anxious seekers for the missing'?[31] After the serious bombing of Bristol in late 1940 the local WVS Organiser in Clifton remarked that the homeless victims 'were still full of British pluck and courage, with sad faces at losing their all but brightening up and saying "After all, we have our lives"'.[32] The WVS Centre Organiser in the London borough of St Pancras, writing after the war, recalled the behaviour of the bombing victims in 1940–1: 'I was so very impressed with the courage and patience of the people who had just suffered the ordeal of a bad raid and loss of their homes. All behaved generally calmly and the old ones were magnificent.'[33] Some witnesses were struck by the displays of fortitude and resilience and determination, others by stoicism or even humour. They saw tragic losses – children who had just been orphaned, a mother killed with a baby in her arms, whole families wiped out – as well as almost pathetic instances of gratitude and docility, especially from the poor. What most influenced Esme Glyn, the WVS author of 'Impressions of the London Blitz', was

the deep humility shown by simple people who without choice found themselves fighting in the front line of the war. I cannot forget how miserable I felt when I heard the story of the charwoman who stayed on dusting one morning at the Admiralty after the other cleaners had left. When the Under Secretary arrived and found her in his room, he asked why she was so late in getting away and she replied that she had just lost her little girl and her house and felt now that her work was the only thing left to her. After this little speech she went on dusting.[34]

CHAPTER 4

RECOVERY 1940–1

British society held together in 1940–1, and solidarities were almost certainly strengthened. However, many citizens were left bereaved, or wounded, or homeless – and clearly in need of social support. Wreckage, human and material, had to be patched up as quickly as possible. 'More and more evacuees are arriving every day . . . all needing help and advice': these were the opening words of the March 1941 Narrative Report from Westmorland. This was the third wave of wartime evacuation in Britain and very different from the first two, as from September 1940 many of the evacuees were not just distancing themselves from danger but actually in dire – and literal – need of a roof over their heads. There were, as well, many needs in the cities that had been blitzed. Damaged sites had to be repaired, at least to the point that some degree of normal functioning could be restored – the routine provisioning of basic necessities and the rebuilding of transport and other essential public services. This chapter discusses the diverse jobs and coping strategies that were found almost everywhere, to varying degrees, in 1940–1 and frequently involved in some way or other members of the WVS.

Britons were better prepared to deal with the challenges of evacuation than they had been in September 1939. Lessons had been learned and it was hoped that certain problems, such as timely medical examinations of evacuees, would be handled more effectively. A government circular of 25 March 1940 acknowledged bedwetting with a new sensitivity:

> Bedwetting is more frequent when the child is frightened or nervous, as for instance immediately after arriving in a new home. If further evacuation has to take place it must be anticipated that a number of the new arrivals may suffer from bedwetting during the first few days, though the condition will tend to disappear as the children settle down. Billeting Officers should, therefore, see that householders are well supplied with mackintosh overlays. A simple leaflet on the subject for distribution to householders has been prepared by Women's Voluntary Services.[1]

The context for billeting had also changed. From September 1940 it probably aroused less hostility than a year before since those now to be re-housed were usually evacuees from necessity, not choice. As the Organiser of heavily bombed Portsmouth put it in December 1940, 'It pays to acquaint beforehand the hostess with some description of or particulars regarding the family to be billeted ... People who have *seen* the destruction caused to homes are more sympathetic and willing to accept and overlook the shortcomings of the poor folks billeted on them.' There was a heightened sense of unity, greater acknowledgement of the importance of pulling together, and an awareness that sacrifices needed to be made by all in pursuit of their national duty. This sort of thinking was already embedded in the sense of mission that Lady Reading had assiduously fostered in the WVS, and many members were girding themselves for the times ahead. On 14 September 1940 one WVS member wrote a letter from Alton, Hampshire about a room that she was furnishing at the back of her office: 'in the event of many refugees coming to Alton I shall find it a great boon for them. I have been able to collect a number of garments and also some baby clothes, and already I have had people from London who have arrived in Alton with nothing but the clothes they have on their backs.'[2]

Similar preparations were underway, or already in place, in hundreds of communities, and tens of thousands of people had by this time become evacuees. In Ely, by the end of October 1940, it was said that 'there are over 1000 known evacuees in the town and nearly every house has either relations or friends from the East Coast or London'. Half a year later, in April 1941, it was estimated that evacuees had increased Ely's normal population of eight thousand by around 33 per cent. By February 1941 a little over 1.3 million persons were living as evacuees in the reception areas of England and Wales, and in getting there and settling in it is probable that most of them (especially those officially evacuated) had some contact with the WVS.

In Bath, much of September 1940 was consumed with the reception, housing, feeding, and clothing of refugees from London, as well as from Hastings and St Leonard's in East Sussex. Lists of billets had already been prepared, largely in case local people were made homeless; now these lists were used to house outsiders, a change that was not universally popular in Bath. Some needs remained unmet, however, notably those of larger families and individuals who were considered 'unsuitable to be billeted upon others'. To accommodate those without billets the town clerk made available houses and rooms owned by the city, on condition that the WVS furnished them. 'We pride ourselves in getting a house ready to be slept in at 48 hours,' said the Centre Organiser, according to a newspaper account attached to the Narrative Report for October.[3] Appeals were made for donations of bedding and furniture, and when the response proved inadequate the clerk empowered the WVS to make the necessary purchases. Welfare workers checked on the evacuees' circumstances, bought any additional items required to make the billet habitable and added the newcomers' names to the existing list of people to be visited on a regular basis. (This was all being done at a time of when private evacuations added to housing pressures, for many residents were taking in relatives or friends from cities at risk.)

Most of these displaced people would have arrived in Bath with few personal belongings, and the WVS clothing depot's admirable state of preparedness made possible the supplying of clothes to newcomers without disturbing the ongoing work of clothing those evacuees who were already in the city. The front page of the *Bath Weekly Chronicle and Herald* for 19 October 1940 featured a large photograph of a young child being newly clothed by a WVS member, along with a message to readers appealing for clothes for evacuees. Meanwhile, a lengthy report on the clothing depot in the daily *Bath and Wilts Chronicle and Herald* for Tuesday 17 December highlighted the growing need for clothes as more bombed-out people arrived in the city. Much of the depot's stock in Bath, as in many places, was in fact supplied by the American Red Cross.*

While coping with the sudden influx of evacuees in September and October 1940, Bath's WVS managed to continue with other work. It was negotiating with female ARP

*See also Appendix A.

wardens to establish a Housewives' Service in the city, supplying cars and drivers to take troops from the Emergency
Hospital to concerts and other recreations, and providing
workers at two canteens, one run by the YMCA, the other at
the Friends' Meeting House. Members also handled a large
volume of clerical work, including tracking every ounce of
wool issued by the Admiralty for knitting sailors' boot socks.
They also made items for the hospital supply depot, as well as
armlets and comforts for the Home Guard: in mid-November
1940 a notice was published by the WVS working party in
nearby Bathampton giving detailed statistics on the more than
one thousand articles they had produced during the previous
year.[4] The WVS ran the only authorised aluminium depot in
Bath; it provided helpers in the kitchen at the emergency hospital, 'scrubbing tables or cleaning vegetables'; and some
members worked regularly at the ARP office, fitting, repairing and disinfecting gas masks. By September 1940 about 2100
women were enrolled in Bath's WVS, a city of some seventy-
nine thousand people.[5]

In some reception areas the huge influx of uprooted people
was almost overwhelming. In Oxford the WVS Organiser
reported in September 1940 that 'it is difficult to give any
coherent report of the work of the last month as the flood of
refugees and evacuees has absorbed all the energies of the local
authorities and the WVS'. As a well-facilitated city close to
London, Oxford attracted many new residents. The roughly
nine thousand evacuees in Oxford were distributed temporarily in halls across the city and another five to six hundred
unaccompanied schoolchildren were housed in the town hall.
These were soon followed by a stream of unofficial refugees –
people who had self-evacuated rather than been requested to
do so – many of whom were housed in a large cinema just
outside the city. The WVS helped out with food, logistics and

the collection of fruit, vegetables and donated clothing. Their members cared for mothers, children and old people; transported people and luggage to billets; helped with children's activities; provided forty-four meals a day for an ARP rescue squad; staffed the mobile canteen that was 'finished just in time for use in the emergency'; and, at the request of local doctors, conducted a door-to-door canvass of streets near the Radcliffe Infirmary which identified 250 potential blood donors.

Over the remaining months of 1940 most evacuees in Oxford were found billets locally, or were moved to homes outside the city. The WVS refined and expanded its services, particularly in ways that would brighten the lives of its newest and youngest residents. Clubs for mothers and children were set up across the city, and by November nearly all of these clubs had started working parties to encourage mothers to make their own and their children's clothes. WVS members helped in nurseries to entertain infants as their mothers worked, chatted and enjoyed tea. A Mrs Labey, herself recently evacuated from London, took over the management of the rescue squad kitchen to serve emergency workers. New Rest Centres were set up; a WVS-staffed control room canteen was opened in the town hall to be available for air raid casualties; and WVS cars were 'kept continuously busy' acting as escorts to billets, railways and hospitals, moving furniture, driving VIPS and other officials and transporting everything from blood to blankets. As 1940 drew to a close, Christmas parties took 'pride of place' in the city. The parties were officially run by the Evacuation Committee of Welfare Organisers, but the WVS gave its services in support of nearly all of these festivities, including an event for over five hundred at the Majestic Cinema, a party for evacuee children at which Polish airmen stationed nearby were scheduled to perform, and the serving of full Christmas dinners for both shifts of the ARP rescue squad.

Evacuees also poured into Cambridge, as the WVS noted in October 1940: 'Our work has grown so much in the last month that we have been trying to reorganise our permanent staff so that running of the office shall be as smooth as possible.' The Centre Organiser was freed to focus on policy and make visits to the various WVS enterprises to check on their progress and assure them that their services were valued; the paid secretary focused on typing and the sorting of enrolment forms; and other leaders were given clearly enumerated responsibilities and each a designated deputy in recognition of the fact that few volunteers could devote full days to their work. One person was to be responsible for all the interviewing of potential staff and the crucial task of fitting the right person to the right job, as 'we found that people interviewed were too often left without the right job or, worse still, given the wrong one'. The Centre Organiser now reviewed each new enrolment card daily and passed it on to the person in charge of matching a woman to appropriate work.

Not everything worked smoothly. A last-minute change of plans had the Cambridge WVS scrambling to care for three hundred evacuated mothers and children for forty-eight hours while a replacement was found for the intended reception centre that had just been taken over by the Addenbrooke's Hospital. That first night sirens so alarmed one or two mothers 'who had expected Cambridge to be completely peaceful' that they needed special reassurance. Much luggage was lost and necessities such as nappies and toothbrushes had to be found quickly. Wartime emergencies were quick to break down social barriers and provide new perspectives, and Cambridge was no exception, as the Centre Organiser described:

We had a very mixed band of helpers: one might see on one side a woman Professor gravely mixing a baby's feed, a

Member of Parliament's wife rushing out to buy a dummy, which the mother insisted upon having in spite of all the tactful persuasion that such things were unhygienic. The helpers enjoyed the experience very much and were quite sorry when the last family – three brothers' wives and their 11 children – were seen off on a bus.

Other work was more trying. The twelve billeting officers (WVS members working on behalf of the local authority) were overwhelmed by the surge of evacuees and new officers had to be appointed when senior voluntary workers refused to perform the unpleasant task of compulsory billeting. Many people's nerves were, understandably, on edge, and the WVS leader in charge reported that 'It is becoming increasingly difficult to supply them [billeting officers] with full-time friendly visitors, of whom more and more tact is demanded!' Despite these strains, the WVS was successful in establishing social schemes that were an important supplement to official evacuee provisions, helping evacuees settle in and boosting their morale. Four city wards held mothers' clubs, two had nursery centres and two provided laundry facilities; one offered a keep-fit class along with lectures, sewing, knitting, community singing, speakers and other entertainment, and another opened a weekly pensioners' club for men and women. One dinner club was set up to offer communal meals every weekday, and a second was in the planning stage.

Nearly a year later, in September 1941, the WVS and its twelve ward billeting officers had been partly relieved of the job of finding new accommodation by the six survey officers newly appointed by the Chief Billeting Officer who made lists of all possible billets. This was a necessity now that accommodation pressures had increased with the arrival of large numbers of war workers and their families. Around five thousand evacuees from the raids of late 1940 remained in Cambridge, some hundreds were accommodated in fifty requisitioned houses and others in three hostels. (One hostel was for 'difficult' children and the other two were buffer hostels for mothers and children; these were meant to provide housing until other arrangements were made: perhaps, for example, while a pregnant woman was waiting to have her baby or until she was fit enough to travel after delivery.) By this time the Cambridge WVS was well enough organised to ensure that all evacuees were visited once a month and a clothing liaison officer regularly looked into the garment situation in each of the city's seventeen Rest Centres. Much had improved, but there were losses. Two WVS workers were killed while on warden duty early in 1941; many younger part-time workers were called up for official national service; and more women were finding it hard to commit as much time to WVS work, especially if billeted evacuees or war workers increased their domestic workloads.

In the spring of 1941 Cambridge's WVS reported that there was 'a tremendous amount of work to be done on all sides and not enough first-class full time unpaid women to go round'. 'Too often', the report added, 'we find the very capable woman has not the tact to get on with other people' and that 'women are getting tired and feeling the strain of war-time conditions, especially in getting food', given the growing challenge of coping with rationing.[6] Indeed, staffing would become an increasing preoccupation of the Women's Voluntary Services across the country.

A report of 8 April 1941 on 'Evacuee Welfare Work' summarises what had been done in the city of Nottingham. The WVS there had a visiting staff of eight, few of whom had done such work before. Each evacuated family had been visited at least once, partly to advise on their rights and the city's welfare facilities, such as the Citizens' Advice Bureau, and partly to assess the family's needs. 'When clothes and bedding are needed, evacuees are helped by the WVS direct. Londoners bombed out of their homes and in need of clothes are supplied from the National Union of Girls' Clubs, 39 Park Row. Evacuees from other bombed areas are supplied from the clothing store at the City WVS [Centre]. Bedding is loaned to evacuees who have their furniture intact elsewhere, and those whose homes and belongings have been destroyed are given bedding and furniture if it is needed.' The Centre Organiser did not pretend that all had worked out as she had wished. Some evacuees had been in the city for months before they were visited by the WVS, and 'although a special point has been made of visiting expectant mothers first, many have had their babies well on the way to being weaned by the time our visitors had arrived!' There were also problems associated with families 'who had taken empty houses and had no furniture' as well as those with five or more children – 'a billet which could cope with such numbers is most difficult to find'.

In Leicestershire, the WVS was particularly busy as, during September and October 1940, the county received and found billets for thirty-five to forty thousand people from London, Ipswich, and other parts of coastal East Anglia. Efficient reception of the Ipswich evacuees was made more difficult when trains, scheduled to arrive at hourly or two-hourly intervals and for which full arrangements to meet them had been made, were cancelled at the last minute. Still, most of the homeless were received as planned, given refreshments, found overnight accommodation and then served breakfast before they were taken to their billets. In October, a quarter of the eight thousand evacuees from London 'were hop-pickers from Kent, and much extra work was entailed in the reception of these people. Notice was sent to the Medical Officer of Health that they would require bathing and re-clothing.' The response to an appeal in the local press for clothing had been 'magnificent', and included stocks of underwear and shoes donated by local manufacturers. In September, two conferences were held in Nottingham to help the Midlands' WVS Centre Organisers make the most of their resources in serving the refugees.

All the while all the other WVS work continued in Leicestershire – knitting, sewing, canteens, hospital supply, the rapid evolution of the recent Neighbours' League, precursor of the later Housewives' Service, and the enrolment of new members. The County Organiser was very busy; she attended eighteen meetings in six weeks and, tellingly, reported that some WVS volunteers 'have become so seriously overworked that they feel they cannot carry on further with the billeting side of the scheme on a voluntary basis', adding that their services were so valued that, in most cases, 'the necessary adjustments have been made by the Councils concerned'. Work at the clothing depot had become a full-time job and a Mrs Stopper (presumably a former WVS volunteer) was appointed to take charge, with one full-time and several part-time assistants.

Emergency Rest Centres were a major concern during these months. Leicestershire's WVS, working in close cooperation with local authorities, developed detailed instructions for the running of a Rest Centre, which advised that the individual in charge was to 'recruit sufficient staff so that there will be at least ten persons in the Centre on the sounding of the siren'.[7] Meanwhile, looking after the evacuees remained the central challenge. Four bathing stations were opened and a large skip of clothing sent to each. First Aid personnel oversaw the bathing arrangements, assisted by the WVS. Thirty WVS members reported to De Montfort Hall to lay and clear tables and serve meals, and later they were relieved by a second shift. Further teams were responsible for the care of babies and toddlers, as well as their supervision while their mothers bathed. 'Owing to the large numbers of mothers and children, the majority of whom are suffering from the appalling experiences of recent bombing, who are sheltered one night in the Hall', it was decided to have a doctor and two nurses in attendance during the night, along with special constables and First Aid squads 'to cope with any emergency that may arise'. One can imagine the chaotic scene of distressed, perhaps injured, and sometimes traumatised people that this description glides over. The next morning all were fed and some sent to the schools where, after medical examinations, billeting was arranged. Those who remained needed lunch, supper and perhaps another night's accommodation. Entertainment was laid on each evening. 'The ARP Concert Party gave great pleasure to the hop pickers, and we have also had the Salvation Army Band, an organ recital and community singing.' It was thought important to try to distract people from their woes.

Leicester itself was bombed in the third week of November, which concentrated energies on the staffing and organisation of additional Rest Centres. There had originally been nine, later eleven on the night of raids and fifteen would be in place by the beginning of December. A rota system was set up and more volunteers were sought, including people prepared to sleep in canteens in case their services were needed overnight. There were active work parties to make garments from material and wools supplied by the American Red Cross, including many in which evacuee mothers worked along with local volunteers. Instructions were given out to publicise aggressively the locations of Rest Centres so that local people would know where to go in the event of a raid. By now, the vital importance of accurate information was well understood and volunteers tried their best to secure detailed information about families and individuals before passing their charges and the responsibility for their welfare on to others. The 1941 brochure on Rest Centres (included with the Narrative Report of January/February 1941 for Leicestershire) also included advice on the value of hot drinks (almost always hot, strong tea with lots of sugar and milk) to 'alleviate shock, and restore confidence', the desirability of keeping mothers and young children apart from the elderly 'especially if children are fretful', and explicit instructions about clearing the Rest Centre by half-past two in the afternoon, if at all possible.

In September 1940 Bedfordshire's WVS reported a virtual inundation of refugees. By the end of that month at least twenty-two thousand evacuees had arrived in the county, with 70 per cent of them in the four towns of Bedford, Biggleswade, Dunstable and Luton. WVS reports have (understandably) a breathless quality, as it and other welfare bodies struggled to meet the ever-growing demands upon them. The mobile canteen was out every day, and there were 146 work parties, though many were 'waiting patiently for wool and raw material that has not yet arrived'. All this work took a toll on the residents. According to the deputy Centre Organiser in Bedford, 'The September story is one of expansion of services and contraction of the supply of available volunteers who have found their homes filled to capacity by evacuation. Reorganisation on a wide scale is necessary to suit new conditions.' To help ease the strains and maintain as many volunteers as possible, the town's billeting officers 'have agreed to give every consideration to the type of refugee put in homes where women are out on National Service and the women are being urged to send their evacuees to the canteens on the days they are on duty'. This was a problem faced elsewhere: with evacuees in a house, the resident housekeeper was less likely to have the time or energy for outside jobs, which were suddenly crying out for takers.

The arrival in a community of hundreds or even thousands of newcomers put pressure on services of all kinds. In November 1940 refugees in Bedford were 'encouraged to offer their services' at one of the canteens and WVS helpers were engaged to staff a just-opened guest house, run by the churchwardens of St Paul's parish, where 'beds have been booked by London firms for restful weekends for employees'. Bedford became so busy that, by the middle of the month, a journalist visiting from the *Star* dubbed it 'Evacuation Town' and a BBC reporter arrived to take recordings at the busy clothing depot and central canteen, snippets of which were heard after the six o'clock news on 1 December. In March 1941, after detailing the wide range of work done by the WVS in the county town, the deputy organiser concluded with the statement, 'Above all, we act as a centre which can refer bewildered people to an agency which can help them. We try never to turn anyone away without some positive aid, if only advice.'

Leighton Buzzard, another Bedfordshire town, was similarly busy, as the WVS's monthly reports attest. During September 1940 the small town received over eight hundred refugees and 'had to open a temporary feeding and sleeping centre for them, which is being run by us under instruction from the Public Assistance Authorities in Bedford'. Blankets were in such short supply that the WVS sent a loudspeaker van round the town to appeal for them, and 'although we had a very good response, we still need many more'. By the end of October the number of homeless had risen to 1350 and the WVS Centre was open daily 'so that the refugees who are in billets may come to us for advice on many and varied subjects and we assist them in every way possible. We have at the moment about a dozen people living in the shelter and have been unable to find billets for them in spite of

our unceasing efforts in this direction.' Efforts were under
way to set up a recreational and occupational centre for the
displaced women, and by December this club was said to be
'meeting a real need and our numbers are increasingly
weekly. We now have 80 regular members and numerous sets
of underwear have been made by the women for themselves
out of some material given by the American Red Cross.' In
January 1941 this club was said to be 'still flourishing', and
making comforts for the troops, 'which we are holding in
reserve so that we can give them to any men in the locality
who may be needing them', while in March its members
were 'busy making frocks and knickers for the girls for the
warmer weather'.

The WVS in Leighton Buzzard was also lobbying to get a
Communal Feeding Centre* started in early 1941, but felt that
the local authorities were dragging their feet: 'the lapse of time
is very distressing to us as we feel it would solve some of the
billeting difficulties'. (Evidence from August/September 1941
suggests that the WVS had strained relations with the male
members of the Council.) Washing facilities were also required
since the town had no public baths, but despite WVS efforts
their provision was not approved until August. In February
1941 the WVS was called upon to open their canteen to servicemen in the area, 'and several mornings we have had to
serve over 250 troops in a period of 20 minutes. This seemed
very hectic at first, but we are beginning to get used to the
rush.' Here was one of many instances when the needs of those
in uniform were added to the urgent needs of civilians. In
August 1941 it was reported that 'the number of troops posted
in this area has recently greatly increased and we have had to

---

*This naming was disliked by Churchill, and later changed to British Restaurant.
For more detail on the British Restaurants, see Chapter 5.

allot some more volunteers to work in the canteen in order to cope with the rush'.

By the time the heads of departments met at the Bedford WVS office on 11 March 1941, much progress had been made in the county's readiness to meet the challenges of what might prove to be a long war. Between March 1940 and the end of February 1941 the Mill Street canteen in Bedford had served 46,886 meals and was well equipped to continue its work. The Housewives' Service was now fairly well established throughout the county, including in most villages. There were six social centres, mostly kept going by the WVS; two new nurseries had been started; another old people's home was planned; and evacuee women were helping out at one of the canteens. Most of the eighty-five pints of blood drawn each week by the Bedford branch of the blood transfusion service, which was partly staffed by the WVS, went to make dried plasma for use by the armed forces. Bedford's WVS had learned from the experience of others: one leader's experience in Cambridge highlighted the merit of storing emergency clothing stores at each Rest Centre and the practical and diplomatic advantages of wearing a WVS uniform at times of emergency 'as it might help in getting into special areas or help people to recognise you and be ready to ask for help in the street'.

Perhaps the most significant lessons learned or reinforced were those of diplomacy, tact and empathy. The backbone of the WVS was its commitment to face-to-face interactions – keeping people informed, soliciting funds for any number of charities and flag days, straightening out the inevitable frictions between foster parents and visiting parents, trying to resolve tensions between evacuees and those in whose crowded homes they lived. There was also the happiness of soldiers to think about. One woman at this meeting in Bedford 'asked if it was possible to have a list of people willing to put up soldiers' wives at weekends', an acknowledgement of the strains imposed on marriages in wartime.[8]

The sudden influx of people into one place from somewhere else meant that normal services often did not have enough staff to keep them running, and that the WVS was called upon to fill these gaps. It was reported from Swansea in December 1940 that 'eight members go every day from 10 a.m. to 7 p.m.' to the Langland Bay Hospital Annexe 'to help in the wards and with the evacuee block. Two of our members help the Sister of the Hospital Annexe with the stores. They are on duty every day.' There was also a need for special services, including social centres for evacuees. According to Leicestershire's County Organiser in November 1940, such facilities had already been opened in over fifty places and 'the evacuees are joining in the social life of the villages where they are living. The centres are proving most helpful in keeping the mothers in touch with each other and in providing them with occupation.' Other work focused on basic comforts: in November 1940 one WVS Centre was 'harvesting bracken to fill the American palliase covers', which would mainly go to homeless people.[9] From time to time hundreds of evacuees would suddenly descend by train on a town in South Wales, needing immediate assistance (which the WVS provided) before they continued on to their billets. Similar assistance was given in Bristol, where from October 1940 the Housewives' Service was asked several times to meet children travelling through the city, 'to give them hospitality for the night and to put them on the right train for their destination. Billets in all cases [were] found and children met and fed and put on their way.'[10] Meanwhile, in Dewsbury in June 1941 the WVS staffed an 'Emergency Rest Centre for [the] reception and feeding of about 80 London evacuees (mothers and children) who were afterwards billeted in the neighbourhood'.

Occasionally needy members of the forces would descend on a community. This happened in a rural district south of Gainsborough, Lincolnshire in January 1941, when 'a convoy of troops in motor lorries passed through the village almost continuously for two days during the very cold weather' and a temporary canteen was improvised. The vehicles of the convoy stopped from time to time and 'WVS, assisted by most of the village, gave the men hot drinks and all the weekend cakes and pastries they had made for their families. They wished that they had had unlimited supplies to give away.' After the raids on Bristol in late 1940 the WVS was 'responsible for the feeding of troops brought in to guard the Town at night'.[11] This help, whether temporary, as in these cases, or more regular, as when soldiers were stationed for a few months in a community or when fresh produce was sent from the gardens of WVS members to the sailors manning minesweepers, was a means of being patriotic and aiding the war effort, and was almost always a source of much personal satisfaction to the WVS and other helpers.

Some WVS work was heavily dependent on foreign aid: reports are full of references to the practical generosity of Britain's allies, in particular the United States (not yet a formal ally), Canada and Australia. In April/May 1941 Luton received a gift of sheets, pillowcases and quilts from the Canadian Red Cross and distributed them 'with a letter of appreciation to householders who have billeted unaccompanied evacuee children over a long period'; the following month the WVS 'personally distributed 50 Canadian bedspreads' to these 'hostesses' and 'a number of letters of thanks are being sent to Canada'. The tea given to evacuees in Sandy, Bedfordshire in April/May 1941 was sweetened with sugar and syrup donated by the American Red Cross. Food items such as Spam, dried eggs and evaporated milk soon became staples of the British wartime diet, but occasionally instruction would have to be sought as to how to use some of the less familiar donations, such as grits from the Southern United States.

The American Red Cross was indeed a major supplier of goods to beleaguered British civilians. Clothing, bedding and fabrics became ever more valued as domestic shortages worsened and many people's slender supplies of garments were lost to German bombs. By the middle of 1941 60 per cent of the supplies in WVS clothing depots came from overseas.[12] In December 1940 one little boy in Marshland, Norfolk was so pleased by what he had just been given that he 'wanted to go to bed directly he saw his little sleeping suit made from American Ripple cloth'; the wish was not granted since it was only half-past ten in the morning. The more sophisticated children of Ely were less than impressed by a – much-needed – donation of boots in October 1940 because the American footwear was 'different'.

In addition to these gifts from overseas, the WVS and local authorities tried their best to make newcomers feel welcome and comfortable. In Hitchin, Hertfordshire in the autumn of 1940 the county council was providing railway vouchers to enable families to return home, or to travel farther afield to join families or relatives, and churches and the general public supplied fruit, flowers and vegetables. In the Suffolk town of Thingoe, two fish and chip vans were up and running by the end of 1940. They had been started with the idea of giving the evacuees from London 'food to which they were accustomed', as well as providing a nourishing diet in a rural area with a scattered population, in which food could not be cooked at central sources. The experiment was a great success and this archetypical East London comfort food was made available in fifty Suffolk villages.

The Centre Organiser in Marshland, Norfolk thought well of the self-help attitudes of the women evacuated there and in December 1940 regretted that they were not better accommodated. Her WVS had 'rather a lot of trouble this past month trying to make mothers and children comfortable in requisitioned houses that were formerly condemned. These houses should not be used for the unfortunate evacuees, especially as they are not considered fit dwellings for the local inhabitants.' In the same county, in and around Fakenham, which had received almost a thousand evacuees, there was the fairly common problem of finding suitable housing for large families and not splitting them up, and the WVS Organiser reported in October 1940 that she felt the evacuation authorities had erred and caused disappointment in promising these families housing when 'there are not nearly enough empty cottages to go round'. But overall her assessment was positive:

> In almost every single case the country people in this district have given their guests a wonderful welcome. Besides doing all they can to make them comfortable, they have mended their shoes, and one cannot stop them making, giving and lending them clothes. Prams and push chairs are a problem; all available ones have been gladly lent and wherever possible we are getting the mothers to send home for theirs. It is of course the worst time of the year to make townsfolk like the country, and many of them seem almost more afraid of mud than bombs. However, they are thankful for peaceful nights and many are already looking quite different in consequence.

Occasionally one comes across reports from a Centre Organiser who was exceptionally sensitive to the implications of evacuation for the parties involved, and one of these comes from the Frome Rural District in Somerset. In October 1940 evacuees were flooding into the district and housing them was a major challenge; while arms were certainly twisted, so far there had been no resort to compulsory billeting. All sorts of circumstances had to be considered. 'Farms are particularly difficult; frequently several empty bedrooms, but no possibility of separate living rooms, and the busy harassed farmer's wife finds it hard to put up with unoccupied women and children hanging about the place, with habits of behavior and cleanliness far below her own. The evacuees, too, are despondent over the isolation and seas of mud.' While placing unaccompanied children was not too difficult, accommodation for family parties 'is becoming extremely rare'. The Centre Organiser also pointed to the dilemmas facing children in their early teens and their mothers:

> The mothers will not, and cannot be expected to, leave them in bombed areas when they bring the younger children to the country, but they object to having to pay for their accommodation. To obtain factory work, such as they are used to, generally entails travelling several miles to the local town, where wages are lower than those received in London and do not cover their board and lodging. Mother is then inclined to take the whole family back for the sake of the elder ones' employment.

She was well aware of the weight of competing demands. 'Wherever possible empty cottages are taken and furnished, but with so many troops billeted in the neighbourhood, no large houses remain unoccupied, and nothing but the most derelict houses are available.' She ended by noting a happy development in the town: 'An excellent (though small) rest room, with bunks and facilities for washing and some cooking, has been fitted up in Frome, where evacuees to the Rural area may be parked temporarily, until accommodation can be found for them.'

Here, then, was a Centre Organiser who had a good eye for the struggles of city evacuees. While some garments, boots and fabrics had been sent to the area from America, running up new clothes was not so easy, for it was found that 'the local workers, who are very busy with soldiers' comforts and Red Cross supplies, are not enthusiastic about working for the evacuees. Efforts are being made to induce the evacuated mothers to form working parties, but the various social levels of Hastings and East London, Dagenham and North Kensington, the scattered country billets, and the incompetence of so many of the women, make these make-and-mend parties difficult to start.' A few weeks later, in late December 1940 and early January 1941, weekly parties had been organised in some of the villages, but it was felt that 'there is still very little intercourse between the town and country women as their outlook is so different that they cannot mix readily, and the standard of domestic crafts in the country at the work parties and WI [Women's Institute] meetings is too high for the London women to join in.' City women were of course used to easy access to shops, and the Organiser of the Frome Rural District was quick to acknowledge this as a privation. While she felt that unaccompanied children were being adequately clad,

> there is still much hardship among the mothers with children, especially in the remote villages, from which a long walk and an expensive bus fare is necessary to reach the town ... Also, the parents who would gladly and gratefully accept a gift from the American Red Cross strongly object to having to beg for it through the Unemployment

Assistance Board.* The children are thereby suffering as the parents are quite unable to afford overcoats and gumboots [she was writing in the winter] which in any case are frequently unprocurable in Frome. The supply of second hand garments in the villages is so scarce as to be negligible, and is needed equally by the villagers themselves.

The challenges faced by city women suddenly sent to the countryside were also acknowledged by Phyllis Walther, who was in charge of the WVS clothing depot in Blandford Forum, Dorset. 'It is very difficult', she wrote on 14 May 1941, 'for a lot of women to adjust themselves to changed conditions and a Southampton woman transported to the country has no cheap or second hand shops to go to and cannot pick up bargains as she sees them.'

On the whole, the WVS portrayals of evacuees at this time show a disposition toward compassion, an awareness of genuine need, proactive initiatives and only a few signs of reluctance to give aid. Indeed, satisfaction was gained from doing the right thing. Evacuees also helped one another: it was reported in October 1940 that in Hemel Hempstead, Hertfordshire 'social fellowship is a strong point, and many kindly acts of one evacuee towards another could be recorded', and later the same year several evacuees were lending a hand to local people in Westmorland who were sick by visiting them and doing their shopping and housework for them.[13] There was also recognition of the need for a respite felt by some people in raided cities, such as badly bombed Bristol

*The Assistance Board, a central government department, focused before the war on the needs of unemployed people, and later on aid for those whose sustenance was imperilled by bombing and/or evacuation. It worked closely with the WVS, especially with regard to clothing (see Chapter 5).

where the WVS had solicited and made a list of offers from people outside the city 'who are willing to take bombed or over-worked people into their homes for a holiday'.[14]

WVS members showed sensitivity to how the newcomers felt, and recognised something of the legitimacy of their outlooks – in West Suffolk in September/October 1940 it was felt that 'furnishing empty houses is the ideal for evacuees' and they 'are far happier amongst themselves' and thus less likely to leave. This was a conclusion of many WVS leaders: evacuees were usually most satisfied when they could be offered a home of their own, such as an empty cottage. In January 1941 in Rotherham, South Yorkshire a dozen council houses were set aside and furnished for the use of air raid victims; cottages in the Chelmsford Rural District were acquired by the WVS in later 1940 for the use of refugees, along with a house and a hostel in town, and some members 'attended auction sales in order to buy furniture cheaply'. More than sixteen hundred evacuees were sent to the Newbury Rural District and in October 1940 the parish hall in Chieveley, Berkshire was fitted up as a winter residence for twenty-nine mothers with young children, and though they were encouraged to 'see the advantages of communal meals, the women who are in Chieveley Parish Hall prefer to make their own meals', and 'they like the excitement of shopping'. The importance of a degree of independence and being able to get away from others was not to be discounted. Major ruptures in ways of living could not (in the eyes of many WVS observers) be expected to be easy. It was said at the end of 1940 of the London evacuees to Watford that 'they appear to be comfortable in their new homes, although in many cases loneliness is apparent'.[15] In contrast to September 1939, it was now seen as best *not* to move people from familiar surroundings unless essential, and if they were moved to keep families and friends, as far as possible, together.

There was also, it seems, more understanding as to why evacuated women might want to return to dangerous places. In November 1940 it was said that most evacuees in Fakenham were 'settling down, though a number, in spite of all efforts to stop them and being in very comfortable homes, have returned. A good many of these have children just over school age left in London, and they get so worried over them and their husbands, with no one to look after them at home, that one cannot stop them from returning. In a number of cases where the mothers have returned, they have left their children behind in the district.'

These were months in which tens of thousands of people were on the move. In both Edinburgh and Glasgow members of the WVS served as guides at train stations and

helped those temporarily stranded for the night, taking parties to hostels, indicating distances to their destinations and the best means of travel, meeting special families and seeing them safely to their train connections and in cases of hardship paying for snack meals. Through the energies of the Edinburgh Guides a waiting room was made available for those who were awaiting an early morning train and a fire kept in all night. Mention should be made of the willing cooperation of various hostels to take in families at all hours of the night and of the very real friendly care that the Guides have taken to ensure the travellers were looked after.[16]

A WVS office was often the first port of call for newcomers, for it appears to have been well known by 1940–1 that it was there that a family seeking refuge was most likely to find flexible, reassuring and friendly attention – 'homely advice' was one characterisation – relatively untainted by stuffiness and rule-bound officialdom. A report from Bedford in March 1941 concluded that 'above all, we act as a centre which can refer bewildered people to an agency which can help them. We try never to turn anyone away without some positive aid, if only advice.' WVS assistance was geared to all comers, whether locals or outsiders. It was reported from badly bombed Hull in December 1941 that 'a food advice counter under the auspices of the Ministry of Food has been started in the central office and is constantly staffed by volunteers trained in domestic science'; that same month a similar facility was said to exist on market days in Hailsham, East Sussex.

While much of the evidence speaks to the experiences of groups (often large groups) of people, some reports mentioned the timely help that was given to individuals and families contending with their own difficult circumstances. A hostel in the Axbridge Rural District of Somerset had been found unsuitable for mothers with young children, and by March 1941 it had been allotted to 'three related families, including an aged father, who have been able to bring down some of their own things and are delighted to have a place of their own'. In Epping, Essex around October 1941 a bombed-out patient still in hospital 'was visited and helped in making a claim for damage. The Public Assistance Board was informed and money was sent for clothing.' The Centre Organiser then went with her to a local shop and bought an overcoat. A year earlier, in Swansea, the WVS was asked to supply clothes for aged women in a hostel – 'they are too old to be billeted elsewhere' – and 'we were able to give them warm underclothing, etc.'; and the next month 'one of our transport officers conveyed a woman from Langland Bay Annexe Hospital to join her husband at their Swansea billet'. In December 1940, also in Swansea, a small boy quarantined with measles was escorted

133

to Carmarthen to rejoin his mother, and a woman and her newborn infant were driven from the hospital to Pontardawe. In the turmoil of these months some children became separated from any responsible caregiver; in due course a WVS member would take them individually by bus or car or train to a place where they could be properly looked after. In Bedford in December 1940 the family of an evacuated boy on his own in a hostel was located 'and letters sent to restore contacts', while 'children needing sympathetic treatment' – probably those who were often termed 'difficult' – were being reported to a 'voluntary educational psychologist who is in constant touch with our [WVS] visitors as well as with the Billeting Officers'.

Many instances could be cited of WVS attentiveness to individual circumstances. In May 1941 Kendal was pleased that it had succeeded 'in clothing a waiter, bombed out of Hastings, and as a result he got a job in a local hotel'. In the village of Eaton Socon, north-east of Bedford, two evacuated boys who were just leaving school at this time were found jobs and 'suitably fitted out'. After the major blitz in Hull in May 1941, special arrangements were made for three mothers-to-be to give birth in hostels, and it was said that 'the babies born are sturdy and well' – they were proudly labelled 'hostel babies' – 'and the mothers have made rapid progress'. Homelessness ensured that individual cases routinely came to the attention of the WVS, and some of these individuals had special needs. 'We are now dealing with a special request', according to Westmorland's Centre Organiser in December 1942, 'received from York WVS for billets for the Italian wife of a Middle East soldier who wants to bring her children to the Lake District, having originally been bombed out of London. The Catholic priest has given us names in Windermere.'

Individuals in need of help (or sometimes reprimands)

appear repeatedly in Helen Lloyd's Surrey diary. In 1940–1 Miss Lloyd was very busy responding to the problems and needs of evacuees in the Guildford Rural District, many of whom had come from London. On 31 October 1940 she learned that 'our billet for Mrs Halpin and the three younger children had not materialised. Went out to the Ridges to explain matters but found they had already gone, and could do little except examine a stained mattress with a lachrymose hostess. Then followed stormy interviews, first with Mrs and then with Mr Halpin. He was taking the matter up with his union, the woman should be prosecuted for slandering his wife and turning them out, while even the stains on the mattress must have been put there by her.' It seems Miss Lloyd managed to cool him down and relocate the family. Then, on 18 December she was told of 'the iniquities of the Styles' evacuee', a Mrs G——, who the following day 'had a van full of luggage from her bombed house which she was trying to force into Posford cottage'. On 22 December this troublesome woman 'wouldn't accept a look at any billet we provided for her and refused to move from the Styles' though abusing them all the time', and was evicted from Chilworth on 23rd. 'After many adventures her luggage was deposited in the Salvation Army Home'; that evening, 'after more lengthy argument she was given one more chance as regards a billet and was finally deposited in Send'.

Such exceptional and demanding cases were bound to be draining for those who had to deal with them. Other challenges involved delinquent or runaway children, serious illness and accidents, and broken families. In mid-1941 Helen Lloyd settled the case of a two-year-old evacuee whose mother had vanished from London in October and was later located in prison. After sleepless nights the child's foster mother, a Mrs P——, resolved to try to adopt him, and on 16 July Miss

Lloyd met with her and the mother 'straight out of prison'. 'I have never seen such a hard and yet tragic face. A few tears rolled down her impassive face as she assured me she only wanted to do the best for her child, and for herself she wished to take up war work and go straight. I hurriedly composed a legal document' and arranged for the child's temporary care and eventual adoption.

Such family ruptures, each with its own sort of dark shadow, were staples of WVS welfare work. Helen Lloyd wrote once of the illness of Arthur Gill, an evacuated child, and his subsequent death, of attending his funeral and of speaking afterwards with his family, one of whom she found alarmingly aggressive. The heartbreaks of strangers could not in such circumstances be readily overlooked. In December 1940 nine-year-old Joan Elizabeth Hunt from south-east London – her father was a railway worker and she was an only child – died in Horsham, West Sussex, where she had lived since being evacuated in September 1939. The child was said to have loved the countryside, and at her parents' request she was buried in Sussex. The mourners at her funeral included two prominent members of the county's WVS, one of them Lady Dunning.[17]

Occasionally – to make a final observation – one reads of imaginative if unusual initiatives. The Bath WVS paid particular attention to the welfare of those evacuees who had just reached or were soon to reach the school leaving age of fourteen. In February/March 1941 an 'after care' programme was set up in an effort to see that these youngsters remained in satisfactory billets or were able to find new ones, that they secured suitable employment and were helped to join some appropriate youth organisation such as the Scouts or a youth club.[18] Achieving the desired objectives meant identifying and locating the teenagers – Miss M. E. Lewis, the WVS volunteer in charge, constructed a card index based on information supplied by welfare visitors, teachers, the education authorities and sometimes foster parents – and later visiting schools to talk with the prospective leavers, and working with the Employment Office to help match young people to jobs. Follow-up assessments found that while some newly employed youth were doing well, others were not, and thus efforts were made to get them different and more appropriate jobs, or to alter their living arrangements. In a wartime economy finding jobs for teenagers was not usually difficult; getting them involved in what adults regarded as healthy free-time activities was more of a challenge – several boys were reported to be uninterested or non-compliant, and some foster mothers preferred that the girls in their care not go out at night, which was not unreasonable in blackout conditions. The project was a notable example of the WVS functioning, or at least trying to function, *in loco parentis*, and the actual parents were not always appreciative or cooperative, especially if they were keen to have their children back at home and contributing part of their wages, however meagre, to a precarious household economy.

Is this emerging portrait of the WVS and its activities excessively positive? Are we too captivated by its members' reports on their own work and the work of their associates? Perhaps, a doubter might suggest, there is an inherent bias in WVS-generated sources that is not being adequately recognised? After all, one would not expect these sources to highlight bumbling and ineptness, even if and when they happened. If the best descriptions of reality portray warts and all, are the warts of the WVS being under-appreciated?

The WVS was indisputably filling a void. It was meeting needs that had suddenly arisen at a moment of national crisis, needs that no other organisation was equipped to meet: Women's Institutes, for example, had little presence in cities.

In striving to carry out this work – and enjoying at least some degree of the success – the WVS was appreciated by people who benefitted from its services and gave satisfaction and pride to its members, whose efforts were manifestly of value to others. It would be simplistic to assert that the WVS was bound to succeed; many of its successes were a result of strong and intelligent leadership, and dedication by tens of thousands of women, and these were not preordained. Still, the work expected of the WVS in the early 1940s was recognised to be so vital that it would have been remarkable had its members not risen to the occasion. There was little to hold it back, though occasionally men in local government were unsympathetic to women doing public work of importance and even giving orders – or perhaps, to put it more kindly, some of these men were just slow off the mark or over-burdened. Most of what the WVS did was uncontroversial. Indeed, it usually agreed to do whatever established authorities asked of it, or negotiated with them to agree and achieve goals as effectively as possible. In short, the WVS was pushed both by circumstance and human agency – perhaps foremost among the latter was Lady Reading's drive and charisma – to succeed.

Success was rooted in other conditions, too. One was the fact that the WVS was non-bureaucratic, for this gave it a flexibility to respond effectively to requests and instructions and to adapt to changing circumstances. In many localities its numbers were large and its organisation sufficiently robust that, if an emergency did occur, there was a good chance that members could assemble quickly and deal with immediate needs. The WVS, to its advantage, was unburdened by rules and red tape, though its record-keeping was thorough and intended in part to foster learning from experience. It was also important that the WVS drew heavily upon women's domestic skills and their experiences with care-giving. What was done at the local level at this time did not usually assume much in the way of specialised training, for most mature women knew something about serving tea and snacks, or knitting and mending clothes, or looking after children, or catering to young men, or attending to the needs of the infirm and the elderly. Much WVS work was an extension of classic housewifery and mothering, heretofore carried out without the pressures of being bombed.

If the WVS had not been created before the outbreak of war, it certainly would have had to be created sooner or later. If later, there would have been a lot more suffering and dislocation than there actually was and public morale would not have been well served. It was important to Britain's war effort that an inexpensive welfare organisation run by women was in place in 1939, especially women who were sufficiently well-off to be accustomed to some leisure; an organisation committed to establishing itself as a disciplined body that could be depended on to get jobs done. This did not happen right away, as experience was needed to teach lessons and demonstrate what worked best, or at least adequately. As a result of these initial trials and errors, by the middle of 1941 the WVS had matured, developed a repertoire of effective practices, shown flexibility and compassion, and earned the respect of both civilians and soldiers. Its efforts were widely lauded, including by American observers,[19] and the American Red Cross made most of its very substantial contributions to Britain through the WVS. 'The Women's Voluntary Service', wrote the head of the Urban District Council in Brentwood, Essex in a private letter in early January 1941, 'is a grand organisation and has done magnificent work in dealing with our bombed out, and with the homeless drifting here from nearer to London'[20] – and this was an attitude widely shared by those who had observed first-hand the WVS at work, such as the Mayor of Stepney.[21] A woman from Hampshire, visiting

Plymouth in June 1942, heard criticism of how the authorities had handled the bombings there, but 'all the people to whom I spoke were grateful for the help given, especially to the WVS for their food service'.[22]

This is not to deny that there were failures. WVS Centres probably felt overwhelmed at times by the tasks they confronted, but few, understandably, wished to disclose these feelings. One that did open up was in Wellingborough, Northamptonshire, reporting in February 1941 that 'Many evacuees are still here – we are inundated with problems all day long about unsuitable billets, and we have the greatest difficulty in helping them. Many of them have for months been waiting for houses, but the Local Authorities do not seem to be able to requisition any. The cases are most pitiful.' It is clear, too, that in some parts of the country the WVS, if it existed at all, was ill-organised and lacked capable leadership. Sometimes deficiencies only came to light when new appointees arrived on the scene, bringing welcome firmness and energy to their jobs. In Arnside, Westmorland, to take one example, the WVS representative was found in June 1940 to be very much wanting – the situation there was said to be 'deplorable' – but a few months later, in October, Arnside's WVS was flourishing, pulling together and hard at work thanks to a new and effective leader.[23] It was only to be expected that some women who first offered themselves for leadership roles were not suited to what was required of them. Both Nella Last and Phyllis Walther wrote of the inadequacies of the WVS leadership in, respectively, Barrow-in-Furness and Blandford Forum; similarly, in Warwickshire in 1940 the diarist Doreen Wright was highly critical of the local leader; and the perfunctory character of many of the monthly Narrative Reports suggests that some organisers may not have been deeply engaged in their centres' activities. It is likely, too, that irritability and frustration and personal squabbles were much more prevalent than official reports revealed – Helen Lloyd's diary certainly testifies to the pervasiveness of these ordinary human weaknesses. While a degree of self-sacrifice was often displayed, heroic qualities could be expected only very occasionally, if at all.

Still, there are enough reports that exude a sense of vigour, enthusiasm, thoughtful improvisation and managerial competence to indicate how and why the WVS came to be in such good standing. A lot of useful and important work got done.[24] Emergencies or semi-emergencies created needs – some unanticipated – that WVS members acted quickly to address, on hundreds if not thousands of occasions. Numerous timely experiments were associated with the WVS, such as sending mobile laundry units to bomb-damaged cities.[25] As testimony to the reputation that the WVS was gaining in 1940 and 1941, it was receiving more and more requests to expand its functions, to plug new gaps in welfare services and to respond creatively to the insistent and ever-changing demands of the war at home.

By June of 1941 the cities of Britain had endured almost nine months of raids. No one could know whether they would continue, or where the enemy might strike next, or how severe future raids might be. We only know with hindsight that the following three years were, with a few notable exceptions, such as the Baedeker attacks in spring 1942, comparatively raid-free. However, even with this welcome pause in hostilities there was still every reason for people to expect, and be properly prepared to cope with, renewed attacks. With the German invasion of the Soviet Union in June 1941, many people realised that Nazi aggression would at least temporarily be redirected to the east and that Britain might well enjoy some respite. (Hull was an exception; at a time when almost all the country experienced no attacks it suffered several raids during the mid and late summer of 1941, which killed some 250 people.)[26] But it could prove to be merely a brief lull. For a while it looked as if Russia – and most Britons preferred to think of their new ally as Russia rather than the Soviet Union – would succumb to Germany's military might, and that when it did Hitler would in all likelihood turn once again to bombing Britain and trying to bring her to her knees.

It was therefore essential, most people agreed, to continue to be vigilant in the interest of civil defence, and to be as well prepared as possible to meet the threat of invasion. As for the WVS, its tasks did not let up even as the sense of imminent emergency abated.

CHAPTER 5

LIFE'S NECESSITIES 1941–4[1]

Helping people with food and drink continued to be a high WVS priority. Canteens were found almost everywhere, some fully run by the WVS, some operated by others – the Church Army, the Red Cross, the RAF, the Army, the YMCA – and staffed fully or in part by the WVS. They were a staple of WVS services, for they were in demand not only for emergencies but also for the everyday needs of evacuees and other people away from home; workers at outdoor sites (docks, some construction projects); special public gatherings such as a fund-raising 'War Weapons Week'; the Home Guard during weekend exercises; and troops on the move or stationed at out-of-the-way locations or simply desirous of friendly visitors to their camp. In 1942 there were said to be 940 static and mobile troop canteens scattered around the country and a grand total of 1500 canteens of all sorts;[2] most of these would have been partly or fully staffed by the WVS. Some were used only intermittently and perhaps catered to only small groups of customers – they may have been little more than tea wagons. Others were very busy, opening early in the morning and still open late at night, with thousands served each week. The Forces canteen in Dartmouth, a naval town, was a hectic, throbbing place, with (it was said) nearly two thousand patrons a day by August 1942. In September 1943 it was serving at least four hundred hot meals each evening, plus 'an enormous number of sandwiches', and two months later the various canteen services in the town required thirty-one helpers every day, 'and in a very small place like Dartmouth this means drawing heavily on our WVS personnel, but the response is wonderful'. In October 1941 approximately four thousand men were served during two days at the station canteen in March, Cambridgeshire, and in late 1945 it was reported that the WVS canteen in Kendal had served some 480,000 soldiers and ATS in the course of the war, most of them during halts on their journeys.[3]

Some of the busiest canteens were certainly at train stations, and one of these, at York, was described in a post-war memoir by Hilda Appleby, who had worked there. The canteen was located on Platform 8 and was open, apparently, twenty-four hours a day throughout the war. Miss Appleby was usually on the midnight to eight in the morning shift, which 'was the longest shift and very often the busiest, as much of the troop movement took place at night. A taxi picked us up at a quarter to midnight, and the people we relieved were taken home in the same taxi.' She recalled everyone working very hard:

We served tea and coffee, pork pies, sausage rolls, and sandwiches ... Everything was sold at very low prices. I can still remember standing there, chopping up Spam, and adding cans of cold beans, at 3 to 4 o'clock in the morning. The air in the canteen was so thick with cigarette smoke that I could hardly see across the room. I have never been able to eat Spam since then.

The canteen was usually forewarned of a troop train's arrival, perhaps with five hundred aboard:

They would only wait in the station for half an hour. This meant that we had to get stacks of food and urns of tea and coffee ready so that they could be served very quickly. We often had to resort to jam jars as we would run out of cups – our cup losses were enormous, 500–600 a month. If we had a lull we would take a walk up and down the station, collecting cups from the floor, luggage barrows, window sills, in fact every conceivable place. I was collecting cups early one morning when I came across a group of soldiers on their way to Malaya – they were playing and singing and invited us to join them. I served men of all nationalities, especially from the Merchant Navy. German prisoners fastened to their military guard also came in for tea.

The canteen at York station remained busy for a few months after the war ended since lots of demobilised servicemen were passing through. Over the years it 'made thousands of pounds and this was shared among charities. It was a very long time before I could get used to seeing Platform 8 without the canteen. As a souvenir I bought the old scales from the canteen, and I still have them.'[4]

The Narrative Report from York in December 1942 is consistent with this recollection, and also gives a sense of the day-to-day challenges of running such a canteen. It had been 'a difficult month for the staffing at the station canteen. Enormous number of absentees due to illness and Christmas holidays, which tie helpers to more household duties. Have been greatly assisted by two members of the clergy and students on holiday, who have undertaken night work.' There had been an air raid on the city on 17 December that had cut off the supply of gas. 'Military authorities [were] asked to supply Soyer Stoves and soldiers to work them and this was done. This arrangement continued till January 4th when the gas returned to normal.' The canteen was open daily throughout the holidays and 'the crew of a torpedoed Danish steamer were served on Christmas morning. They were extremely cold and hungry and appreciated all that was done for them. Many men expressed their appreciation at finding the canteen open over the Christmas period.' On one day 6660 men were served, the largest number since the canteen's opening. Keeping it going was a big job. On the following page of this report it was remarked that the Centre Organiser had 'heard from a man in the Middle East that they had a ballot on the best station canteen in England, Preston got 28 votes and York 21. The rest were "also rans".' Such acclaim was not likely to go unnoticed.

Of course, those in need of refreshment were not always gathered at one site, and so refreshments had to be brought to them. These were the roots of the by-now flourishing mobile canteens, of which there were hundreds by 1942. In Lincoln in September 1943 a mobile canteen served tea to five hundred ATS attending an anniversary service in the cathedral. In Boston, Lincolnshire in May/June 1942 the mobile canteen was called out to feed arriving Irish labourers 'before they were taken out to the places where they are to work', while at Southend-on-Sea the two WVS mobile canteens had been 'in constant request for serving cricket and football matches (the Unit providing the rations)' in August through October 1941. In August 1941 the director of a Ministry of Information film being shot in the Crowland area of Lincolnshire and starring Ralph Richardson made 'an urgent appeal for a mobile canteen as it was impossible to get anyone to do catering in that district', and though the WVS could not oblige 'as our mobile canteen is needed for the troops', it did agree to supply the cast of sixty with sandwiches, cakes, etc. for a week. And in 1943 the mobile canteen in Weston-super-Mare, which visited women on barrage balloon sites, found that their customers were eager to acquire hairpins and Kirby grips, and that 'cosmetics went with a rush, and we all got quite adept in advising them as to the right shade of lipstick and powder'.

Some mobile canteens operated according to a more regular routine. The London, Midland and Scotland station in Chesterfield was regularly served by a mobile canteen, which in October 1944 was catering to some nine hundred servicemen a week, plus airborne troops 'when leaving on early morning trains. These men have to walk in for some miles and appreciate a cup of tea.' In Glasgow there were several mobile canteens for the men who worked on the docks and the troops who embarked or disembarked there. A surviving log book for 1941–2 reveals something of the details of their operation: complaints about the tea (some legitimate: on one occasion the water had been boiled in a newly galvanised tank and picked up a foul taste), grouchy customers, days with no fuel and large quantities of unsold food, a shortage of soup spoons, a canteen with a dead battery, punctured tyres and other mechanical failures, complaints about the food tasting of petrol, stolen money, police objections to a vehicle showing a white light, minor collisions, bureaucratic obstacles to registering a new van, lost keys and, of course, the weather. On 19 November 1941 'Mrs Hunt phoned from Prince Dock at 4.20 p.m. The fog is so dense at Docks that she finds it difficult to carry on. Has quantity of food left but no men coming to canteen. Will leave shortly to go to Graving Dock. She is afraid to wait much longer in case she is unable to make her way back.' Later the van's battery went flat and a mechanic had to be summoned. The next day's weather was cold and miserable, and the volunteers wondered if 'it would be possible to arrange for the men to buy tea food at lunch time in order to let the ladies home earlier. Many are complaining of the blackout.' Over the following few days it proved difficult to find a paraffin lamp to help the servers see what they were doing as dusk fell. Clearly, there were challenges in running a busy mobile canteen – and this is not to mention unexpected demands for service, a few in the middle of the night, and the many last-minute requests that crews had to deal with.[5]

Canteens, especially those in fixed locations where patrons could relax for a while, were important places for men and women in the Forces to put their work (which was often boring) aside, enjoy a few modest physical comforts and have a bit of fun. According to Nella Last, who volunteered there for part of every Friday, Barrow's canteen was usually a lively place of bonhomie, chatter, teasing and jokes, some of which she recorded in her diary. Canteen society was bound to gen-erate humorous episodes – and help sustain good feelings. The fondness of young boys for peashooters enlivened the spirits of the WVS members working at the still very busy static canteen in Oakham, Rutland in February 1945. According to the Organiser's account of this 'amusing episode', several 'small boys locked themselves into the Gents lavatory, and bored a hole through to the Ladies. They then went out, bought themselves a lot of dried peas, returned and locked themselves into the Gents lavatory again – and proceeded to pepper any ATS, WAAFs or Land Army who made use of the Ladies lava-tory. We soon stopped their fun.' Whatever these ladies' disapproval, it was clearly offset by amusement.

One of the most interesting wartime creations was the 'Communal Feeding Centre', later renamed British Restaurant at Churchill's insistence – he disliked the word 'communal'.[6] This was very much an innovation rooted in the realities of wartime, for increased numbers of people were not in a position to get a hot dinner at home, including men who were mobile or working away from home, husbands lacking a housewife (because evacuated), groups of evacuated schoolchildren, those who lacked access to adequate kitchen facilities (the victims of bombing, some evacuees), and women newly in the work force. British Restaurants, the first of which were launched in early 1941 under, as a rule, the auspices of local government, were designed to provide a hot, full-course midday meal for a shilling or less, usually with cafeteria-style service. Since eating there did not require the patron to give up any of his or her food coupons, they supplemented the rigours of wartime food rationing.

At their peak, in 1943, there were 2150 British Restaurants around the country. Most served at least two hundred meals a day and normally drew their unpaid workers from the WVS. By May 1944 Leicester had fifteen British Restaurants, the largest of which catered for 1500 people per day, assisted by teams of WVS helpers of a dozen or so at a time as well as three supervisors. When Rotherham initiated a British Restaurant in January 1941, the WVS was tasked with ordering the food and engaging the paid staff along with organising teams of volunteers. If the estimate that seventeen thousand WVS members were regularly serving as helpers in 1943–4 is correct, then on average each British Restaurant had a contingent of eight WVS women.[7] Certainly the many references to these restaurants suggest that WVS involvement was more the norm than the exception, and that this involvement was often substantial and ongoing. When Dewsbury's third British Restaurant was opened in November 1942, the local newspaper reported that 'much of the credit was due to the WVS, who had served at all the Communal Feeding Centres and the mobile canteens', and recognition was also given to the WVS for similar success in Guildford.[8]

The work of one British Restaurant, in Bexhill-on-Sea, East Sussex, is particularly well documented. Mrs Clare Turpin, its WVS supervisor, oversaw the borough's British Restaurant from its inception in 1941 until it reverted in early 1945 to its former function as a council-operated public restaurant. With its favoured location in a pre-existing restaurant that was part of a larger municipal facility, the De La Warr Pavilion, an elegant modernist structure on the sea front, opened in 1935, this British Restaurant undoubtedly had more charm than most.* But despite the grandeur of the surroundings, the jobs undertaken were much like the ones anywhere else. WVS helpers acted as 'peelers', preparing fruit and vegetables for the paid cook and her assistants, and also as servers in the dining area. By 1944 Mrs Turpin supervised six paid workers – a cook, deputy cook and washers-up – and a daily average of fifteen WVS volunteers.[9]

This Bexhill restaurant was a business success. It ran at an overall profit, after paying 5 per cent of its takings for heat and rent and, from late 1943, another 5 per cent to help cover the costs of the pavilion's renovations and upkeep. For the fiscal year ending 31 March 1943, the borough accountant reported an income from meals of £2096, and £2659 in 1943–4, the increased revenue being the result of a rise of about twenty thousand in the number of meals served. Based on figures reported for the last six months of 1943, the number of meals

*The De La Warr Pavilion is included in Dan Cruickshank (ed.), *Architecture, The Critics' Choice: 150 Masterpieces of Architecture* (London: élan press, 2000), pp. 264–5, and is also featured on the dust jacket. Most British Restaurants were housed in more modest premises, such as church halls or trade institutes.

provided annually would have been around seventy thousand. Mrs Turpin and her staff seem to have forged an effective team that had a close and cordial relationship with the local authority. The restaurant bought much of its fresh produce from the borough's Parks Department, which managed its plantings of crop rotations to help meet the restaurant's needs, though a local greengrocer was engaged to supply what the town could not grow. Documents held in the East Sussex County Record Office testify to amicable and frequent communications between Mrs Turpin and the town clerk, Edward Smith, who was generally supportive of her requests for equipment, staffing changes, wage increases, holiday closures and other routine matters. He was also supportive when an angry constituent complained to his local councillor that Mrs Turpin had asked his wife to keep her rambunctious children from disturbing other diners. On 18 March 1943 Mrs Turpin wrote to Mr Smith to give her side of the story:

> Owing to complaints received from working diners about noisy children, Mrs Freeman was asked to see that her children did not annoy other people during their meal. We have asked other mothers to do the same as it is somewhat trying after a hard morning's work to hear a lot of screaming. I am sorry Mrs Freeman has taken exception to our request, but I think it was necessary in the interests of at least 100 people [a common number of daily diners] to make a protest. We have always done our best to feed the children and welcome them as the next generation but we expect a give and take attitude on the part of the parents.

The next day the clerk wrote to the councillor, enclosing a copy of this letter and suggesting that no further action be taken. Later, in 1945, when the restaurant was reinstated as a 'normal' eating facility, the well-regarded Mrs Turpin was invited to hire the new paid staff, replacing the WVS volunteers who were starting to leave.

Managing a British Restaurant was no sinecure and Mrs Turpin was the regular recipient of directives, via the town clerk, from the Ministry of Food. These included reminders to lay on adequate coal supplies for the winter, advice on nutrition and novel recipes including prune fritters and mock orange cream,* thoughts as to how to reduce the pilferage of cutlery, instructions on the proper heating of plates, hints about how to popularise the new National Wheatmeal Loaf in 1942 and thus reduce the demand for white bread, praise for the potato and suggestions concerning interior décor – many British Restaurants strove to be cheerful places and their walls were often covered with posters and even original works of art. It needed a capable and efficient woman to keep on top of all these pressures.

The roles and responsibilities of the WVS in British Restaurants varied from place to place; there was no single model for success. Where the WVS was an active player, it probably contributed in at least one of three main ways. First, it sometimes provided the necessary leadership and supervisory skills, at no or minimal cost. Second, by depending heavily on volunteer helpers and thus keeping overall labour costs low, many British Restaurants were better able to offer good meals at modest prices, and thus become a hit with hard-pressed consumers. Third, since in some places paid help was by the middle of the war hard to find, volunteers were essential to keep restaurants functioning. In January 1942, one of the two British Restaurants in Cardiff's dockland was said by the

---

*This involved carrots and mashed potatoes with a little sugar and spice, and was served with watered down custard in order to curb the excessive use of milk.

Centre Organiser to be 'very popular with all types of working people, especially with staffs of the various banks, who have had great difficulty before in obtaining meals that are not too expensive'. The WVS was never the sole force behind British Restaurants, but it was frequently – perhaps usually – an important contributor to making them function effectively and economically. It is noteworthy that the 1941 government publication *Community Feeding in War Time*, an enthusiastic how-to guide, was prepared by the WVS and included a foreword by Lady Reading. While excessive claims should not be made, WVS aid to these eateries certainly did contribute to the nation's nutritional standards in wartime and introduced tens of thousands of people, many from the working class, to the novelty of cafeteria-style eating.

In addition, the WVS was, with the support of the Ministry of Food, running what was referred to as 'the pie scheme' from 1941–2. This allowed for and encouraged the distribution of affordable and nutritious meat pies in mainly agricultural areas, which meant that rural workers could enjoy some of the benefits conferred on town-dwellers by British Restaurants, which were usually unsuited to serving scattered populations. Many farm workers had to take their meals outdoors or in farm buildings, where they were working; to have palatable, off-ration food delivered to them around midday was undoubtedly valued, especially in seasons when the working days were long. Most pies were prepared by private bakers and marketed or delivered by the WVS. In Brigg, Lincolnshire in 1943 the WVS was selling over a thousand pies a week from a stall at the town's Thursday market and also took them to other villages three days a week. By the spring of 1944 the pie scheme was operating in 2734 villages nationwide, selling over a million pies a week.[10] It was calculated that in the year June 1943 to May 1944, the large rural district of Kesteven in Lincolnshire sold 676,413 pies.[11]

Numerous commentators lauded the pie scheme – though sometimes with reservations. It was said in October 1942 that the pie scheme in Thorney, in the Isle of Ely, 'is much appreciated by the inhabitants' and that 1500 to 1600 'pies are distributed weekly. This commenced week ending August 6. May it soon end.' Her final words are telling. The scheme often demanded daily work from volunteers, sometimes in bad weather, absorbed scarce petrol and could be time-consuming though the demands declined significantly in the winter as workers spent more time at home. This last was reported in the town of Ely in November 1942: pies were 'not so much in demand now that the harvest is over. The great difficulty is to squeeze one gallon of petrol per week out of the Government for delivery. It might be liquid gold for the difficulty we have in getting hold of it. I hope that we shall be able to get it fixed up soon; otherwise we shall have to employ a pool car.' In a few places home baking countered the appeal of the pie scheme – home supplies might be readily available wherever women were not employed in factories, or in the fields – and there the scheme was liable to fold or not get started at all.

Some of the tasks of the WVS from 1941 were a continuation of responsibilities spelled out early in the war, others were relatively new. In reception areas, evacuation and billeting continued to loom large, even at times of little or no bombing. While some evacuees returned home, as they had done in late 1939 and early 1940, and the total number dropped to just a little over 260,000 in March 1944,[12] others stayed in the safer regions where they had found refuge – after all, the Blitz meant many of them had no homes to return to – and thus their presence was bound to be a continuing concern. At the end of 1941 Houghton Regis in Bedfordshire opened a 'Help Yourself Club' for evacuated mothers and their babies, to be open two afternoons a week; a WVS member who was a dressmaker attended regularly 'and helps mothers with mending and making up their own materials' (a sewing machine was provided). It was said in December 1941 that in Kendal 'the billeting officer constantly calls on us for help; our Deputy Organiser being specially gifted in this work, having such a wonderful knowledge of suitable houses in Kendal. She has been most successful in settling a Dutch family in comfortable billets. Two expectant mothers returned to London, one has come back to us, and the other is coming back shortly.'

Helen Lloyd's Surrey diary for the months after mid-1941 is full of references to billeting matters. On 26 August 1941 'an anxious husband from West Clandon brought in a medical certificate to say his wife must give up her evacuees'; a family was to be moved from Chilworth to West Horsley, 'and I had to break the news to a very surly husband that the move could not take place till tomorrow'; and she discussed with a billeting officer 'how a child of 14, at work but billeted Form E, could obtain clothes'. On 3 September she had 'tea with Mrs Harvey to discuss the billeting of a school in Compton – an inordinate number of staff, 19 teachers and matrons and 11 other staff for a school of 75 children; sat up till 11.30 apportioning the billets'. Three days later 'Lady Isabel Browne, who has eight evacuees, had a tale of woe to tell on the telephone. She has whooping cough, the parlour maid is having an operation, the housemaid going away on leave, the kitchen help away with tonsillitis, the official Helper called away at a moment's notice by the Education Authorities, and now she thinks two of the children have scabies! Had nine telephone calls trying to get her a nurse and a Helper. Lady Isabel rang up four times getting angrier and angrier!' Every week Helen Lloyd, as Centre Organiser, wrestled with such issues. And sometimes she needed the patience of Job.

In January 1944 the Centre Organiser in the Frome rural district offered an evocative portrait of the challenges of finding enough housing to satisfy the legitimate demands of uprooted people, which had increased in the region after Bath was blitzed. 'Housing a great difficulty,' she wrote, 'especially for the privately evacuated.' She had

> followed up many reports of empty cottages but always they have been found to be tied to farms and not available, as the farmers live in hopes of obtaining additional labour and must be able to offer a cottage, or they have been booked by local people long before they were vacated. One example is the case of a soldier's wife, with six children, all of whom are becoming sickly from living in a three-roomed hovel and which is causing the Centre Organiser much anxiety. The local authority is sympathetic, but there seems little they can do. Neither the local householders or the evacuees will consider billeting where there is a large family, as this invariably ends in unhappiness for both parties.

It was always much easier to accommodate unaccompanied children, single adults such as the elderly, and women with only one or perhaps two children. It is likely, too, that the opinions of the WVS commonly played a role – even a key role – in determining who got what. For example, in June 1941 there was 'keen competition' for any available cottages in Higham Ferrers, Northamptonshire and the clerk and billeting officer 'always confer with the WVS before allotting them, since they think we can fairly judge which is the most deserving case. Last week, by WVS recommendation, a small two-roomed cottage was rented to the young wife of a soldier, who is expecting a baby in a few weeks' time, and who has been twice bombed out in London.' On 11 September 1941

Helen Lloyd spoke with an evacuee 'and told her she could have the requisitioned house at Peaslake. A charming woman and with her five children a far more deserving case than any of Mr Lockwood's protegées' (Lockwood was the chief billeting officer for the district). On such matters there was lots of scope for preferential treatment, and WVS members, particularly when uniformed, were women whose views could really matter.

Clothing was a perennial concern for the WVS as old clothes wore out, others were damaged or destroyed. Overalls might have to be sewn for children at a nursery, as was happening in Wembley in May 1942.[13] New clothes were rationed from June 1941, and often difficult to find. Large numbers of people were poorly clad, so WVS clothing depots were catering to many in need, mainly evacuees, refugees and other displaced people, those who had been bombed out of their homes and families of men in the forces. The depots were sites of emergency supplies intended for the really hard up, who were in some ways victims of wartime damages and disruptions. Supplies of clothing for applicants were usually conditional on some kind of means test or at least a recommendation from a reputable third party, such as the Assistance Board. In other words, most claims for assistance were carefully investigated. By mid-1942 dealing with clothes and the valuable stocks in clothing depots, not to mention the rules of rationing and the coupons needed to acquire new clothes, had become sufficiently complicated that the WVS published *The A.B.C. of WVS Clothing*, a twenty-five-page booklet to guide members' conduct at the local level. Each person had an annual government allocation of coupons for clothes – the number varied from year to year: it stood at forty-eight in 1943 – and these coupons had to be given up not just to buy new clothes but also to get 'free' ones from the WVS. As this booklet put it, 'It is only fair that people who receive gift clothing because they are in need should not also be able to buy an extra supply of clothing in the shops, which they may be able to do if they receive their gift clothing coupon free.' Here as in other respects, strict rules constrained any excessive tendency towards liberality.

While the parents of unaccompanied evacuated children were expected to keep their offspring properly clothed, some were clearly too poor, or too negligent, to do so. Consequently, foster parents and the WVS in reception areas sometimes struggled to cope when, with the advent of clothes rationing, the coupons required for new garments were unavailable. In September 1941 this was a problem for many evacuated Londoners in Gelligaer, Glamorganshire, 'leaving children definitely under-clad, in weather which is getting more wintry every day'. Parents in some cases, it was added, could not be traced. 'Local stores of warm second-hand clothes are almost exhausted and insufficient material for make-and-mend parties is available – it is useless to spend time and trouble on remaking cotton garments now. We shall shortly be reduced to cutting up [Rest] Shelter clothing to cover these children. THEY MUST BE CLOTHED ... This situation cannot continue. If only we could get extra coupons we would raise a fund and buy if necessary.' Some WVS Centres spent a lot of time salvaging and recycling fabrics and other soft materials. In Plymouth in 1942 seamstresses were 'repairing clothing which would otherwise have had to be discarded and altering some of the less practical garments. Converting nightgowns with worn-out tops into children's petticoats and knickers, old-fashioned nightgowns into babies' wear, and partially worn coats into boys' shorts and girls' skirts are among a few of the alterations successfully undertaken.' This work was a staple of make-do-and-mend working parties.

The 1941–2 diary of Phyllis Walther, who was in charge of the WVS's clothing depot in Blandford Forum, Dorset, gives a sense of the nitty-gritty of wartime clothing. The stock of emergency clothes was actually kept in the attic of her parents' large house, to which she had self-evacuated with her young son at the beginning of the war while her husband remained in London. Her diary testifies to some of the challenges of managing a clothing supply: stocktaking; receiving and sorting donations, mending some and labelling garments; sometimes having insufficient supplies; distributing material to working parties and dealing with knitters; dispensing layettes; ensuring that Rest Centres had adequate reserves of clothes; and adjusting to new directives regarding coupons and applications for aid. (Other clothing depots mentioned their struggles to keep moths at bay.) Mrs Walther also had direct encounters with women in need from elsewhere, some the wives of soldiers posted nearby, others evacuees. On 7 November 1941, after a request from a visitor for some clothes for evacuees, she remarked that one boy 'has a most unsatisfactory mother who sends rubbish not fit to put on him and then only at great pressure from the London County Council and the foster mother. I gave him out the essentials and they are going to get the forms filled in later. Her other family had run out of coupons so we fixed them up with second-hand pyjamas and pants and socks which will hang on until the New Year. It was a family of three boys with a splendid foster mother but she could patch and darn things no longer.' Then, on 2 January 1942 she had 'a small boy to clothe. He seems to be billeted with evacuees and to have been in hospital and come out with very little. I gave him a suit, vest, stockings and boots. He had an overcoat of sorts. I hope the billeting officer will succeed in getting me the coupons.' And on 1 June 1942 she was 'asked to supply clothes for a small boy evacuee living on a farm and helping with the work. He only brought good clothes with him and has no coupons left.' By virtue of some fudging of the coupon account she was able to supply him with shorts and boots.

Occasionally the military authorities solicited her help. On 4 February 1942 the ATS at the Blandford Camp 'applied to us for some clothes for a girl who was being discharged after conviction for a civil offence. She would be allowed to keep her underclothes and a pair of shoes but nothing else and as she was an orphan and destitute when she joined, they were at their wits' end to clothe her. I fitted her up very easily from secondhand things.' Some months later, on 24 June, she dealt with another ATS case when she was asked to clothe 'a girl being discharged and coming from Southern Ireland. Again I was able to fit her up very well with a frock and a coat but as the coat was rather thin she had a little green jacket to go under it, which went very well with the green silk frock which had just come in.' Such details were important to the giver and, one assumes, the receiver as well. They also show the sort of discretionary authority that a WVS 'officer' might wield.

Footwear presented a major headache and was mentioned repeatedly in the Narrative Reports – and had been from almost the beginning of the war, when many city children evacuated to rural districts were quickly found to be poorly shod. The problem persisted, and for various reasons. It was said in July 1943 that in Weston-super-Mare the supply of wearable shoes for unaccompanied evacuee children was a 'great concern':

> We have frequent calls to supply second-hand shoes to chil-
> dren who in more than one case have not been able to leave

the house for a fortnight, or even longer, because they have nothing to put on their feet. Enquiries show that some foster mothers have used the children's coupons for themselves, leaving none for the rightful owner. This is never discovered until the case is completely desperate.

Such deceit was surely uncommon, but weather-related challenges were not. In December 1942 the Centre Organiser at Ely noted that Wellington boots 'for folk in the Fens are tremendously sought after. If they live on a road I have refused the application, but of course any road in a Real FEN village such as Prickwillow is miry to a degree totally unknown to urban dwellers ... The mud is just unbelievable. I'm told also that the school playgrounds are so wet that *all* children really need rubbers, as otherwise they have to spend the rest of the session with wet feet. If there really are more to spare I'd love to give them to all applicants.' She was making much the same plea at the end of the summer of 1944: 'We are continually asked for Wellingtons for children. The Fen Country is very badly served with hard roads, and the soft farm droves down which the children go to school too muddy and wet to be believed if not seen. Therefore if any Wellingtons are available these Fen villages really in justice should have priority.' Naturally, other regions were making their own well-grounded claims for Wellingtons. Surrey's Dorking Rural District noted in January 1944 that 'This is a very muddy part of the world and many children have long walks to school through fields and so-called lanes.' Local parents were 'thrilled' to receive an allotment of Wellingtons, while in November 1944 in Oakham, Rutland, 'the demand for Wellingtons has been enormous, both for the evacuees and local children qualifying for them'. The hard reality was that, given the military's demand for rubber, a scarce commodity, civilian needs were bound to be sacrificed and parents were routinely in quest of adequate boots for their children.

When boots were forthcoming, the WVS frequently played a role in identifying recipients. In 1943–4 Wellingtons from the American Red Cross 'were distributed to all children in Kesteven who were found eligible by having to cross fields or walk through muddy lanes to reach school. Every case proposed by the school teacher was verified by a WVS representative.'[14] Establishing the criteria for who would or would not get boots was no easy task. Writing in January 1944, the Centre Organiser in the Frome Rural District observed that issuing American Red Cross Wellingtons 'to the rural children has been one of the outstanding jobs of the last few weeks'. While the Somerset County Council had declared that only children who had at least a mile and a half to walk to school were eligible to receive boots, 'in this very rural area, where many children walk up to three miles to school and many others have to cross wet fields or live in extremely muddy situations, not nearly enough pairs were available for all. One hundred and fifty pairs have now been issued and, in general, all children with over two miles to walk have been supplied.' She thought that the head teachers in the twenty schools involved had 'cooperated nobly in attempting to achieve a fair distribution, but it has been a difficult matter'. Praise was lavish for the North American donors; the boots arriving in the Chard Rural District of Somerset in January 1944 'have been a real godsend'. 'In some cases children have had to stay away from school as their parents have been unable to procure adequate footwear for them.' The mood was likely to be celebratory when Wellingtons were made available. Haslemere, Surrey did 'a roaring trade' during October 1944 and the clothing depot 'sent away many a happy mother, clutching her Wellingtons to her bosom. The Centre

Organiser feels she needs police protection when she collects them from the store.'

A further, inevitable issue was that children outgrew still-serviceable clothes. As they could be handed on to others, from 1942 the WVS set up clothing exchanges. The idea was simple and, on the whole, the implementation successful. Mothers would bring to an exchange good quality clothing that had been outgrown; this clothing would be assessed by WVS members and given a 'points' value; these points, or credits, could then be used to acquire from the exchange's stock an item of equivalent points value; and the garment or garments turned in would become available to some other mother with a smaller child, as long as she had clothing of at least the same value to give to the exchange. If nothing suitable was in stock at the time, the points could be saved for future use. No money changed hands. To get started an exchange needed a nucleus of second-hand clothes, perhaps supplied by WVS make-and-mend parties, some of whose members also helped with alterations once an exchange was up and running.

Various protocols determined how these exchanges operated. In Grimsby there was a rule that football boots could only be exchanged for football boots, and Wellingtons for Wellingtons, 'due to the dearth of these articles'. The clothes offered to the exchange in Gainsborough were not to circulate there but rather were to be sent to other towns in the area, from which Gainsborough would get its supplies – this was presumably designed to guard against the embarrassment of having one's neighbour see *your* child wearing one of *her* children's cast-off garments.[15] The reports on clothing exchanges in 1943–4 often indicated that they had value for some women, such as evacuees and those for whom tailoring was a chore. It was said in November 1944 that the clothing exchange in Oakham 'has been more popular than it ever has been', though it was struggling a little since 'we have lost our permanent helper and have had to manage with temporary helpers'. Managing a clothing exchange or clothing depot was a rather specialised job, so a resignation or illness (the latter was very common) might jeopardise ongoing work. It should also be noted that clothing exchanges were not for everyone. As the report for January–March 1944 from Ely pointed out, 'the poorer people find it difficult to produce articles good enough to be up to the standard required'.

By this time, there were around four hundred clothing exchanges nationwide. While they were in many ways undoubtedly a good idea and cost almost nothing to run, they did not catch on as widely or as fervently as was hoped for and might have been expected. The large numbers of poor and near-poor, with their shabby garments, were often not in a position to make use of them, for a clothing exchange was interested in receiving only items of a quality that were likely to attract customers. Perhaps, too, for many women the whole idea of clothing one's children from the hand-me-downs of strangers remained hard to digest. Here, then, was an aspect of wartime recycling that, while innovative, enjoyed only limited acceptance.

CHAPTER 6

COMFORTS, COLLECTIONS AND CONVIVIALITY 1941–4

During the middle years of the war the work of the WVS extended well beyond basic material necessities. Nurseries, some residential, some not, were a continuing concern, and the most ambitious of these ventures were intended to support the war effort by helping women with young children to hold down full-time jobs. In Surrey a residential hostel for mothers with children under five was opened in later 1942 at Ryde House in Ripley, and in December Helen Lloyd described how this social experiment worked:

> During the day, the mothers work in a munitions factory while the children are cared for in the hostel on the lines of a residential nursery. The families come from danger areas on the coast and thus the dual purpose is served of bringing the children into safety and releasing their mothers for full-time war work. The hostel is run by a paid staff who

have been engaged by and are under the direction of Mrs Liddell of the WVS Centre staff. In addition, a great deal of voluntary help is needed and this is being provided by WVS members. The mothers work extremely long hours – a 12-hour shift three days a week and 10-hour shift the remaining days. Consequently, except at weekends, the hostel has entire charge of the children and in addition has to provide breakfast at 6.30 and supper at 8.30 for the mothers.

A project of this sort would have been impossible without voluntary labour. 'The WVS has taken over all the catering arrangements and provides members to take the children for walks, to provide occupation for them, to do housework and give help in the kitchen, to undertake the mending and innumerable other duties', which occupied some twenty-five members during the first week the hostel was open. 'I went over twice myself to wash up and scrub!' she noted in her diary for 17 January 1943. Less ambitious nurseries also benefitted from WVS efforts – volunteers made overalls, slippers, or toys for the children – and in February 1943 in Huntingdon, where women were making curtains for a soon-to-be-opened nursery, it was said that 'this is no mean task as it involves some 120 curtains and is being undertaken by members who are unable to go out to working parties and are doing the sewing in their own homes'.

Almost all of the accounts of these nurseries say that they were well run and that the children seemed happy, though whether this was actually the case is almost impossible to determine. Unlike adults, most children were not in a position to articulate any grievances they might have had. Many were undoubtedly too shy to say what was really on their mind, or too confused to make sense of their feelings. Adults enjoyed hearing from children what they wanted to hear, including words and other tokens of gratitude, but it is not clear that adults were good at noticing the symptoms of loneliness, anxiety and other miseries. To be thoughtfully attuned to an individual child's needs and desires was often close to impossible in an institutional setting, especially those that were residential. At least day nurseries were usually linked to a more-or-less normal home life (however stressful for those families that had been evacuated) and the continual presence of a mother, even if she was employed outside the household – and possibly missing her conscripted husband. It is possible, too, that a few of these children were in fact escaping from unhappy homes. WVS sources tend to be biased towards documenting cases of apparently negligent mothering, and of children who seemed happier with their nursery care (or foster parents) than with life with their own families. These are matters on which there is never likely to be much certainty, but what is clear is that quite a few mothers, mainly those with large families, faced serious hardships and were really hard-pressed in their efforts to discharge their parental responsibilities.

Pretty much from the start of the war the WVS had been serving as a source of practical guidance, such as supplying leaflets and providing directions to other sources of support, and it is certain that this function expanded as many more people came to be on the move, passing through and staying in unfamiliar places; some were even of no fixed address. The office of a Centre Organiser was the usual venue for seeking and dispensing such aid, but not always. In Glasgow the demands from travellers, mainly servicemen and their loved ones, were sufficiently persistent that the WVS staffed an office at the Central train station for 'Station Guides' and, happily, one of these guides kept a log of her activities. She usually worked at night, from around nine o'clock (give or take an hour) until three or four in the morning and her notes, which start in October 1940 and end in April 1942, reveal the diversity of the requests she was obliged to handle. Many of these involved giving directions to the thousands of people in transit who did not know or could not find their way around (the blackout never helped) – people in search of a hostel or billet or cheap but respectable hotel, women in search of their husbands and men in search of their wives or sweethearts, foreigners who struggled with their English. A few Canadians were once in search of an understandable meeting place, the Beaver Club; a soldier wanted advice on how to divorce his wife; some Chinese seamen were lost; a sailor needed help in finding a lost money belt; drunks had to be pointed in some direction; a dog accompanying a soldier might be cared for while the man did other things; and lost dogs were reunited with their masters. Occasionally, an elderly traveller was given refuge for the night in a volunteer's home.[1]

There was a wartime adage 'When in doubt, turn to the WVS', and functioning as a source of information and guidance was yet another service that confirmed the point. Since in many places public social services were inadequate or even non-existent, the WVS was undoubtedly filling a void. Its members were not, however, always glad to play this role: in May 1943, under the heading 'Information Bureau', the Centre Organiser in Exmouth, Devon reported mixed feelings:

We are still kept busy with numerous enquiries, but during the last month it has been particularly noticeable that the enquiries made are really irrelevant and feeble, and it would appear that some of the general public expect to be spoon fed by the WVS – for example, 'Where can I get the best sausages?', 'Which is the best cleaner in town?' We are all keen and interested in this part of our work when it is of a genuine nature, but it becomes irksome to those who give their time and have to neglect more important work.

It is unsurprising that a matter of importance to one woman might seem frivolous to another. A more compelling problem was brought to the WVS in Weston-super-Mare in March 1944. An unmarried officer in the ATS 'approached the Centre Organisers, having no one else to turn to, to ask advice and help as she was expecting a baby. We were able to put her in touch with a good local doctor, obtain her priority rations etc., and arrange for a member, living in the country, to make a home for her for several months, between leaving the Service and going into the Nursing Home. She greatly appreciated our help, owing to an unhappy home life.'

The middle years of the war were also marked by some new activities and approaches on the Home Front, for as the conflict wore on new needs were identified, new proposals for service put forward and priorities were rearranged. Systematic collections of rosehips and nettles were started to supplement meagre commercial food supplies; the rosehips were processed into a syrup rich in vitamin C, which was otherwise scarce. Collecting other items of value, which began early in the war, was greatly expanded, and 'salvage' came to have new connotations. Children were enlisted to help, notably through the 'cog scheme', a programme designed to harness the energies of schoolchildren to do jobs of which they were capable. In particular, children were organised to help combat the enemy that was waste, perhaps by hauling a barrow or cart from house to house in search of, from their point of view, a kind of booty. The participating children were encouraged to think of themselves as cogs in the mighty wheel that would win the war, and teams of these junior salvage stewards were specially motivated by being put in competition with each other, with prizes for the winners and badges to be earned as they sought to rescue as much as they could from the nation's dustbins.[2]

The WVS also played a major role in salvage collections, with members in some places driving a council's salvage lorry. In other places they had wagons or carts, and in the country the work could be strenuous. North Witchford, part of the Isle of Ely Rural District, reported in January 1944 that 'this is a scattered rural area so the problem of collecting the house-holders' salvage is not an easy one. Those WVS members who trudge round with a handcart sometimes walk miles in order to collect from a few houses.' Many volunteers served as sal-vage stewards – and sometimes lamented the poor support they received from local government or uncooperative men: it was reported in June 1943 that a WVS member from the Frome Rural District, 'appalled to find that the local haulier was dumping both tins and broken crocks together in the adjacent quarry (contrary to the Local Authority's latest orders), organ-ised a band of housewives who picked out all the metal. She then badgered the Local Authority's Salvage Officer till he arranged to collect it.'

From 1941, and especially in 1943–4, one of the most wide-spread activities was collecting books, which resulted in millions – perhaps tens of millions – salvaged: in many places WVS collectors and the youngsters they supervised were get-ting three or four or even more books per head of population. In Bath alone in a fortnight in June 1943 some 450,000 vol-umes were collected. The books were sorted and the best items sent to libraries that had been bombed. Others were distributed to members of the Forces and their libraries; books deemed of poor literary quality and donations in bad condition were pulped. Occasionally something of real value was found: a letter from Lord Byron, 'written from Venice in 1819', turned up in

the Frome Rural District in June 1943, while four months earlier a 'beautiful brass Bible' had been given to an RAF
regimental depot by West Kesteven; and when some seven-
teenth-century books appeared on a salvage dump in Wales, 'A
representative of the Welsh National Library was called in to
confirm the fact that these objects were of considerable interest and the owner's consent was obtained for them to be sent
to the National Library rather than to the paper mills.'[3]

A miscellany of other tasks was taken on by the WVS. This
work included responding to requests for help from the local
Food Office; conducting billeting surveys; assisting illiterate or
marginally literate people to write letters to loved ones in the
Forces; organising blood drives; helping in hospital laundries;
making camouflage nets – this was generally regarded as messy
and unpleasant work; promoting national savings such as
through 'Wings for Victory' and 'War Weapons' weeks; interviewing candidates for the Women's Land Army; and planning
'holidays at home' in their own localities – this programme was
intended to discourage people from travelling for pleasure since
trains and tracks were needed by the military. The list could be
extended: running mobile libraries; collecting books to lend to
troops at isolated camps and even medicine bottles for the local
Medical Officer of Health; distributing fruit juice or cod liver
oil to young children, especially in regions of scattered population; assisting some branches of the Women's Institute in
jam-making and the canning of fruits; organising bins for pig
food; arranging parties and presents for children at Christmas;
and of course knitting, knitting, and more knitting.

A visitor to almost any region would be able to find WVS
members engaged in some worthy and perhaps even agreeable
activity. In Minehead, Somerset the WVS did book-binding
for naval libraries; in the Llandeilo Rural District of

Carmarthenshire pillows for evacuees and for 'Rest Centres in the case of emergency' were made from feathers collected from farms by the WVS. Meanwhile, in some parts of London members formed 'shopping squads' that took orders from women in factories, cycled round the shops and eventually left the goods at the homes of the working women. In May 1942 in Shipston-on-Stour, Warwickshire a working party was 'making covers with shoulder straps for the thermos flasks which Land Girls take to work with them on the bicycles', for it had been found that 'the flasks were always getting broken and these cases have been much appreciated'.[4] The volunteer car pool in Chertsey, Surrey had two jobs almost every day in May to July 1944: one was 'collecting pathological specimens from five or six nearby hospitals' and delivering them to the Botleys Park Hospital, the other was transporting a masseuse. In Westmorland work parties appealed through post office counters for buttons (which by then, February 1943, were in short supply), which 'brought us in an avalanche of much-needed buttons' for clothes-making, though 'they take a lot of sorting'. The desires of children were also taken into account. Toy-making was valued – and popular with makers as well as recipients – since manufactured toys were increasingly unobtainable. In Birmingham in August and September 1943 it was 'progressing following the present of large pieces of wood from Messrs Emlyn Williams of Aston'; in Cardiff in January 1942 one ambulance depot (as air raids declined, its members were probably by then under-employed) was 'making toys for wartime nurseries, partly with the aid of money from the American Red Cross and partly from scraps of wool and material provided by themselves'; and in August 1944 Chesterfield's WVS was distributing to local nurseries the output of a joiner who 'had made the most lovely cots and climbing horses, porter's barrows, pull-along trucks, hobby horses, etc.' The list of projects undertaken, somewhere or other, is a long one.

No district did almost everything, and some of the jobs mentioned above were taken up only here and there, depending on local needs and opportunities and the dispositions and energies of the WVS leaders. In March 1942, during the 'Dig for Victory' campaign that promoted home gardening of edible produce, the WVS had a stall in Rotherham town hall 'with samples of vegetable salads and bottled fruit'. When in July 1942 an infants' hospital was moved from London to a requisitioned house in Puttenham, Surrey, within the Guildford Rural District, the WVS scrubbed floors and moved in furniture from storage, and everything was 'prepared for the babies in three days'. In January 1943 Huntingdon reported that, at the request of the Ministry of Labour, concerts had been arranged for workmen on one isolated site, and were enthusiastically received. Occasionally the WVS helped to set up a youth club – in many places there was not much for teenagers to do. In July 1944 the WVS in Boston, Lincolnshire undertook the catering for a party of boys and girls from Bolton in Lancashire who were visiting for a few days 'at the invitation of the Holland Youth Committee', and members were pleased by how much the young people appreciated 'the good meals provided for them'. The WVS in Derby was asked in the summer of 1944 to find someone to cut hair for the wounded soldiers at a large hospital, and of course it found a willing and efficient member to take on the job. In East Sussex in 1942 the WVS opened six depots for the 'breaking down of dry batteries' for the Army;[5] and in parts of Northamptonshire in 1943–4 the WVS was doing military outwork, which members particularly enjoyed: assembling and packing parts of Bren and Tommy guns 'under the supervision of a Sergeant', and packing spare parts for the Ordnance Department.[6]

Military men and others in uniform were also to benefit from WVS efforts. In Luton in January 1943 the Army 'appealed for help with the billeting of officers on exercises in this district' and places were found for thirty of them; WVS 'bath hostesses' opened their homes to servicemen (and women) eager for a hot bath; and young Scottish wives of servicemen and their babies arriving early in the morning in London on overnight trains were sometimes met by WVS members and helped to find their destinations.[7] In East Horsley, Surrey in October 1943 the WVS 'was asked at very short notice to change the flashes on 200 battledress tunics belonging to the local Canadian unit; several working parties were formed and the work was finished in four days'. The WVS helped to furnish a WAAF convalescent home at Stamford, Lincolnshire (September 1942) and later established a club for Land Girls in Faukland, Somerset which 'is a great success. A weekly social evening is held, the members taking it in turn to be responsible for the programme. And from this a Youth Club is developing among the lads of the village who join in with the girls every week.'[8] In Wolverhampton the 'great event' of November 1941 was the opening of a hostel for service women, 'either those on leave, or those passing through the town on duty ... Although we have only been open for three weeks, we have had 145 guests, including four married couples, for whom one room is reserved, labelled "Married Quarters". Friends and mothers of the service girls can also have accommodation, and we are allowing the Ministry of Labour to send in girls for rest when they arrive very early in the morning, as long as there is room.' Birmingham had a similar hostel by

July 1943, and it too had a room set aside for married couples as well as a much-appreciated laundry.

Perhaps understandably, WVS workers sometimes became emotionally attached to the troops they served, as the accounts of canteen work sometimes attest. Numerous reports suggest satisfaction from mothering young men in uniform, helping them to keep decently clothed, fed and perhaps entertained, possibly visiting those who were ill, and sometimes contributing a little sparkle and colour to their bleak living quarters. Throughout 1941 the WVS in Weston, near Spalding in Lincolnshire, was providing services for one hundred soldiers stationed near the village, many of them 'searchlight boys'; according to a letter from the WVS village representative,

> I found the village people was able to get to know and make friends with the lads and several of them found real homes from home to go to when they got a pass out for the evening instead of wandering around alone. We have seemed to be like one large family. I used to visit the camp every week to fetch the mending and return it – the lads always looked forward to my visit; they called me the fairy godmother when they had news from home or loved ones . . . If anything was added or any improvement made to the camp they always took me to have a look and see what my opinion was.[9]

Across the county, in Epworth, it was said in March 1943 that several WVS members had 'adopted' the local searchlight unit, supplying them with books and magazines and doing their mending.

A few WVS organisers had fun describing how they came to the aid of needy soldiers. A charming write-up from Chesterfield in February 1942 reveals both a fastidious concern with mundane details and playful sentiments beyond any rule book. The Organiser spoke of making a set of curtains 'for a military unit stationed locally, and providing furnishings and books for their "Quiet Room". The same unit has entrusted the WVS members with the additional honour of embroidering their battalion colours.' She noted that three pounds of 'darning wool has been received from Army Ordnance, but the sock darning scheme is still in abeyance, the local military authorities having failed to produce any socks. However, the secretary of the local military football team heard of the WVS willingness to darn, so he brought in the stockings of the whole team, in a terrible state of disintegration. They were so successfully darned the team won their next match 11 goals to 2. These stockings were a sideline and not done with Army wool so it will not show in the Army Ordnance accounts.' A similar rescue operation was performed in Woodhall Spa, Lincolnshire in the autumn of 1944 at the request of a local Army unit. The men's football kit had been lost and 'the only socks they had were cast-offs of another luckier regiment ... As usual we took pity on them and our faithful work party members undertook to repair them, and the result is most pleasing.'

The WVS was the official darner of socks for the Army – no doubt hundreds of thousands of socks throughout the war. 'We have carried out our routine mending for Grange Camp, over 100 pairs of socks weekly,' reported Kempston, just outside Bedford, in April 1943, 'besides repairs to coats, shorts, etc. We still mend and repair for the Pioneer Corps too. We have our weekly work-party of about 30 members who do the bulk of the work, as well as knitting and hospital supplies and any rush work the County WVS gives us.' These work parties were virtually ubiquitous for they tapped into skills that almost all women of a certain age possessed, some of whom may have felt nervous about more visible and unfamiliar assignments, and allowed them to make their own patriotic contributions. Occasionally, though, this willingness met with frustration, such as in March 1942 when the WVS in Rotherham offered to sort and mend socks for all local Army units but found that the practice was to mark the men's clothing and send it to the laundry, returning it to them in individual bundles, and 'in many cases the men have moved to other sites and the bundles follow them unsorted and unmended. Thus the Sergeant we deal with in each case tells us he often has not enough to bring in.' The Centre Organiser was vexed. 'We have a great many offers of help from older members but unfortunately we cannot regiment the Army!'

Numerous branches of the WVS were sensitive to the importance of 'social amenities' in wartime – of the merit of visiting and bucking up lonely men who manned searchlight units, of befriending outsiders and helping them to feel welcome, of finding ways to encourage strangers to connect with one another. Necessities of life were seen as psychological as well as material. The WVS in Dewsbury, Yorkshire helped organise a cabaret and dance given in July 1941 by the local detachment of the Royal Army Service Corps, and the volunteers ran the buffet and decorated the hall, 'the flowers, plants and ferns being loaned or given by WVS members', while in Gainsborough, according to a 'personal report' by the Centre Organiser in October 1942, the WVS was approached 'by officers of a Polish squadron stationed nearby to see if it is possible for us to arrange hospitality in members' homes – and otherwise – for lonely Polish airmen and officers'. She thought that she could arrange something 'for some of the ranks' at a local club, 'but parties of six to ten officers to be entertained with the same number of ladies (as requested by the officers) would be a very tall order, situated as we all are in Gainsborough, minus domestics.' Many of her colleagues, 'who would not possibly think of six to ten men and partners', would be happy to entertain a couple of officers; 'somehow some of us must make an effort to brighten the lives of these men whose unhappy country is now so sorely tried'. During the later months of the war the Overseas Club in Gainsborough was a very busy place.

While North American servicemen – mainly the Americans, who were well paid – were renowned for their generosity to, in particular, British children, they were themselves sometimes the beneficiaries of WVS outreach. This might take the form of assistance at hospitals for US troops, or invitations to teas, dances and other social events, or answering a request to make blackout curtains, which happened in Weston-super-Mare in February 1944. In some regions, including parts of Scotland,[10] the WVS were significant providers of hospitality for Americans, who usually arrived suddenly, more or less en masse, and departed just as abruptly. In these localities a 'Welcome Club' might be set up – there was an active one in Tiverton, Somerset at the end of 1944 – parties organised and dances arranged, sometimes with members of the WVS chaperoning the local young women conscripted to be dance partners. Of course, British women did not necessarily look to the WVS to facilitate their introductions to GIs. In April 1944 the Centre Organiser for the St Thomas Rural District in Devon – by this time the West Country was packed with US troops – made a passing remark that acknowledged their impact: 'My representative at Whimple was very anxious to do something for the Women's Land Army hostel, but soon discovered they could offer no attraction comparable to that offered by the company of American soldiers!! How can we compete with the attraction of an American soldier on each arm?'

Overseas servicemen were also shown hospitality on an individual basis, usually by receiving them in private homes for conversations and refreshment. In Swindon in early 1944 the WVS was cooperating with the American Red Cross to arrange home visits for some thirty American soldiers every Sunday. At Christmas in 1943 US soldiers were hosted by WVS members in Weston-super-Mare and in Cleethorpes, Lincolnshire, in 1943: 'Two days before Christmas we were asked to find hospitality for four American soldiers for the whole of Christmas Day.' Although they 'had already made arrangements for many of our own men' and 'exhausted our lists of hostesses', the WVS 'were glad to find two homes and to know that the men had a good time at each'. On the Saturday of the August Bank holiday weekend in 1944 Cleethorpes was again appealed to, this time 'to find hostesses for four Canadian Air Force men for the holiday period. They were to arrive on the same evening. We were fortunate in finding two of our members willing to do this and the four men were given hospitality.' In June 1944 in Landscove, Devon a Mrs Burrington had just given weekend hospitality to two Canadian sailors. 'These bring her total of Canadians entertained to twelve. Two of them spend all their leave with Mrs Burrington, one having returned four times.'[11] In Witham, Essex there was a nicely equipped club room for members of the Forces, and in October 1944 it was reported that the books it housed (given by the British Council) 'are greatly appreciated by one particular American who comes regularly from Sudbury and often spends hours on end at the Club. He now has friends in Witham and often spends the night there.' (Military life was unlikely to suit bookish, introspective people, and the WVS tried to keep in mind the interests of more inward-looking members of the Forces.) All these incidents were expressions – widespread from 1942 until the end of

1944 – of that 'British Welcome', whether official or unofficial, that WVS members were being asked to extend to Allied
troops, of whom Americans were easily the most important.

The presence of large numbers of foreign troops posed all
sorts of dilemmas for British civilians, as was found in the villages around Frome, an area which, according to the Centre
Organiser, Dorothy Day, in early 1944, 'has suddenly been
inundated with American troops. The rowdier element,
coming in for evening leave from adjacent districts, had
aroused much resentment and antagonism. Especially rife
were the tales of deplorable behaviour of stray men who had
"blown in" drunk to the village dances, whist drives, and
even to the Church socials, and all feelings of good will and
welcome were lost.' She set about planning some WVS-
hosted social events and called a meeting with six young
American officers – who, she observed, 'coped most gallantly
with the rather daunting mass of 26 middle-aged women of
all types' – to discuss 'the various forms of hospitality that
could be offered by the villages and the means of inviting the
right type of man who would appreciate it'. Soon she was
'asked to bring a dozen or so girls to an officers' dance at the
camp. This was very difficult owing to the scarcity of girls left
in the neighbourhood, but by augmenting the numbers with
young marrieds a very cheerful party resulted.' Later she 'was
asked to arrange upwards of 40 girls for a men's dance, with
an older woman to accompany them from each village', an
event that was deemed a success, 'and the word soon went
round the villages of what an enjoyable and well conducted
affair it had been. In each case the Centre Organiser piloted
the American transport from village to village, being blown
completely inside out in a jeep.' (Similar social interactions
with US troops were reported in August 1943 from Wantage,
Berkshire.)

All this work seems to have broken the ice and laid a foundation for constructive social reciprocities. 'Several villages have arranged return hospitality. Parties of men have been invited to tea in individual houses and have later all joined at a dance; officers have been asked to tea or supper on Sundays at various houses; sightseeing parties are being arranged; mending is being done for some units; and other plans are afoot.' New American units continued to arrive, and the Centre Organiser took pains to welcome them. Dorothy Day concluded with the reflection that 'Real friendships are resulting, and though the unruly element continues to make a bad name for the whole force, the solid antagonism has been broken down and the nicer men are finding a welcome in the cottage homes and seem to be appreciating it.'*

What is rarely revealed are the tensions and disagreements that must have arisen within groups of WVS members discussing what to do about some matter. Sources tell of outcomes and decisions made, but usually not what preceded them. One exception is found in Dewsbury, from Dorothy Dixon's diary entry for 23 November 1942. At the WVS meeting that evening,

> we discussed how we should use the money we had in our hand. Our President said she had been asked to subscribe something to the Christmas treat for evacuees and proposed

---

*There were already in later 1942 large numbers of Americans in parts of Northamptonshire (Rushden, Kettering, Higham Ferrers), and the WVS was active in arranging dances for them – 'suitable local girls' might be invited – and other orderly entertainments. Finding dance partners for the men at American military bases, and perhaps transporting the women there, were standard WVS practices by 1944; and it was said that sometimes 'the boys' later visited 'the girls' at their homes.

10s. There were several dissentient voices, one saying that the evacuees were getting far too much now, that they had oranges any time while we hardly saw one, and that if they broke crockery they had nothing to do but get more from the Town Hall while we couldn't buy it in the shops. Another said why couldn't we do something for the soldiers billeted in the town? Dewsbury did not seem to bother about *their* entertainment. In the end the 10s was voted for the evacuees but grudgingly.

(There was a tendency in some places to look more favourably on the needs of billeted British soldiers than on those of billeted evacuees.)

One experiment that is well documented is the setting up in Gainsborough in 1942 of a social club for young women who had been sent there to work in munitions, with the assistance of the Ministry of Labour. Such facilities for healthy recreation, socialising and self-improvement were widely commended; they were focused principally on the needs of young adults whose links with home and neighbourhood had been ruptured, and quite a few such canteens and clubs had appeared since 1940 – in November 1940 in Horsham, West Sussex, for example, a YWCA canteen partly run by the WVS opened for all women in uniform 'and their men friends'; it included space for games and a bedroom for any girl that might be stranded in town.[12] Gainsborough's Centre Organiser had two meetings in October 1942 with many of these working women (there was both a day and night shift) to plan what attractions might be offered in the evenings:

I asked them what they usually did at parties, and one poor girl said, 'Mrs, I've never been to a party and I don't know

Lady Reading (*left*), Chairman of the WVS, is shown leading by example. No time to waste, no task too small, always ready and willing to serve, Lady Reading embodied the spirit of the wartime WVS. By 1942 the organisation had a million members from across the country. *Below*, uniformed members in Mablethorpe, Lincolnshire. (Many members were identified simply by badges or arm bands.)

In September 1939 the WVS escorted many children from cities to parts of the country thought to be safer (*above*). *Below*, one of the countless parties arranged to cheer up the young evacuees during their first Christmas away from home (this party was at Wisbech, Cambridgeshire).

Mobile canteens were hard at work in all sorts of circumstances, and serving all kinds of people. *Right*, a WVS canteen outside a bombed-out London hotel. *Below*, WVS members can be seen serving tea to thirsty demolition crews.

Feeding the population at a time of scarcity and rationing was a major challenge, and the WVS helped in various ways. *Above*, a produce stall in Wisbech run by the WVS. Much time was also spent preparing for the consequences of possible air raids. *Below*, WVS members are practising emergency cooking in Gainsborough, Lincolnshire, September 1942.

Collecting salvage was one of the regular tasks of the WVS, whether kitchen waste for pigs (as shown on the cover) or aluminium for making aeroplanes (*bottom right*). *Top*, door-to-door salvage collection – with the help of local children; *bottom left*, WVS members weighing and processing salvaged material.

Women volunteered for a wide range of tasks, some mainly for the benefit of civilians, others for the armed forces. *Top*, a soldier selects a book from a WVS mobile library. *Middle*, members garnishing camouflage netting. *Bottom*, a work party knitting. Knitting was an important contribution to the war effort, from clothes for children to socks for troops.

New clothes and footwear became scarce and children, of course, quickly outgrew theirs. The WVS responded by setting up clothing exchanges (*above*). No money changed hands; clothes were exchanged after being assigned a points value. The sign on the wall says: 'Ladies May Attend ONLY ONCE During Each Month For the Exchange of Clothing'. *Below*, a boy is fitted for new boots.

The WVS was a major provider of hospitality for men and women in uniform. *Above*, appreciative customers leave a social centre in Rickmansworth, Hertfordshire.

At the end of the war, tens of thousands of homeless people in the south-east, the victims of V1 and V2 attacks, were furnished with household goods from other parts of the country. The WVS played a major role in this 're-homing' scheme. *Above*, residents of Sutton, Surrey receive donations from Nottingham.

how to dance'. So there and then we promised dancing lessons and the meeting brightened visibly. Some of these girls come from London, and seem to have had few advantages in life. Miss Clixby is making enquiries in the town with a view to a dancing class at the Club for an hour every week. The girls are too shy to go to a public dancing class, and many say that Gainsborough girls are horrid and won't speak to them ... The girls were obviously thrilled with the idea of a party, and are now left entirely to themselves to arrange the social side of the evening.

The WVS took a further step to make the new club attractive: 'We have now purchased a hood hair dryer, and engaged a new hairdresser, a Mrs. Cook, who will take 50 per cent of the takings and hand over 50 per cent, as we shall have *all* overhead charges to pay for, including heating, electricity, gas, towels, etc.'

During the last weeks of 1942 there were favourable reports on the launch and initial activities of this 'Liberty Club', and the Centre Organiser, Mrs Alice Ridley, was heavily invested in its success. Understandably, there were teething pains as all interested parties strove to find the right social chemistry. A weekly dancing class was up and running, but there was little demand for either a keep-fit or make-and-mend class. By late November Mrs Ridley had concluded that for a club of this type 'to be really successful and used to capacity we shall eventually have to open it at *all* times to members and a friend of either sex. Miss Townsend, Welfare Officer of the Ministry of Labour, does not take this view, saying that men do not like women in their clubs and women do not like men. My view and experience is that men strongly object to women invading their privacy at their clubs, but girls, working girls who have *few*, very few hours of leisure, like to spend it, I feel, somewhere where there is at least the possibility of meeting someone of the opposite sex.' On 20 November the County Organiser toured the 'small house' which had been taken over and 'ingeniously adapted so as to make the Club look and feel, as it were, a home for these girls and women to come to'. She described 'the drawing room or rest room containing comfortable chairs, papers, books, writing desks, electric lamps, pictures, china, etc.'; the adjoining café and 'very nice little kitchen'; and upstairs the games room, which was also used for dances, and the well-equipped hairdresser's shop with its 'very nicely fitted up bathroom'. The club's homely feel was deemed the major attraction; Mrs Ridley had gone to view 'a club on similar lines in a neighbouring county, but it was rather grim and forbidding, and consequently not very well patronised'.

On the whole the WVS was pleased with its efforts and what they had achieved, as Mrs Ridey wrote at the end of December:

> We now have 76 members and during the month I have arranged four social evenings for the girls, also a Christmas party in addition to the dancing classes on Wednesday evenings. On Christmas Eve Mrs Scott, Miss Donson and myself were presented with bouquets of chrysanthemums from the girls, who also sent the WVS members a calendar and Christmas cards. I was very pleased and gratified by this action on the part of the girls, and it does show that they really appreciate the work that the WVS are doing to make their lives brighter.

But Mrs Ridley did not stop there, with the agreeable signs of being appreciated, for she was aware that there was only so much that the club could do. 'I have yet to make the acquaintance of a transferred war worker who likes the life she is called upon in wartime to live, entailing transfer from home, and long hours spent in noisy engineering workshops without any of the compensation of a communal life as experienced in the ATS, WAAF, etc. They one and all are longing for the end of the war.'[13] A major reason that young women soon to be called up for national service – as so many were in later 1941 and 1942 – volunteered for, say, the Land Army or one of the women's military auxiliaries was to avoid being forced into munitions work. At the least, a social club might have helped to mute their pain.

The WVS often functioned as de facto social workers to individuals in distress or with just a personal request, and these opportunities for personal and sometimes intimate aid seemed to provide particular fulfillment to its members. In Luton in January 1943 visits were being made to a number of old age pensioners: 'It is really a pleasure visiting these old people, and does one good to see their faces light up when these visits are made.' A few months later, in May, it was reported that a member took a blind person every day 'to and from the bus stop, thus enabling her to go to work in safety', and that two members of the Housewives' Service took on 'an unusual duty. It was brought to their notice that a woman with pneumonia was being left alone while her husband was at work, so the housewives took charge of the invalid, doing the housework and cooking required.' Similar aid was rendered in Poulton-le-Fylde, Lancashire, when in January 1944 'a sailor appealed for someone to sit up with his wife at nights as he had to rejoin his ship. The wife was very ill with pneumonia and incapable of looking after their two small children. Neighbours helped during the day but at night no one was available so WVS came to the rescue.' Similarly, a worried soldier in Chesterfield was said to have asked for someone to sleep in the house with his pregnant wife, and a member of the

Housewives' Service did this until the baby arrived (March 1944). In December 1943 the WVS in Cleethorpes persuaded a local newspaper columnist to print a public request for 'a perambulator for the wife of a serviceman. She has been ill for six months, and has a family of three young children. Can any reader help?'[14]

Many people were struggling, and WVS members often tried to soften the blows of fate. It was reported from Weston-super-Mare in February 1944 that the WVS hospital visitor was 'acting as a "relation" to a girl from Camborne who is very ill in hospital, and whose parents were killed in a raid. She writes letters for her and does everything possible to help cheer her.' On 13 September 1941 Helen Lloyd and her colleagues in Surrey were absorbed in one family's miseries:

> Molly and Sarah [two colleagues] in a great flap. A family sent to us from Bristol by the Ministry of Health, consisting of a woman with six children, proved to include a husband dying of cancer. The party were to go Ockham Park. The husband was taken so ill on the journey that he was taken from the train at Salisbury. The wife and six children were in hysterics. They had been promised a cottage where the man could die in peace, and instead they were to be lodged in 'a mansion' and the man sent to Warren Road [a hospital]. Molly was last seen taking Dr Haine with her to soothe the wife's hysterics.

Two days later the Chief Billeting Officer 'thought of a Council cottage at Shackleford which the family could have. A great to-do getting it ready.'

Along with such sad circumstances were situations that had happier outcomes, thanks to WVS interventions. In Higham Ferrers, Northamptonshire in October 1941 an Irishman working at an aerodrome returned from a holiday in Ireland, bringing his wife and three small children back with him, but his displeased landlady refused to take them all in. Since the family could get no support from either the billeting officer (as they were not official evacuees) or Public Assistance (as they were insufficiently destitute), they were tramping the streets in search of lodgings, finding their meals at a WVS canteen, and then tramping the streets some more. The police sent them to spend a night at the train station, and they again sought out the WVS. 'Though they have been very foolish, they are clean, self-respecting, and plucky, and the woman and children are taken in by one of our members till accommodation is found at a farm-house. All seems to be going happily – the woman most grateful and of real service to the farm.'

There were other small acts of kindness. In December 1944 flowers were delivered by the WVS in Weston-super-Mare, 'at the request of a soldier in Holland, to his wife on her birth-day'. In Westmorland in November 1943 the WVS in Windermere was asked by the WAAF if they could lend 'a wedding dress for a very nice but hard-up WAAF and our Miss Pennington lent a charming bridesmaid's dress and hat for the bride and this had given intense pleasure to the WAAF (and to us!).' It is likely that, when it had the chance, the WVS enjoyed playing cupid. In June 1944 the WVS in Stamford received a letter from a sailor 'who wanted to get in touch with a Stamford girl whom he had met on a train', and from his description of her 'we were able to find the girl and put them in correspondence with one another'. On another occasion the WVS was pleased that it had been able to come to the rescue of a Wren who had walked 'very disconsolately' into an office in Scotland 'because she had missed her train to London and therefore would not be able to go to a rendezvous she had arranged "under the clock at Waterloo" with a young

Canadian soldier and she had no way of letting him know she would not be there'. Naturally, the Centre Organiser telephoned London, a WVS member was dispatched in search of the Canadian and, 'with the assistance of Toc H', he was located 'in the Canadian Forces Hostel and a happy reunion took place in London the next day'. Even if embroidered, this was a story, published in the *WVS Bulletin* for October 1942, which was bound to gratify its readers.

Here, to conclude, is a brief portrait of the wide range of WVS activities in one well-documented area: Sleaford in Lincolnshire, and the countryside around it. A report of 18 November 1941 noted some 3500 evacuees in this part of Lincolnshire with a further 115 expected that week. The main clothing depot was in Sleaford, staffed by four women, plus 106 clothing officers in the rural areas and twenty in the town of Bourne, who had distributed 2500 garments from the American Red Cross during the first eight months of the year, and almost certainly more from other sources. A boot and shoe repairing scheme had been set up with the cooperation of local cobblers and WVS clothing officers authorised the repairs to schoolchildren's footwear. The WVS was 'instrumental in having evacuees who are "bedwetters" removed to hostels, for otherwise the inhabitants of the villages are reluctant to take evacuees'; there were four mobile canteens, and the canteen at the Sleaford station was open daily from eight o'clock in the morning until ten at night, serving up to five thousand people each week. The WVS in the district was also involved in collecting rosehips for vitamin C syrup, making hundreds of garments for the Central Hospital Supplies Service and dozens of stretcher straps for the Public Health Department – an appended list reported 601 pairs of socks dispatched from the district since May 1941, along with 470 other items of clothing – soliciting money for the Red

Cross, supplying and staffing Rest Centres, lining up blood donors, producing jam in villages where there was no Women's Institute, and helping to put out new ration books and place bins for kitchen waste in and around Sleaford. Some villages offered to make camouflage nets, 'but difficulties have arisen owing to not being able to obtain suitable premises or a demonstrator'. Salvage was also said to be disappointing, despite the 'vast amount of time and energy' invested in it, and the blame was put on local authorities who failed to make regular collections. As a result, 'erstwhile enthusiastic housewives in many villages now burn their paper because it is not collected, and dispose of bones for the same reason, to avoid rats. In many villages there are insufficient or no bins.'

The women in the Sleaford area were proud of some unusual ventures. There was a RAF hospital near by and 'the WVS is undertaking to make a particular type of bed jacket to be worn by spinal cases under plaster-of-Paris. They are also making special pyjama coats for cases of burns.' The pregnant wives of servicemen were helped to be admitted for their confinements to emergency hospitals and after the babies were born special provisions for their welfare were sometimes made from a WVS services maternity fund. It was said that 'Within the last two weeks the committee have purchased three new prams. They are a beautiful apple-green colour with "WVS" painted in an inconspicuous place. These will be hired out at a small cost. The reason for this purchase is the scarcity and expense of prams, cheap and second-hand ones being almost unobtainable.' As we have seen, numerous innovative projects were devised in other WVS branches, who were always pleased when they could imagine of new way of alleviating or resolving some difficulty.

Clearly, the work of the WVS covered a very broad spectrum. Some of it was akin to that traditionally practised by the Church:

helping the poor, consoling the weak, relieving those in distress. But WVS work was made more demanding and much more complex by the realities of modern warfare: the movements of masses of people; extensive property damage, mainly in cities, resulting in widespread homelessness; the rationing of consumer goods on an unprecedented scale; and the substantial presence of war-workers and members of the Forces, many of them for-eigners, in parts of the country where outsiders had previously been little seen. These were facts that determined the context in which the WVS planned and acted. One of the major con-sequences of this reshaping of social life was that poverty and deprivation were brought face to face with comfort and privi-lege. Aspects of city slum life penetrated the countryside; the hard luck and miseries of strangers could not be so readily kept at arm's length when these strangers were billeted in your town or village. War meant that people from different backgrounds had many more opportunities to look one other in the eye, and often they had no choice but to do so. And social barriers were bound to relax when some of the traditional privileges of gen-tility were eroding: domestic servants were vanishing, private motoring was eliminated from mid-1942, the power of money to acquire desirable goods was constrained by the fact that these goods were hard to get or not available at all, and certain advan-tages, such as a large house, were apt to be transformed into liabilities if a housewife had to look after it with little or no help. Perhaps the uniform of the WVS was some sort of compensa-tion for these significant losses.*

There are only occasional hints of WVS discontent, such as unhappiness about frivolous enquiries and requests to do jobs deemed to be time-wasting. Official documents were unlikely to disclose much in the way of personal grievances, but private

*For more detail on the WVS uniform, see Chapter 9.

papers might, and a few did. In Dewsbury the diarist Dorothy Dixon remarked several times in late 1942 and early 1943 on the apparent inadequacies of the recently resigned local WVS leader, and even when her capable replacement took over members were sometimes displeased with what they were asked to do. On 11 November 1944 Dixon remarked on a recent sore point: 'WVS women are grumbling because collecting for Poppy Day has been palmed off onto them the last three years, which formerly was done by the British Legion'. Two days later she was talking with the local WVS leader, who was tired and thinking of resigning, and offered the view that 'the WVS seem to be the mugs for every group in the town which has an unpleasant job to pass on'.

In Surrey, Helen Lloyd gave voice to different frustrations. In April 1944 she was getting annoyed at what she saw as excessive and unreasonable demands from headquarters. On the 8th she complained in her diary that since early March 'the WVS grew almost neurotic in its appeals to us to be prepared. I worked like a beaver trying to organize the [Car] Pool, the Enquiry Points [see below, pp. 217–18], Rest Centres, Clothing Depots etc. up to standard.' Three weeks later, her irritation resurfaced: 'The WVS Powers-that-Be flood the Centre Organisers every day with circulars to do this and that ... I have come to the conclusion I have been too weak minded in paying meticulous attention to their hysterical outbursts.' We cannot really know how common such feelings of being hard done by were. Certainly they were rarely voiced in Narrative Reports, though the fact that women felt run down and over-worked often was. In fact, in the second half of the war some had to take leave of the WVS for a while in the hope of recovering their health.

We conclude with a caveat. The evidence from WVS reports cannot necessarily be taken to suggest typicality. While some activities were certainly standard WVS fare, such as staffing canteens, knitting and mending, others were not, stemming instead from peculiar local circumstances and the personalities and priorities of individual leaders. The impact of the WVS was bound to be rather hit and miss, for its work was unpaid and not mandated and enforced by legal sanctions, and most of what it did was dependent on established authorities whose dedication and competence were highly variable. Salvage, for example, was almost always determined by what these authorities were or were not prepared to do. We are well informed about the thorough and effective welfare work that was carried out in some places, but we know little or nothing about the places where this work was neglected or poorly executed. Caution must be exercised in order not to generalise about wartime society on the basis of individual reports. Two or three like instances may not be representative of a larger pattern of behaviour; they may point in a particular direction, but such indicators require further investigation. The experiences of evacuees, for example, were tremendously diverse, as was the conduct of billeting. In WVS records (and other wartime sources) there are reports of negligent inner-city families and abusive foster parents, but also cases of the opposite. Evidence can often be cited in support of generalisations that, if stated baldly, would contradict each other. On the other hand, some generalisations clearly do have sturdy roots. Rest Centres did usually work well, especially after 1941; the WVS was, throughout the war, a major dispenser of clothes and footwear to civilians, and this service was valued almost everywhere. And the frequent appearances of the elderly in WVS reports undoubtedly testify to a recurrent problem that was not always particularly visible: in the 1940s large numbers of aged and infirm people were on their own, struggling to cope, often overlooked and desperately lonely, and needing but getting little in the way of meaningful support from established institutions.

One dimension of the activities described in this and the preceding chapter is missing: the work of the WVS at times of emergency and raids. For while there was never again the sort of country-wide bombing that had been endured in 1940–1, from mid-1941 there were dozens of relatively isolated raids, as well as the bombings in 1942 that targeted several historic cities. Then there was the 'little Blitz' of early 1944 and the V1 and V2 attacks from June and September of 1944 respectively, which mainly affected the south-east of the country. These were events that called upon other resources and other initiatives from the WVS, as we shall see in the following two chapters.

CHAPTER 7

CASUALTIES – ANTICIPATED AND ACTUAL 1941–3

Until 1944, the possibility of an invasion could not be ruled out. The enemy was still at the door. Raids might recur; indeed did recur, in numerous places after mid-1941. It was vital to remain alert and be as well prepared as possible to meet these threats. Should a community be attacked, it was crucial to be able to respond effectively, buffer the blows and minimise the damage. In almost all of these scenarios the WVS had an important role to play.

A great deal of time was spent preparing for events that might or might not happen. These possible futures embraced further air attacks, and from 1941 the task at hand was to devise plans to deal with such grim, or at least disruptive, happenings. One job was to canvass for billets and make lists of available accommodation: the WVS in Cromer, Norfolk was asked to find lodgings for as many as 250 homeless people in case of a major raid on Norwich – 'this was hard work', according to the Centre Organiser, but by March 1943 they actually had collected 415 offers. Much practical training took place, mainly in the Housewives' Service, which continued to recruit new members – this recruiting was a major WVS activity during the middle years of the war.[1] The Housewives' Service was the bedrock of the WVS's commitment to civil defence. Members were expected to attend lectures on First Aid, basic ARP, gas attacks, the decontamination of clothes, and incendiary bombs. There were instructions on effective communications and the reporting of information; lessons in emergency cooking and the repair of respirators; exercises in fire-fighting, including the use of stirrup pumps; and plans made for the reception of casualties. The WVS fire-fighting practice held at Dewsbury on 17 August 1942 was, according to Dorothy Dixon, made up mostly of 'middle aged, stout ladies who, like myself, had never handled a stirrup pump before. They pumped and sprayed energetically if not to much purpose.' Bath had been badly blitzed in April 1942, and the following December dozens of the Housewives' Service attended special lectures on plumbing and the repair of windows and kitchen utensils. Housewives were encouraged to complete basic training, a structured programme of instruction that would qualify them to exercise responsibility if called upon, and to wear a WVS armband to signal their proficiencies to others. Tens of thousands did just this between 1941 and 1944, with the aim of being able to stand confidently on guard in their own communities, almost always in partnership with ARP wardens and fire-fighters. Much decision-making was decentralised and it was expected that women's local knowledge would inform the choices made.

There were two major dimensions of the Housewives' Service. One was to assist the wardens, if needed and asked; the other was to function as 'good neighbours' in the event of a raid. A document from 1942 listing the Housewives' duties in Newhaven, East Sussex reveals this breadth of concerns, along with the minutiae that were given close consideration. Among other things, the WVS Housewives were expected 'to lend rakes, shovels or spades etc. should Wardens require' them; place 'a bucket or buckets of water *outside* the front door directly the air raid warning is sounded for the use of the Wardens in initial fire-fighting'; know enough about the probable movements of neighbours after a warning sounded that they could inform the warden concerned if these people had taken shelter; and allow wardens 'to temporarily house injured persons while waiting for the required service'. Neighbourliness included providing special assistance to expectant women, the aged and the infirm; making available hot drinks, hot water, hot-water bottles and blankets; assisting in the use of the 'baby protective helmet' if a mother was struggling; and looking out for children playing in the street when a warning sounded. With regard to this last point, it was stressed that if these children lived nearby they should be '*sent home at once and not taken into houses*, as such an action might mean that mothers would go out searching for them. Children should only be taken in if it is first ascertained that they cannot reach home in time to be safe.'[2] Such attention to detail was a common feature of WVS planning during these years, and is confirmed by a similar three-page statement from Sutton in Surrey concerning the purposes and recommended operational practices of the Housewives' Service.[3]

Rest Centres, a staple of civil defence, were seen as immediate refuges for civilians in distress, and from 1941 a great deal of energy was invested in establishing Centres in suitable places – schools, village and church halls – and equipping them with the essentials, such as food, clothing (often lots of it) and blankets. For almost eighteen months from the middle of 1941 Helen Lloyd was regularly concerned with organising and supplying Rest Centres in the Guildford Rural District. On 29 March 1942, with spring arriving, she was contemplating the renewed prospect of a German invasion: 'I laid awake another night thinking of Rest Centre preparation I had not made, and the next day organised a hurried transport of blankets to East Horsley and a distribution of paper towels and cardboard cups.' Then, on 13 May – the time of the Baedeker raids – 'The great preoccupation of the Council is the village Invasion Committees which are being set up by Mr Sellings [clerk of the RDC]. WVS is being most active – plans for our mobile canteen which will be stationed at Ewhurst, the new Basic Training in Civil Defence for all the Housewives' Aid Points, and hideous new regulations for applications for uniform and monthly returns.' By late 1942 she was no longer dealing with evacuees, who had demanded so much of her time in the early years of the war, and was concentrating almost solely on other WVS duties. 'Now I have become obsessed with preparations for bombing', she wrote on 2 November 1942, 'emergency feeding plans, Housewives' Service, Basic Training course. With the help of the Guides, demonstrations of camp cooking plans have been held in nearly every village and field kitchens have been put up in most. The Volunteer Car Pool, which was started in July, takes up a great deal of time.'

Numerous WVS organisers reported on their preparations to ensure that Rest Centres and other emergency arrangements worked satisfactorily. On 26 August 1942 there was a Rest Centre exercise at Bury in Lancashire that tried to anticipate all the problems that would have to be contended with in dealing with homeless people; this resulted in a three-page evaluation of the effectiveness of the preparations by the WVS Regional Organiser.[4] During a civil defence exercise in

Lincoln around March 1943 members of the Housewives' Service 'were brought into action, both acting as casualties and taking casualties into the houses for treatment', and apparently pleased the local authorities 'with all they did'. In Penrith, Cumberland two evening practices were held in June 1943. 'Centres worked in pairs; the personnel from one centre visited the other, acting as homeless people during one practice and roles were reversed at the second practice. The emergency clothing for Rest Centres has not been moved from the clothing stores to Cromwell House (our residential Rest Centre) as it will be able to be kept better aired there.' On 25 February 1944 the WVS in Prestwich, Lancashire had a practice, 'Exercise "Vision"', for all six of the main Rest Centres. While the 'call-out was partly satisfactory', not all went well – people acting precipitately, people not being at the right place at the right time, a delay in opening one Centre. Of course, the point of all this was to identify problems early and thus be better prepared should a real emergency happen. One day in July 1942 in Plymouth the WVS held a 'blitz practice' involving thirty-one members, which focused on issuing clothing to potential air raid victims. 'Several weak spots in the running of the clothing centre were revealed and some helpful improvements suggested by those taking part. It was generally felt by the staff that, though it is impossible ever to create blitz conditions at a practice, enough had been learnt to make it an afternoon well spent.'

While one should always be cautious about claiming typicality, one account of an ARP exercise in 1942 does have the ring of experiences that must have been replicated in other places. It was reported by Evelyn Shallcross, the Centre Organiser, that 'a practice on a large scale was held on Sunday, 29th March for the area of Mablethorpe and Sutton', on the Lincolnshire coast:

Messenger service in full use, officials from Lincoln and Skegness, Relieving Officer, Divisional Relieving Officer, also raid welfare officers, which are Mr Shallcross and myself. Gas was used and an amount of benefit has been derived from this practice. Many officials acted as umpires. We had a debate at 16.15 hours in the Council Chamber and we were able to find the weak spots of the practice. The Rest Centre was opened and satisfaction from our personnel has been reported by our Relieving Officer, but even here one or two improvements can be made.[5]

In this way, learning from trial and error, when further raids occurred later in the war the work of the WVS and other welfare agents was undoubtedly better than it would otherwise have been.

The WVS routinely played a role in preparations to deal with invaders, as Helen Lloyd recorded on Sunday 13 December 1942:

Today there was an Invasion Exercise in Compton, Shackleford, Puttenham and Seale. The Home Guard and Civil Defence Services took part. Invasion Committees functioned, and our Rest Centres were opened. Molly [Assistant Billeting Officer] and I went round as umpires. I was very impressed with their preparations and especially with the field kitchen at Shackleford, which was cooking merrily. Throughout our drive the Home Guard was not much in evidence, but Civil Defence workers were everywhere. One constantly met ambulances with pathetic-looking figures on stretchers. Obviously their only form of wound was broken legs as all the corpses had their legs tied firmly together with bandages.

During a later exercise, in September 1943, the WVS from the Guildford Rural District 'produced teams of people to play the part of bombed-out person at rehearsals of eleven of the Rest Centres in Guildford Borough. The performances were made as realistic as possible and the parts included brazen pregnant women, drunk and blind people, deaf people and people with no teeth, unfortunates in their night clothes, bombed-out persons covered with soot and others mentally afflicted from their terrible experiences. Dogs and canaries were part of the cast.' Miss Lloyd stressed the important lessons to be learned from these realistic exercises: 'For example, nothing drove home to one more forcibly the need for adequate clothing and washing arrangements than when the Centre Organiser was left for three-quarters of an hour in her pyjamas covered in soot and no attempt was made to wash or clothe her.'

During these middle years of the war, when most regions experienced prolonged lulls from bombing or no bombing at all, exercises were going on all over Britain, and it was normal for the WVS to be involved in some supportive capacity. The WVS at Cleethorpes, Lincolnshire was called out to cook for the Home Guard during an invasion exercise on the weekend of 24–5 July 1943, less than a fortnight after the town was blitzed, and was said to have gained valuable experience. 'On the Saturday the cooks were confronted with fish and chips to be fried for about 100 men'; and the following day, after setting forth at half-past five that morning, and despite some unavoidable delays in getting the cooking operational, 'the dinner for over 200 was served punctually to a minute. The Colonel was extremely pleased with the achievements of our ladies, the men all cheered them as they left, so that they returned home hot, tired and terribly dirty, but very cheerful and willing to go again at the next call.' On 22 February 1942, outside Barton-on-Humber, Lincolnshire, 'the Home Guard were exercising with live ammunition in and around a large chalk pit and we went to man the Church Army mobile canteen from New Holland.' While this was said to have been 'a really good day out', there was one awkward feature: 'I regret to say that one of our members, who was old enough to know better, deserted the tea urn she was supposed to be minding and spent the morning standing in a snow drift watching hand grenades explode. However, she returned in time to do a spot of work at the dinner hour.' These remarks were probably offered more in jest than anger, for a few lines later, after describing (partly tongue-in-cheek) some of the military exercises being conducted, she recalled a moment when 'I regret to say one of our husbands walked straight into an ambush. However, he survived.'

Emergency cooking was expected to be required if civilians were in peril, and much effort was invested in learning how to use specialised stoves and demonstrating what could be done with regard to field cookery. It was said in December 1941 that in the villages around Hailsham, East Sussex, 'cooking in the open has been demonstrated on camp fires. In some places, permanent open air stoves are being installed under the advice of Army cooks.' In Chesterfield in October 1943 two groups erected such stoves and 'entertained the Chief Warden of the Borough, the Head Warden of the Group, and representative wardens to excellent meals cooked on the stoves ... These excellent meals were successfully produced in spite of very damp weather, and the wardens' service seem satisfied that the people of Chesterfield will be adequately fed in the event of an emergency. One Group have also successfully experimented with a lighter type of stove to provide hot water for tea, etc.' Setting up and learning how to use emergency stoves was the principal activity of the Housewives' Service in and around Chelmsford, Essex in 1943; one of these stoves was actually put to use after a raid.[6]

To be ready for the worst was vital. Pamphlets were printed showing how to cook outdoors with a minimum of equipment; one was published by the Girl Guides, and the WVS issued at least one leaflet on how to build an outdoor cooking stove (from bricks and old building materials). WVS members learned how to manage these stoves effectively, and practices like those at Chesterfield were widely conducted – and often photographed, a noteworthy fact given the scarcity of film. During an exercise at Harwich in Essex on 7 December 1941, designed to deal with fifty homeless people, 'Gas and electricity were not to be used for cooking or lighting, it being assumed that the mains were damaged, and these services not available.' The cooking was done on coal ranges. Some women were trained to improvise cooking arrangements in quite primitive post-raid conditions.

Here, then, were some of the many very practical ways in which communities, with WVS participation, prepared to defend themselves. Even if the worst never happened, these efforts helped people to feel that they would be able to cope in the face of danger, that they could usefully help one another and that they were not entirely at the mercy of the enemy. This, clearly, was the view of the women attending a two-day training school in Lincoln on 30 June and 1 July 1942, who wrote enthusiastically about what they had learned.[7] The attendees from Cleethorpes were said to have been 'extremely interested in all the lectures and came back very much re-inspired for WVS work'. They appreciated the opportunity to attend a WVS meeting 'away from their own town'. July's report from the Southern Louth Rural District spoke of the two-day school as 'marvellous': 'We all learnt a lot and thoroughly enjoyed it. Mrs Porter of Bilsby and I had a most amusing time there demonstrating an Emergency Cooker, and were so relieved when the smoke came out of the chimney.'

While preparing and planning were matters of efficiency and prudent policy, pleasures occasionally intervened. On 29 April 1944 Helen Lloyd wrote in her diary that

> My personal form of activity is in visiting all the WVS Chairmen and discussing emergency plans. It's a good occupation driving from end to end of the District in this lovely spring weather. The country is unbelievably beautiful. The green of growing grass, of budding hedge rows, of young birch and newly opened beach leaves make a colour so vivid and exhilarating that I wonder why green has even been described as a restful shade.

Planning was one thing, responding to actual attacks was bound to be different. After a lull of close to a year, concentrated air raids resumed in late April 1942. These 1942 raids were mainly on historic cities, notably Bath, Canterbury, Exeter, Norwich and York, not on targets of military-industrial significance. The damage was substantial and the demands upon civil defence consequently heavy. With thousands made homeless, the WVS had a lot of urgent work to do. Rest Centres were in high demand; emergency feeding was a priority everywhere – a Queen's Messenger Convoy was called out from Cambridge to go to Norwich and spent forty hours there, and others operated in Bath and Exeter; clothing depots were exceptionally busy; and all sorts of personal crises and private losses cried out for and received attention.

The Narrative Reports from the blitzed cities had a lot to say. In Bath the Housewives' Section

> was thoroughly tested during the severe raids in April [25th and 26th], when every group was called to action. Reports from Group Leaders have shown that the Sector and Street

Leaders have done splendid work, both with the Wardens and as Street 'Mothers', realising to the fullest extent their responsibilities, and organizing cooking and washing facilities etc. A few Street Leaders wavered but in the main the spirit behind the Housewives' Service was not lost and the morale of the Leaders was unshaken ... In every case the first line Rest Centres called on the Housewives' Service for assistance. Several Street Leaders built outdoor cooking stoves in their streets, of which they had seen as demonstration only a week previously.

Rest-Centre work was the first priority after the all-clear sounded:

We heard that three unofficial halls had been opened to take the people off the streets. WVS volunteers went in immediately and took care of the homeless, feeding and clothing them. Unfortunately, the raiders returned in about an hour's time and the work during the next raid in these Centres was no easy matter. Work was continued in the official Centres during the week, volunteers going whenever they were needed to relieve the organised rota.

WVS helpers were dispatched to all emergency feeding centres and mobile canteens; 'at the request of the National Fire Service, we sent in workers who fed the firemen night and day at the various feeding stations already arranged'; and food vans were sent to rescue squads and demolition workers. It was claimed that on one day twenty thousand meals were served.[8] A mobile canteen from the Frome Rural District spent some of its time in Bath taking 'refreshments to the crowds spending the night in the woods'. Homelessness was extensive. Finding housing for some nine thousand de-housed people was 'a gigantic task in a town that was already too full', and the WVS was active in assisting with temporary billeting, local transport (about 160 volunteer cars were used), and moving some children and the elderly away from the city, in part to relieve the pressures on accommodation. Likewise, in post-blitz Norwich WVS cars and drivers spent ten days transporting people's salvaged belongings to new billets, assisted by some grammar-school boys.[9]

A report to the WVS Regional Organiser for the South-West, dated 3 May 1942, vividly detailed the work in Bath of a brand-new mobile kitchen, a gift from the people of New South Wales and named in their honour:

> I wish you could have heard the cry of 'Good Old Australia' as dozens of tired, dusty men, many of whom had been at work with pick and shovel and bare hands for 14 hours without a break, swarmed round the mobile kitchen with its NSW flag painted on its side. Some 600 people were fed the first day, including parties of weary people waiting for their relations or belongings to be dug out of the smoul-dering ruins of their homes.

Twice more the kitchen put in fourteen-hour days, serving at least two thousand persons daily. She had high praise for the new vehicle: 'it is so very maneuverable as well as so conven-ient to work', and above all it carried large quantities of hot water so did not require frequent refilling. This benefited not only tea drinkers, for 'doctors working to save the life of some victim would send along to *New South Wales* for boiling water. Many a poor body was made a little more presentable for its relations to claim by being washed with water from the mobile kitchen.' This was a rare reason for praising a canteen. Her next sentence was perhaps anticlimactic, though certainly truthful to the gritty realities of reacting to a raid: 'Also, the dust from the old Georgian freestone lying on everything made all the workers on their different jobs so thirsty.'[10]

Getting clothes quickly to people who needed them was another top priority, and the WVS took pride in being able to meet these needs. In Bath there 'were more than enough clothes', partly because few garments in storage were lost in the raids, and partly because 'a tremendous amount of clothing was sent into Bath by societies and private persons'. Norwich, which was raided just after Bath, also received gifts of clothes from outsiders, and in May 1942 it was reported from Plymouth that 'a van load of clothing was sent to Exeter after the recent blitz on that city'. Some fifteen thousand garments were given out by the WVS in the three weeks after Exeter was raided in late April. Occasionally, there were problems with due process and fairness, such as a complaint from Norwich that 'some organisations appear to have brought in stocks and dealt them out without reference to coupons, etc., which caused some ill feeling and made the work of the WVS more difficult'. Supplies of new clothes were supposed to require coupons, supplied by the Public Assistance if not by the individual actually in need. 'Repeated visits to the Rest Centres showed that anyone insufficiently clad to visit the Assistance Board was given clothing on the spot.' Gift clothing was also available though apparently few in straightened circumstance knew about it. It was thought that 'the policy of conserving coupon-free secondhand clothing for those not in a fit state to leave the Rest Centres proved a very wise one. It is important to stress the need for economy in issuing secondhand clothes; otherwise the supply would not equal the demand.'[11]

Re-clothing was always an important aspect of recovery, and it was a high priority for the WVS. A later account of post-raid actions in Norwich reported that new clothing depots had been open for four weeks and that slightly over twenty thousand coupons had been used there up to 3 June. In York, which was attacked on 29 April, clothing coupons worth five thousand points were distributed from the WVS clothing depot for the acquisition of new clothes, 'and in addition 115 people have been supplied with secondhand clothing ... The Rest Centre stocks were replenished as soon as possible after the raid and further clothing is being sorted out to send to new Rest Centres'; and a little later, in May, secondhand clothes were delivered for distribution in bombed areas of the city by the Housewives' Service. It was added that 'the Clothing Officer considers that the prompt issue of soap had a very great effect on the morale of the bombed people and was a most important service'.

The WVS was involved in other aspects of post-raid work. In Norwich members fed the men responsible for the city's emergency mortuary and in Bath some fed the men digging graves and others reassembled body parts of the dead so that relatives could identify them.[12] After the 27 April bombing of Norwich the WVS 'undertook the whole of the Forces' air raid enquiries' under the supervision of a military officer. 'All telegrams of enquiries to police and to town clerk came to us and we dealt with them.' More or less immediately 750 telegrams of enquiry arrived from servicemen concerning their families, 'so we had a pretty hectic time, especially after the second blitz and the two later raids'. The report from Norwich in the following month indicated that this work did not let up. The WVS 'dealt with close upon 3000 enquiries about families, about property, about compassionate leave for men in the services and their families. For over a fortnight it meant working at full steam. Thirty grammar school boys did the searching for us and eight of the WVS workers dealt with the replies and sent telegrams, working ten hours a day. We have even had 150 further enquiries this last week in May when a ship with a large number of Norwich men on it put into a faraway port.' Information was precious, and the WVS was sometimes charged with collecting and conveying it to those who might be frantic with worry.

York was the victim of another raid, on 17 December 1942, which affected over twelve hundred houses and 'involved a considerable amount of work for welfare'. This work included visiting the widows of the two men killed, distributing necessities (soap, blankets: the latter because damage was done mainly to the top part of people's houses), and putting some families up in a hostel for one night – they couldn't remain at home because of unexploded bombs. As usual, food and drink were major concerns. 'On the night of the raid three canteens were out serving hot drinks to firemen and demolition workers and also to 200 night workers in a factory who were without any means of obtaining a hot drink during their break', probably because the gas mains were broken. During the following week hot meals were taken round the city in the WVS's mobile canteens and Ford vans – the Ford Motor Company was a prominent supplier of vehicles to the WVS. Immediately after the raid, four emergency feeding centres were set up to serve hot meals, and the British Restaurant opened for extended hours, serving breakfast and teas as well as the usual midday meal. While every raid would have given rise to its own peculiarities, and each place had its own ways of doing things, this sort of attention to essentials was fairly universal. These and other incident reports highlight both the challenges faced – vehicles breaking down, damaged Rest Centres, no water, insufficient staff, illness and exhaustion, WVS members distracted by their own personal losses – and the many resourceful and improvised efforts to make the best of a stressful situation.

While extensive evacuation was not an outcome of these 1942 raids, on a few occasions people were evacuated to country areas. In May, four Rest Centres were opened in the Frome Rural District to receive two hundred refugees from Bath. 'There were ample volunteers to staff them both by day and night, and in spite of the rather overcrowded and inconvenient villages halls and chapels that were used, the spirits of the people remained most cheerful. They were appreciative of what was done for them and many even said what a jolly time they had had.' Some evacuees made private arrangements for accommodation, others were billeted; some were still there in November, and the total number of official evacuees from various blitzed and endangered towns was around five hundred. There was also evidence of sorts of temporary evacuation, such as in Bath in 1942, where it was found that 'many cases have come to our notice of families who were injured during the Blitz, and who are now in need of holidays and convalescence. We are making arrangements for them to go away, finding accommodation and generally fixing up everything for them as they are not in a fit state to help themselves.' Similar holidays were arranged in 1941 and 1942 for some of the survivors of the raids on Bristol.[13]

There were also relatively isolated and scattered raids during these years: sometimes called tip-and-run raids, they were attacks by a few planes or a single plane here and there, particularly on or near coastal regions in the east of the country. One of these targets was Cromer in Norfolk. At 11.35 p.m. on 22 July 1942 it was badly damaged by four bombs dropped on the main streets by a dive bomber, causing terrible destruction and several deaths. Many had miraculous escapes, and the death toll would have been far heavier if residents over their shops had not moved into the country after last year's raids. The Rest Centre was not opened as all the homeless found sanctuary for themselves with relatives and friends, and the wounded were taken to hospital. Were able to clothe several from our WVS clothing depot, and everything was returned to us later, with expressions of gratitude for the help given. We were asked to provide tea and sandwiches for the rescue squads and demolition workers, as the mobile canteens coming from Norwich had broken down, but they turned up later.

Towns in various parts of the country suffered bombing 'incidents'. On 17 October Cromer had its third blitz, which caused considerable damage to Upton House, the local WVS headquarters, and demolished the house opposite, but resulted in no personal injuries. The Centre Organiser was full of praise for her members:

Almost before I had time to turn round, a party of them turned up with overalls, mops and pails, got down on their knees and never stopped except for meals and sleep each day until the whole house was absolutely clean and clear of all dirt and debris. So well did they work that we were able to meet here as usual on the Friday, very little the worse except for the damaged windows.

After a raid on the north-west London suburb of Sudbury on 19 October 1943, 159 people spent the night at the WVS Rest Centre, even though it was only designed to take around a hundred.[14] From time to time a raid disclosed a noteworthy social fact. On 27 March 1944 bombs fell in a part of the

Bridgewater Rural District, damaging a house and two cottages even though only one bomb exploded, and after a man of eighty was rescued from one of the cottages 'the rescue party were implored by him to go back and fetch his mattress from off his bed as he had £300 hidden in it. How', the writer wondered, 'can we persuade our people to lend their money to the Government, and so increase their capital?' (Whatever weight such populist suspicions of institutional savings may have had, the WVS was in fact mightily successful in its ongoing campaigns to raise money for the war effort.)

The WVS was called into action in the aftermath of other relatively small raids – though 'small' was perhaps not a word on the lips of those at the scene of most bombings. After a raid on Great Yarmouth in Norfolk just before Christmas 1942 the WVS manned Rest Centres, accompanied people to billets, and 'some of us took people to the Assistance Board who were too upset to think for themselves. Our canteen was out all day and of course the clothing depot was kept busy.' After a raid on Mablethorpe on 6 January 1943, within two hours every damaged house had been visited and accommodation found for some of the fifty people made homeless. Hot drinks and comforts were provided, and 'several people waited at the Depot for news of buried victims ... Families in a nearby street were kept in touch with the finding of relations under debris by Raid Welfare Officers. As soon as news came, these people were informed.' During the following week the WVS fed a hot meal at midday to the roughly two hundred men working on the demolition squads.[15] After bombs were dropped on and near Weston-super-Mare in late March 1944 the mobile canteen was sent out to serve tea in one village and it was thought that 'the drivers had some hazardous times driving over fields in the black-out to avoid unexploded bombs on the road'.[16]

Other accounts reveal the attention paid to various practical details. An unexploded bomb in Stamford, Lincolnshire in the spring of 1942 meant that lots of people had to leave their homes 'in night attire and were subsequently clothed by WVS in order to go to work next day'; a mobile laundry and bath unit was stationed near damaged parts of Hull after raids in August and December 1942; in Hertford around June 1943 a member of the Housewives' Service 'in a large house' took in people who had just been bombed out of their homes, most of which were promptly cleaned up; after Cleethorpes was raided on 14 June 1943 'a small amount of clothing was issued from the Rest Centres', which was later 'all returned when the people were able to return to their own homes or obtain help from the Assistance Board' (after a raid on 17/18 August 1943, Woodhall Spa, also in Lincolnshire, had a similar experience with clothes lent out and soon returned); and in the following month after another raid on Cleethorpes the WVS for ten days staffed the official Citizens' Advice Bureau and Information Centre, dealing mostly with problems connected with the raid. Some rescue efforts were very small scale, but presumably not insignificant for those in trouble, such as when, in August 1943, two families were bombed out of their homes in the Blyth Rural District of Suffolk: one of a man and his wife and six children, most of the latter with measles, and they were temporarily sheltered in a Rest Centre. A couple of days later 'an empty cottage was found for them' and night clothing given to the children. There must have been dozens of such relatively minor incidents during these middle years of the war, when an explosive – usually randomly delivered – jarred people out of their normal rhythms of living, leaving them or their housing damaged in some way, and calling for a practical response from the WVS.

Air raids had receded in importance since mid-1941, but

this respite was not to last into 1944, especially for those in the south-east. Indeed, from June of 1944 this corner of the country was to experience some of the most terrifying moments of the war on the home front.

CHAPTER 8

EMERGENCIES IN 1944*

The final air attacks of the war were mainly in the south-east of England, concentrated in and around London. They were terrifying, and often deadly. The little Blitz early in 1944 was followed by the menacing V1 flying bombs from June and the V2 rockets from September. As ever, the WVS was quick to respond in the aftermath of attacks. Egham in Surrey suffered its heaviest blitz on Tuesday 22 February 1944, and over the following two days the bombing 'was repeated on Egham and some houses were set on fire etc. We opened the "Limes" Rest Centre on Friday, where we fed the homeless (14), clothed them from the American Gift Store, and arranged for the Public Assistance officials to meet them at the Rest Centre and settle their claims. We were able to house them all before night.'

In the Guildford Rural District Helen Lloyd was pleased with how her members dealt with scattered raids. On 31

*A few examples later in this chapter are drawn from before or just after 1944.

January 1944 she wrote a blow-by-blow account of an incident at West Horsley two days earlier, in which four bombs had fallen in the middle of the village; 'it was miraculous that there were not more casualties'. Miss Lloyd's work included lots of telephoning, initiating the funeral arrangements of an evacuee child killed in the raid and investigating what re-housing was needed for the dozen or so who had been driven from their homes. Mrs Kenyon, the WVS clothing officer in the village, 'who is elderly, by her coolness and presence of mind, set a pattern to all WVS members in the district. She rendered immediate First Aid to the dying child and the injured mother, fortunately having dressings in the house as well as at the First Aid Post.' Such attention to detail was always important at times like these. 'Hospitality was arranged for those whose houses were damaged by the WVS village representative. No praise can be too high for Mrs Cameron, the billeting officer, who is also WVS . . . Throughout the incident complete cooperation was maintained between the WVS and the Wardens Service.' It was vital for people to pull together. 'The amount of neighbourly help given was most praiseworthy,' Miss Lloyd added, 'and I asked Miss Gumpert to arrange for two WVS helpers to assist Mrs. Knapp of Vine Cottage as she is expecting a baby and was considerably shaken.'[1]

The death of a child was always horrible – Anne Lee Michell in Somerset said that one of her saddest days in the WVS was 4 September 1941, when she was called upon to drive an evacuee mother to her child's funeral[2] – and Helen Lloyd thought it important to report the orderly arrangements that had been made for the funeral of young Marian Jordan, the child killed in the raid on West Horsley:

Mrs Jordan's brother has taken full responsibility for the arrangements, as Mrs Jordan [still recovering in hospital]

215

wishes the child to be buried at Hither Green [in Lewisham, south-east London], where her grandparents are buried, who were also air-raid casualties. The bill for the funeral will be sent to the Guildford Rural District Council in order that we may make the necessary claim from the Ministry of Pensions. It is hoped that the child's father, who is in the Navy, will be coming home on compassionate leave. The Admiralty are trying to arrange for him to be flown from Alexandria.[3]

Later that year Helen Lloyd reported on the handling of several other raids on villages outside Guildford.[4] On 10 June a bomb fell on a house in Effingham; its thatched roof 'immediately burst into flames'. A woman and her ten-month-old baby were rescued but her husband was trapped and burned to death. On 4 August a bomb demolished a farmhouse at Seale; two people were killed, four were taken to hospital and an old man 'suffering from shock' was looked after. A bomb dropped close to a cottage in Send on 12 August, causing considerable property damage and killing a soldier passing by on his bicycle. In these and other cases members of the WVS were quickly at the scene to provide aid – food and drink, clothing, emergency ration cards, sometimes first aid, perhaps tracking down relatives – and to help relocate those who had been made homeless. Sometimes they arranged to move furniture and valuables from wrecked homes, and to help clean them up. In Ockham, which was bombed on 21 June, the WVS 'spent six hours in cleaning the church, which was covered with fine dust and plaster'. The morning after the 12 August bombing at Send, the WVS village representative 'visited all the neighbouring houses to see if food stocks were damaged and if provisions were wanted for breakfast'. The Harringtons, the family made homeless, were helped to pack up their personal belongings and move their luggage, and a few days later the WVS car pool moved them to relations in Maidenhead. Transport was also provided for Mrs Harrington to visit her husband in hospital.

There must have been dozens of similar incidents during the summer of 1944 involving the WVS. Most of what it did in danger areas then and shortly thereafter was in the south-east, mainly in response to the novel, unsettling, and (for many civilians) demoralising V1 flying bombs, which were also known as buzz-bombs, pilotless planes or doodlebugs. They were first launched by Germany on 13 June, a week after D-Day. Hundreds of these weapons fell on English soil: one day in July at the train station in Reigate, Surrey, where dozens of mothers and children were waiting to be evacuated, 'there was a ceaseless procession of flying bombs overhead, but mercifully none fell in our area'; the author of the Narrative Report added that 'Hitler certainly gave them a sample of what they were going away from.' While the majority of these bombs were intercepted in the air, those that got through were frightening to behold, partly because they flew so low, partly because of the roughly twelve seconds of silence endured in painful expectation between the motor cutting out and the eventual explosion, and partly because their capricious terror emerged at a moment when victory seemed imminent. (How cruel it would be to die just as war was thought to be ending.)

Happily, many doodlebugs fell on open ground. These were not mass, concentrated raids like those of 1940–1. However, there were and were bound to be incidents in which people were killed and more still where property damage was significant. The on-the-spot relief provided by the WVS was of the usual order (canteens, clothes, temporary shelter), and hands-on, personalised, neighbourly aid of the sort described by Helen Lloyd. The main innovation by 1944 was the Incident

Inquiry Point (IIP), commonly staffed by the WVS, which was designed to ensure, during an emergency, accurate record-keeping, reliable sources of advice and information to distressed citizens, and clear lines of communication among those dealing with civil defence. In Region 5, London, 483 IIPs were opened between 15 June and 22 July.[5] A document from Sutton, Surrey in 1944, directed to women keeping house, indicates that by then the WVS took an active role in searching out people in trouble:

> If your house is blasted by a bomb you will receive a visit from a member of the WVS. She will call, as soon as possible after the crash, to see that you and all your household are unharmed, whether you have any problems that she can help you to solve, whether there are any old people or invalids in the house, and if they are suffering from shock and should be moved. She will ask you whether you are staying in your own home or going elsewhere. If you are leaving she will ask what your new address will be. All these details will be taken to the Incident Inquiry Point.

This IIP, it was added, might be 'in a house or shop or at a table in the open air, and, so that no one can miss it, it will be marked with a large board'. The WVS members there would 'take particulars of war damage and tell you how to set about making a claim', and also advise on such matters as billeting, clothing, food, and emergency cooking.[6] Clearly, by this last phase of aerial attacks, civil defence, of which the WVS was a key component, was very well organised.

Most of the relief work done by the WVS in the summer of 1944 is not particularly well documented. Only a few Narrative Reports survive from London, the principal target, though there are some fairly detailed ones from outer suburbs, notably Bexley in Kent, Carshalton in Surrey and parts of Middlesex. From these places and others around London it is clear that the months of preparation and training paid off. The WVS proved to be disciplined and organised in its relief efforts, often on a street-by-street basis – the summer's Narrative Reports from Shoreditch testify to this – and in general it had effective working relations with the other civil defence services, particularly the Wardens and Fire Guard. Rest Centres were quickly opened and Incident Inquiry Points staffed; clothing was issued to bombed-out people; plans for emergency feeding were put into action and some British Restaurants became much busier. Mobile canteens were dispatched to cater to householders in areas where flying bombs had fallen, as well as to clean-up crews and others engaged in public works; at some sites hundreds were served in a day.

In addition to these fairly routine responsibilities, there are also reports of special responses. In a district in Twickenham in July, 'a rota of helpers has been working every night from 9.30 to 11 p.m. making tea in the public shelter – this was at the request of the Post Warden in that area'. Another case that month, in Brentford and Chiswick, involved searching for a lost parrot belonging to an elderly woman in a Rest Centre, who refused to be evacuated to Epsom until her parrot was found (it was). Some WVS members felt they were reliving experiences from the Blitz of 1940–1, though they usually had a much clearer sense of what to do and how best to do it, and with better facilities to support their efforts.

Relief work was performed in trying circumstances. Many WVS members during these weeks had also to think of themselves, the needs of their own families, and coping with their own damaged property (these distractions were mentioned by a number of observers). On 31 August a flying bomb hit the Rest Centre at Lyminge, in the Elham Rural District of Kent, seriously damaging the clothing depot – members worked frantically in the pouring rain to throw tarpaulins and ground sheets over holes in the roof and later removed all the garments, 'some "saturated" with broken glass and splintered timber'. At least half a dozen WVS members had to retreat temporarily from their damaged houses and leave the village. In later June, the staff of the Falconwood Sub-Centre in Bexley had 'been working under difficulties – raids, blitzed premises with splintered glass in clothing rooms and on blankets, office papers scattered through gaping windows and rain pouring through roof into office and through into the clothing room'. There were lots of urgent needs to attend to in a brief period of time. While every incident would have had its own character, what was said of the flying-bomb explosion on the morning of 19 June in St Leonard's Gardens in Heston, Middlesex must have been fairly typical of those urban neighbourhoods: 'The incident was a bad one as the bomb had fallen on a closely built up area. There were many casualties, the majority of which were not serious however, and only three were fatal. This was surprising as a great deal of damage was done to property.' Dealing with people in shock and the consequences of property losses was at the heart of this summer's work for the WVS in the south-east.

We know a lot about the relief work done at this time by the WVS in Croydon, for there those in charge of the Housewives' Service kept a very detailed log of all the V1 raids, day by day, from 16 June until 15 August, and these reports – totalling over ten thousand words – survive in the Croydon Local Studies Library and Archives.[7] They show the active, sometimes almost daily, staffing of Incident Inquiry Points; the dispensing of innumerable cups of cocoa; the relief provided to hundreds of victims; the help given to householders to clean up damaged homes; the comfort offered to people in shock; and the 'many little deeds of kindness ... quietly done'. It was said that after the first flying-bomb attack, on 16 June, WVS members brought 'help and comfort to many frightened people, including two old ladies in a shelter behind an uninhabitable house, one crippled with arthritis, and the other too scared to think'. The women were given hot tea and moved to a more comfortable site, then later driven to stay with friends. The Housewives' Service took temporary charge that day of three young children whose mother was in shock, and minded other children 'while their mothers got on with the clearing up'.

Much was done by the WVS in Croydon during the following weeks. On 27 June an old lady 'was taken from her shattered home and housed with a Housewife'; a heavily pregnant mother of a toddler was taken to Paddington Station 'just in time to catch a train to Chepstow, where she had a sister' (28 June); advice was given on the storage of furniture from uninhabitable houses (12 July); and when on 16 July the Red Cross canteen ran out of supplies, 'bread, margarine, etc. were collected by the Housewives round the area to feed the Home Guard', who were assisting with repairs. Some afflicted citizens were stoical, others needy. After a bombing on 1 August the organiser of the Housewives' Service

went to see what I could do with a difficult woman who was hysterical and in an awful state, her pretty little home having been very badly damaged. The Wardens said they could do nothing with her, and as they wanted to move out her furniture, as the house was dangerous, they asked me to see if I could get her to leave. Mrs Bowman and I went along, and were able to calm her sufficiently to get her dressed – we had a job to find her corsets: she could not remember where anything was – and to pack a case to take away [and be 'settled' with her brother].

In the south-east, these were weeks of urgent need; WVS Centres from around the country sent members to London to help their overstretched colleagues there – this was the one time in the war when large numbers of WVS volunteers, thousands in fact, worked for a week or more at a distance from their home communities. They were employed in various forms of standard relief work and some helped in cleaning up bomb sites.[8] In July one volunteer from Cleethorpes, Lincolnshire was sometimes 'visiting houses [in London] to consider whether the man of the family should be given compassionate leave or not. This was no easy job in a strange place where damage took from a street map much of its value.' In response to a call from WVS headquarters, fifteen members from Weston-super-Mare went to London in July, and a fairly detailed account was given of their activities:

> The jobs they did were very varied: clothing and feeding the bombed-out; helping in mobile and static canteens; driving vans; preparing food for evacuation on trains; acting as escorts on trains as welfare workers; train marshals; and last, but not least, scrubbing out milk churns. One of our members was particularly struck with the good temper of the people. She heard no grousing from anyone.

These women from Somerset were kept very busy 'and hardly knew whether the Alert was on or off. Some of them were very much cheered when Lady Reading paid them a visit and spoke to them in her usual charming manner.* All these helpers say how glad they are to have had this

---

*Lady Reading visited numerous afflicted sites in London, including St Pancras on 18 July, where she talked with the members. 'As usual, after it, we felt better, cheered and renewed in strength.'

opportunity of helping ... and most of them are volunteering to go again.'

Helping the beleaguered capital gave much satisfaction, and some 1971 WVS members came from a distance to work there up to 4 September.[9] The five volunteers who went to London from Westbury in Wiltshire came home in a buoyant mood and eager to return; they had been made to 'feel that all the past months of training had not been in vain because it had been put to some practical use'. In August, two members from Midsomer Norton who had worked in London with the Queen's Messengers for a week returned to Somerset 'full of enthusiasm and would have been very sorry to have missed the wonderful experience'. Indeed, to volunteer for a week or two in hard-pressed London that summer was seen as an act of significance: the front page of the *Derbyshire Times* for 14 July 1944 found it appropriate to inform readers that four members of Chesterfield's WVS car pool had just returned from a week driving in the capital and two more had gone up to help.

Londoners were not ungrateful for this aid from outside. 'We could not have asked for more efficient or willing help than was given by the teams which came to us,' wrote Shoreditch in July. 'They seemed tireless and only too glad to do anything they possibly could. Our first team came from Bristol and, at the end of the afternoon when I left the [clothing] store for a moment, I came back to find Lady Vyvyn sweeping out the entire store in readiness for the next day. We should not have dreamed of asking her to do this, but that was the spirit that was in all the teams who came to help.'

Human relations are intense when people are in crisis. On 17 November a flying bomb fell in the garden of a house in Benfleet, Essex, causing some casualties and driving at least thirty-four people from their homes.

Members were very touched by the attitude of the homeless – never a moan or grumble, simply expressions of
thankfulness that they were safe. There were two large families of children – and such gratitude for the help that was
given them. After breakfast on the Saturday, one of the
homeless in a very nice little speech thanked helpers for
making them all so welcome and comfortable, and there was
a round of applause from the rest. I think most of the
helpers felt a lump rise in their throats.

The report concluded with the observation that 'Ours was a
small incident as incidents go, but we have learnt much from
it, and we found that our five years of training have taught us
to tackle difficulties with confidence.'

During these years, up to mid-1944, people were from time
to time evacuated from blitzed towns, but almost all of these
movements were on a small scale, involving only a few families. In July 1943, after a second raid on Grimsby, there was a
modest evacuation; two mothers and eight children were sent
to Woodhall Spa. 'The Billeting Officer spent three days in
trying to place them satisfactorily, but without compulsion
found it impossible [one assumes he/she was reluctant to use
the compulsory powers permitted, which rarely had good
results]. In the meantime we had housed them comfortably in
our centre. Three bedrooms were set aside, with the use of a
bathroom, and there is a sitting room on the ground floor.'
The WVS was later asked to allow the evacuees to stay on for
a while, 'as the arrangements seemed so satisfactory to all concerned. One great advantage is that they can have their lunch
and tea at our Communal Feeding Centre, which is in the
same building.' The countryside around Grimsby was also busy
with evacuees. 'The neighbouring villages – in fact almost the

whole rural district – have been filled with townspeople. At midnight one night a party of fourteen mothers with children and babies arrived in Healing' and had to be accommodated. Occasionally evacuees arrived somewhere quite unexpectedly; in March 1943 a small number reached Spalding 'as they were afraid of reprisals after the heavy RAF raid on Berlin'. They were temporarily housed at the local WVS headquarters and later found billets. Several reports from the first few months of 1944 indicate that, with the renewal of fairly severe air raids, some people were hoping to be evacuated to the places where they had found refuge in 1940–1. In March, the Centre Organiser at Ely remarked that 'we are pleased (though embarrassed) by letters from former mothers and child evacuees who want to return to us – we *hope* because they were happy, but they *may* prefer the ills they know to those they know not'.

The raids on London and outlying areas from June 1944 resulted in yet another major wave of evacuees – the fourth and last of the war. That summer there were probably close to a million evacuees who received some sort of government support.[10] As ever, the first task was to escort these large numbers of people to train stations for their journeys to distant places. In July two WVS members from Woodhall Spa went to London to help with the evacuation of mothers and children. They were first briefed at 41 Tothill Street, WVS headquarters, then travelled with the children to Truro 'and supplied tea and milk to the people on the train'; after returning to London they accompanied another group of evacuees to South Wales. These long journeys sometimes included a refreshment break, usually at a station stop en route. One day in August the WVS in Somerset was called out 'to feed 520 mothers and children who were passing through Wellington Station on their way to Cornwall. Urns of tea, milk, lemonade, buns and biscuits were provided.' WVS train escorts living in Cambridge left home for London early in the morning and returned the following evening.

In the reception areas the WVS was usually well prepared to deal with an emergency, and this was partly a result of the practice exercises involving Rest Centres that had been widely carried out in anticipation of raids during the previous three years. Members had also sometimes helped in conducting a census of prospective billets, and they quickly swung into action, taking on the sorts of essential organisational tasks that had been done earlier in the war, but now doing them better. The evacuees were usually received at train stations, where firm but friendly measures for crowd control might be called for, and then they would probably be put up temporarily at a Rest Centre until suitable billets were found. In Worcester on 11 July a trainload of eight hundred mothers and children was initially dispersed to sixteen Rest Centres. In Ellesmere Port, Cheshire, two modern schools were used as Rest Centres and the arriving evacuated children 'were able to watch the school pigs, chickens and rabbits being fed, which helped considerably to keep them amused during the short time they were there'.

Billeting was everywhere a central and sometimes a touchy matter, to say the least. In Midsomer Norton it was said in August that 'from the WVS point of view it seems that the hard work commences after the evacuees are settled in the billets'. As in previous years, householders could hardly be expected to be thrilled to have strangers thrust upon them and many evacuees, already stressed, may have experienced personal indignities at the hands of people with the power to decide what should happen to them. Inevitably, some decisions would not be felt to be fair from at least somebody's perspective, and suspicions were sometimes bound to fester. It was easy to feel hard done by, and perhaps surprising that grumbling was not more widespread. In the Wisbech area a significant problem with billeting was that local people 'did not like going to work and leaving their homes in the charge of evacuees'.[11] A remark from Walsingham, Norfolk in August 1944 would certainly have found support elsewhere: 'We have had two batches of official evacuees in the District, about 750 in all, besides numerous unofficial ones. The majority have been nice and have settled down, but there have been, as always, some very difficult ones.' In Long Eaton, Derbyshire 523 evacuees arrived late one evening in July; they were taken to their billets by WVS members and 'a great deal of difficulty was experienced in billeting mothers and children, though there was no difficulty in billeting the unaccompanied children', who were not so likely to lodge protests.

These were times when events moved quickly. Trains arrived with little notice, perhaps with more evacuees than expected, and with special needs that were not anticipated. Fast action was essential. On 22 July the WVS in Mablethorpe, Lincolnshire was asked to clean some disused Army billets, which were very dirty. The next day the first hundred evacuees arrived and were given tea at the Rest Centre. The mothers were then driven to the food office and from there to an appointed grocer to do their shopping (in the meantime, their children were minded by WVS members), before being 'taken by car to their new homes, received by WVS, and shown round and given a feeling of welcome' and asked to sign 'an inventory of the contents of their billet, viz., tables, chairs, beds, pillows, blankets, pots and pans, and cutlery. The people on the whole were most awfully grateful at the reception they had received. Many were in a very distressed state. This work has continued up to date with probably our last batch tomorrow, 3rd August. Some clothing has *had* to be given out. We are holding back in connection with this as far as possible but have received extremely poor people.' Mrs Shallcross, the local Organiser, concluded with the observation that 'we have been so pleased at the result of our efforts, seeing the evacuees so happy and appreciative'. During the rest of August 1944 most of the work concerning Mablethorpe's evacuees involved 'answering questions and trying to resolve their problems. Prams, cots, drawer sheets for expectant mothers, curtains (short), clocks and flat irons are still being asked for. We cope with the whole situation to the best of our ability.'[12] As usual, direct evidence from evacuees is almost non-existent, but there is no reason to doubt the value of the support they got from the WVS at these times of upheaval.

Problem-solving was a priority for most WVS members. Some 120 evacuated children arrived in Ashburton, Devon in mid-July, which (it was said) made for all sorts of issues that the WVS had to help settle. One concerned clothing: 'The Billeting Officer was besieged with foster parents threatening to return the children if some clothing was not forthcoming.' He promptly solicited WVS help and 'we had to supplement the clothing of 50 per cent of the children'. Many were not well provided for and, having spent two nights with them, the Centre Organiser thought 'it was pitiful to see the poor little mites trying to go to bed without removing their top clothes as the "undies" were so unpresentable'. She then remarked on the almost unbounded scope of issues put to the WVS:

This Office is kept busy all day long trying to help people out of their troubles. It's either rooms, a flat or a cottage, a job, a cot or cradle, and an endless string of 'wants'. These poor souls are in a far worse mental state than they were in the Blitz and it seems to help them to be able to talk to someone who will listen and give them a little comforting chat. One dear old man of nearly 70 told me he had come here to get some rest from the 'doodle bug'. His wife was killed by one in June and I had to listen to all the details. He finished up by saying he would not be able to stay down here very long as it was nearly as bad as the doodle bugs – 'the quietness I mean, Miss'. I suggested perhaps a light job might help to pass the time away, and then he calmly said that was what he had come to see me about.

Country life was a strain for some city dwellers. It was said in August that in the Okehampton Rural District, also in Devon, 'evacuees have settled down quite well on the whole, but the real country has got some of them down and London and its shops drew them back in spite of "doodle bombs"'.

Much was done that summer to try to resettle evacuees as well as possible. In Chesterfield, where approximately three thousand evacuees from London were received in July, a lot was done to support them:

All the hostels are visited and helped. The original evacuee club has been re-opened and another two have been started. One of these is called the 'Southerners' Club' and is open every day from 2 p.m. until 6 p.m. Our visitors find this a great comfort. They can make the babies' bottles, have a cup of tea, and talk to their friends. They help to run the club and feel they are doing their part.

Similar clubs were operating in August in Bebington, Cheshire and, the following month, at Beeston in Nottinghamshire. In July a quite sophisticated one was active in Okehampton, which, among other things, arranged to gives mothers regular breaks from childcare so that they could go to the cinema. A mending class had begun at the Chesterfield club; cooking lessons, given by one of the evacuees, were started in August;

and on two mornings each week the evacuees were allowed to do their washing and ironing at the club. After families were billeted, members of the Housewives' Section showed 'these strangers where the shops and parks are situated, and have added many little personal touches, e.g. ordering milk to be in the house when they arrive, getting clothes lines and irons etc.'

Chesterfield's experiences would have been shared by other WVS Centres. The lack of prams was a problem since 'most mothers were told they could not take their prams with them. The Chesterfield people have been very good indeed and have loaned prams to several mothers, but we still have tired mothers carrying heavy children.' In the Mere and Tilbury Rural District of Wiltshire, where prams did accompany the 258 evacuated mothers and children, it took two full days in July to load them on a lorry and distribute them to Londoners in the five villages concerned. Sometimes newcomers already knew of and were well-disposed to the WVS. This was the case in the Kettering Rural District in Northamptonshire, which reported in September 1944 that their evacuees 'have fortunately a good opinion of the WVS (no doubt gained in London) and this has made our work on the whole pleasant'. In addition, relationships between a local WVS and evacuees were not a one-way street: in Chesterfield 'one of the evacuees came in to offer *us* her help and she is coming in to the office three times a week to do typing'. A prominent theme in this report from Derbyshire was cooperation and mutual support. The writer observed in August that 'any problem that arises between billetee and billetor is given prompt attention – hence the reason, I think, our guests are mostly very happily settled'. A welfare worker visited the hostels daily and 'it is surprising the community spirit and good comradeship that exists among these families'.

Even in Chesterfield, where the welfare picture was apparently good, there were awkward moments, as the Centre Organiser recounted. A 'very nice woman with five children' came to the office in tears one day in August 1944 because her husband, convinced that she was leading an immoral life, was threatening to sell their home unless she returned to London:

> She was staying with one of our members and so we knew what a grand little mother this evacuee was, and she begged us to tell her husband she was doing her best and ask him to come to see for himself. We did this, and the next day an irate bully entered the office and wanted to know who was responsible for the message, because he wanted a private talk with her. Our only place was the cellar, so I took him down there and for five minutes he raved and stamped. My knees shook – but I did not let him know I minded. Then for ten minutes I talked to him and told him exactly what I thought about a man who would take his wife and children into danger. The outcome was he stayed for a happy weekend, came into the office and thanked us for what we had done. His wife is still very happily settled in Chesterfield, tells everyone we deserve the Victoria Cross, and that for the first time in six years her husband is being reasonable. During the London Blitz she was evacuated and her husband *did* sell their home, so we felt it was no idle threat, and rather pat ourselves on the back for having brought happiness to this little family.

Many communities in Lancashire – suitably distant from the endangered south-east – received groups of London area evacuees in the summer of 1944, usually between about one and five hundred of them, and WVS organisers sometimes recorded what happened in considerable detail. There was an emphasis on hospitality, individual attentiveness and concern for those practical matters that were likely to affect the women and children suddenly torn from their homes. One senses a lot of determination to execute assiduously plans already in place. 'We, in this Centre [Penwortham],' wrote the organiser in the Preston Rural District in August, 'had made a special point of Rest Centre work, and had produced playlets on that work, presenting them in other villages. This would be our test and our opportunity. We must be a success.' She resolved not to be driven to use an old, drab, ill-facilitated building as a Rest Centre, but rather a new, cheerful and up-to-date junior school, and she succeeded: 'A lovely school in lovely surroundings, lovely weather, and everyone willing to help, even though it was Bank Holiday.' According to the deputy leader of this Rest Centre, 'the dining room was very nicely arranged, with nice cloths on trestle tables, and fresh flowers each day during the time the Rest Centre was in use. Having plenty of room, some of the mothers had a washing day and they were also able to do their ironing.'

At Chadderton on 14 July ninety-six evacuees were received in the Rest Centre there and that evening, having borrowed a small wringer, 'the WVS ladies washed all nappies, thereby saving a lot of individual washing all over the building'. Four cars driven by Haslingden WVS took twelve escorts to Blackburn on 16 July 'to meet a consignment of our evacuees arriving there. These women took the place of bus conductors and escorted the buses to the Haslingden Rest Centres.' That evening twenty-seven London escorts were privately billeted, and the following day 'long mop parties' were kept 'busy cleaning twelve requisitioned houses, putting in fires and curtains up, putting in Ministry of Health furniture and other homely touches'. These and other accounts were infused with a sense of pleasure in work competently done.

After evacuees were billeted, care was taken to ensure that

they settled in as well as possible. In Ashton-under-Lyne some were placed in empty houses and members of the Housewives' Service 'were appointed Friends of the Evacuees and helped them to solve the innumerable problems that arise on entering an empty house ... Members of the clothing depot and others were kept busy making pillows for families which could not be supplied in billets. Now they are making curtains out of gift materials for the empty houses.' In Westhoughton WVS 'visitors' checked on unaccompanied children to see that they were doing well; a few days after the evacuation in Haslingden the WVS 'sent a special letter to every adult evacuee inviting her to attend an afternoon tea and bring her little ones with her'; and in Eccleston and Windle several young people home for the holidays 'were most enthusiastic and helpful, running messages, talking and playing with younger children – in fact took a great deal of the drudgery from the older people'. It was reported from Eccles in September that in the fortnight after five hundred evacuees arrived much welfare work was undertaken, 'to adjust small and large difficulties, and many of our visitors were found to be very understanding and helpful'. Perambulators 'were borrowed for the youngest babies so that mothers could walk the 20 minutes to the shopping streets' and cases of particular hardship received close attention, including the needs of an exhausted woman whose three-week-old twins were cared for in hospital until she recovered and was found 'a very comfortable home'. Hers and other urgent cases, said the WVS organiser, 'were an hourly anxiety until they were solved'.

Reports from Accrington in Lancashire during the second half of 1944 portray the WVS's responses to the arrival of about eight hundred evacuees after a journey of ten hours 'during which time there had been no water or milk on the train and only two tins of biscuits brought by the [three WVS] "stewardesses", who wired to one station for water, but even then there was not a sufficient supply'. Six Rest Centres received the evacuees, many from Ilford in Essex, and a great deal of work had to be done to accommodate them satisfactorily (which sometimes involved resettling families), arranging for personal belongings to be sent from their homes, cleaning some quarters, coping with illnesses and helping to supply household essentials such as crockery. Setting up a social club for evacuees was again a WVS ambition: one was opened in a Sunday-school hall in Accrington on 6 September, with considerable ceremony and in the presence of numerous dignitaries and officials. There was

> a small room upstairs where there are toys and books for the children and we have a writing room and magazines for the mothers, and also an ironing room, but we find that they prefer to do their own knitting and just meet for a talk over a cup of tea and cake. Milk and biscuits are provided for the children. We were very fortunate in having had a Uni-relay wireless set installed as a gift from the Company; another kind friend had given us a loud speaker. The clubroom is very bright, catching any sun which shines in Lancashire, having windows on two sides, and altogether the atmosphere is very cheerful. Flowers from the Park also add to the brightness. We are allowed the use of the room three afternoons per week. In spite of the rush back to the south [this was written at the beginning of October], we still have over 600 evacuees in the borough.

Attentiveness to evacuees' needs, material and social, was a matter of pride. By the end of October 1944 five babies had been born in Accrington to evacuee mothers and each was given 'a cot cover, cot blanket, tiny pillow and woolly ball', and lots of time and effort were put into arranging two Christmas parties that, by the austere standards of late 1944, were fairly lavish in their treats, edible and otherwise. Some toys had been made by members, others were donations from America. Evidence of evacuee contentment was duly noted. One day in November a mother and her child billeted in Accrington returned home, but the next day she sent a telegram 'to her hostess ... saying she was returning that night!! She arrived at the club today and said she could put up with all the friendly chaff of "Who couldn't take it" etc. rather than the perils of her home town.' (The numbers of evacuees nationwide were in steady decline from September 1944; still, around a million people remained in billets that October, some of whom had no home to return to.)[13]

In recounting all these activities of the WVS, it is worth recalling that it rarely acted entirely alone. Naturally, WVS sources highlight its members' own contributions, their extent, effectiveness, the people helped and the thanks received. But other players were almost always in the picture, perhaps ARP or Public Assistance, or other arms of local government; perhaps the Ministry of Health or the Ministry of Education or an Army welfare officer; perhaps some other public-spirited body such as Toc H or the YMCA or the Red Cross. Some of these partners were in the background, others very much centre stage. British Restaurants, for example, some of which became extremely busy after raids and offered extended hours of service to meet the needs of people suddenly uprooted and on the move, commonly brought together a variety of contributors, of which only one was the WVS. The crucial fact was that the WVS was designed for maximum flexibility – to supplement services that suddenly needed more staff, to fill in chronic gaps in the provision of welfare, to compensate for scarce supplies of waged labour and to be prepared for and able to help with almost any kind of urgent demand that might arise on the home front. In August 1944 the Mayor of Bath appealed to its citizens to give up their Morrison shelters for the use of people in bombed parts of Britain, and the WVS helped prepare and distribute six thousand letters publicising the initiative, work that was seen as essential to a good response. Such fruitful partnerships were normally a precondition for success. WVS efforts were most effective when its own leadership was both effectively committed and well supported by the local authorities, which, it seems, was by 1944 usually the case.

Evacuation was almost bound to be a time of tension and frayed nerves, and while most centres said little about these stresses, observers in Westmorland did. Many of their comments would surely have been applicable to other places. It was a mixed picture, as indicated by a report of 21 July 1944 from a social worker in Kendal, which was based on her interviews of thirty-three mothers at two Rest Centres.[14] She found them all rather tired 'but mainly reasonable and patient. A minority feeling resentful that they were still waiting' to be billeted, but a 'general appreciation of their friendly treatment at the centres'. She found some attitudes that were commonly held: 'There was a feeling that this evacuation was likely to be of short duration, and that therefore one could put up with fairly uncomfortable conditions as a temporary measure. The main reason for evacuation seemed to be a desire to get some rest and respite from the strain of constant alerts – many comments about being "nervy".' False rumours about available accommodation and empty houses were regrettable since it was thought that they 'accounted for most of the resentment rather than any feeling that the individual householder of Kendal did not want them'. As happened almost everywhere, large families were hard to settle, regardless of everyone's best intentions, for suitable houses were at a premium and women were determined that their families not be broken up. 'The women with large families especially were emphatic that they did not mind how primitive accommodation might be as regards furnishing, but that they did want a place on their own.' Billeting was a delicate matter, and it must often have been emotionally charged. It was said in August in Westmorland that 'one mother wept with gratitude to the billeting officials' the day after she had been settled. 'She never dreamt that anyone would really want her and four little girls, but she had had a wonderful welcome from a lonely spinster at Arnside that she would remember all her life.'

Then there were issues of class and class consciousness. Most of the evacuees were to varying degrees poor – this was a time at which around 80 per cent of the population was working class. Some were considered less 'respectable' than others; and many were felt by those in more comfortable circumstances to practise inferior standards of hygiene and orderliness. The social worker in Westmorland thought that a key difficulty in billeting would be 'Kendal's fear of folk with a low standard; a close second was the evacuees' fear of poshness'. She thought that this latter concern, if scrutinised, 'usually consisted either of a fear of damaging the hostess' furniture, or not being allowed to do washing for the children as and when necessary (this arose from the two facts that they had not enough clothes to send them to the laundry and that they could not afford the cost)'. Here was one of a number of acknowledgements that there might be and sometimes were problems on both sides: perhaps concern among householders about slatternly and rude evacuees, perhaps a fear among uprooted women of a loss of independence and of being looked down upon by their (often) genteel hostesses, who had the biggest houses and thus usually could not avoid accepting billets. The August report from Kendal tried to be balanced in its assessment, pointing out that while there were 'misfits' and some evacuees who were unreasonably demanding, 'they are the minority and on the whole most of them have settled far better than was expected'.

General statements about class relations are tricky to put forward, partly because almost all of the evidence is anecdotal. It is easy to compile both a list of incidents of class hostility and another of examples of class harmony and cooperation. On the whole, it seems that the stoicism of the evacuees was both noticed and admired, as evidenced by a WVS observation from Norwich in April 1942, just after its Baedeker raid: 'I think all our people worked splendidly, and the people who were bombed out were very brave and uncomplaining.' The astute organiser in Chesterfield got the balance about right when she wrote in July 1944 of the clothing depot there, which was open six days a week, and its efforts to help the approximately three thousand evacuees just arrived from London: 'Obviously, some of the applicants are scroungers, pure and simple, but the genuine cases are easily distinguished by their good tempered demeanour and their gratitude is pathetic.'

Other kinds of emergencies were also experienced and dealt with. In both Bath and Huntingdon, outbreaks of influenza in December 1943 prompted the WVS to offer the afflicted domestic support: cooking, shopping, washing up, and the like. The flu epidemic in Westmorland prompted a similar 'Home Helps' scheme for stricken individuals: the objective was to ensure that no one in the countryside was 'left stranded through illness'. There were numerous other instances of the WVS coming to the rescue of people in perilous circumstances, two of which were reported from Kendal in December 1942. On one occasion, the WVS received a letter from a soldier stationed in the north of Scotland who was worried about his wife and children. They were visited and found to be 'in a very poor condition, having been bombed out of their home, and the wife had not known where to turn. We were able to put her in touch with the proper authorities.' On another occasion a WVS leader was asked 'to visit a farmer near Kendal whose wife was very ill and had to be rushed to hospital', and arrangements were made to look after her children. In July 1943 this same WVS member was confronted with what must have been an unusual case, 'that of a soldier in the Middle East who wanted leave on compassionate grounds as he and his wife were approaching middle age and both longed for a child', for they had none despite having been married for some time. The soldier's commanding officer 'wished the matter to be investigated, and Mrs Pennington was asked to obtain the wife's consent and the doctor's assurance that this was a genuine case. This she managed to do.' In a few instances the sense of emergency might be mainly in the eyes of one or two beholders. One day in June/July 1944 an airman and his wife in Cambridge 'came in with a baby which they wished to leave with us for a long weekend while they returned to London for their belongings. Their train left in half an hour. The Canteen Organiser took the baby to her home and looked after it. We were a bit anxious that these light-hearted parents would not return, but they did.'

Unanticipated and pressing demands of one sort or another were bound to occur, and there was a fair chance that WVS members would be among the people best placed to respond. According to a report from York in October 1943, the Housewives' Service there 'had an SOS from the Ministry of Agriculture in the middle of the potato-picking campaign. It appeared that the children who were sent out potato picking had no supervision at the bus stops where they were collected in the morning', and so the WVS was asked to fill the void by supplying, as the writer put it, 'the right sort of "sheep dog"' (which they did: this was a case of nearly literal mothering).[15] During the flying-bomb emergency in the summer of 1944, the Shaftesbury WVS in Dorset received 'an urgent request from the Army for rags to clean the Anti-Aircraft guns', and vast numbers were promptly supplied.[16] In July 1944 a WVS canteen in Boston, Lincolnshire was called out to serve tea and sandwiches to men searching for survivors of a nearby air crash. Likewise, on 31 December 1942 two planes had collided over Gainsborough, one of which fell in flames on some houses, and the WVS was called out to open a Rest Centre and staff a snack bar (though uncooperative behaviour by one WVS leader was responsible for a less than ideal service); another member was credited with serving tea and soup from her home to the men assigned to guard the second crashed plane just outside the town and near where she lived. One of the most lethal accidents on the home front occurred on 27 November 1944 when there was a massive explosion of an RAF underground munitions storage depot in Fauld, Staffordshire, which caused extensive damage and killed at least seventy-five people. For the next two months WVS canteen teams visited the site daily, serving soldiers, civil defence personnel and clean-up crews. 'There are large numbers of men to be catered for who appreciate the service enormously,' stated a report from Burton-on-Trent in November. 'In fact, the thanks we receive are just too embarrassing.'

Other incidents, while much less critical, still benefited from having WVS hands to help out. In July 1943 in Huntingdon a WVS member in charge of an ARP auxiliary canteen – a private car equipped with several dozen mugs and a thermostat urn – 'received an unexpected emergency call to serve tea and sandwiches to Home Guard and police in search of an escaped Italian prisoner. She was ready in record time and spent from 9 p.m. to 5 a.m. going round to the various "searches" and serving over 150 teas!' And on 15 October 1943 Helen Lloyd composed in her diary a can-do account of a fire in the kitchen of a factory works at Compton that got out of control and generated noxious fumes that overcame the regular staff: 'Dr Haine came down to see me and asked if the WVS, at a moment's notice, could take over the cooking and serving of the dinner for 80 men.' Naturally, the local WVS rose to the occasion, quickly providing seven volunteer replacements, including at least two cooks. 'Lunch and tea were served up to time and the full production of the Works continued without interruption.' Life on the Home Front was littered with mishaps of this sort, some small, others more substantial, and it was common for the WVS to be on the spot to help put things right.

In June 1944, shortly after D-Day, the WVS in Portsmouth was asked by the port authorities to maintain a twenty-four-hour canteen service in the dockyard to receive returning sailors and the ships bringing in survivors from the invasion beaches, and one of the participants wrote a heartfelt account of the work she and others did. One canteen was operating within an hour of the request, but 'it took us a day or so to find our bearings and the routes to the various jetties, for we were switched from one jetty to the other to meet these small ships, and the driving at night, especially over the narrow dock bridges, was very difficult'. At first the arrivals from France were mostly hungry sailors.

> On the third night we were suddenly asked to serve ships bringing in the wounded ... We served all walking wounded either in the ambulances or coaches, or as they were waiting to enter them, with free tea or cocoa, cake,

chocolates and cigarettes, the latter given by the WRNS and local inhabitants. Many of the men were cold and shivering from sea-sickness and felt much better for the hot sweetened tea. Some of the stretcher cases were also served with tea, and after the wounded came the turn of the weary sick-berth attendants and the RAMC [Royal Army Medical Corps] personnel, including the stretcher bearers.

One night they toiled through torrential rain. Sixty-eight shifts were worked over a fortnight 'to cope with the present emergency, and by their willing cooperation and determination to surmount the innumerable difficulties, such as flat tyres, breakdowns, arrangements of personnel, and so on, which mean so much at the time and yet can later be dismissed with a smile, this round-the-clock service has been maintained. The work is at all times interesting, and we are more than compensated for our endeavours by the knowledge that we have been given the opportunity of doing some small service for those who have sacrificed, and are still sacrificing, so much for us in order to hasten the end of the war.'[17]

The casualties that resulted from Allied advances after D-Day sometimes called upon other WVS services, such as driving to hospital injured soldiers arriving home and doing relief work (or just visiting) at hospitals, both British and American. There was also an increased need for blood transfusions, and here the WVS had a long-standing commitment. A report of 26 September 1944 from Bristol took pride in recalling the contributions since 1940 of WVS Housewives to careful record-keeping at the city's blood depot, and the efforts to meet the urgent need for blood transfusions after D-Day 'for our men in the beaches. The Depot was working night and day in a supreme effort to keep up with the demand. Factory workers, city workers, housewives, everyone who could in this West Country city of ours

gave freely to the Blood Bank.' The WVS was active in helping to ensure that these processes ran smoothly. 'We made up
800 filters and drippers each week, besides preparing test tubes,
putting draw strings through bags – hundreds of them!! – and
cutting up yards and yards of linen', work, she emphasised, that
'must be carefully done and kept very clean'. She also mentioned the letter of thanks received from Major Laycock. (Praise
for services rendered was always appreciated, and perhaps particularly so when the jobs done were unglamorous and out of
the public eye.)

From time to time the WVS encountered situations that
caused women particular distress, a few of which revealed the
indifference of men to women's needs. Hygiene and toilets
were usually not a big deal for men, and rarely a source of
emergency, but women were disposed to think differently. It
was said in October 1942 of the clothing depot in Swindon
that 'our rather serious difficulty is the lack of any sanitary
arrangements', and the letter-writer appealed to the city for
improved facilities.[18] In Woking, Surrey in June 1944 the WVS
had the new task of serving refreshments from a mobile canteen
to the workers who were loading and unloading hospital trains,
which were arriving regularly, but 'the whole organisation has
been extremely complicated owing to the advanced stage of the
war which we have now reached, with consequent difficulties
of finding staff and food.' Since no 'sanitary accommodation
was provided for the numerous women personnel working at
the loading site', the Centre Organiser pressed to have something done, and she encountered other women whose welfare
was being overlooked: 'There are 15 nurses to each of these
trains and they live on them entirely, with their train parked in
a goods siding between journeys. Their life is consequently not
a very easy one.' So the WVS acted to help them out:
'Everything possible has been done to let the nurses on the

trains know that we have their interests at heart, and we have arranged baths for them at nearby houses where there is constant hot water – a somewhat unusual amenity in these times.'

One almost unobtainable item in reception areas was rubber teats for babies' bottles, and the WVS was sometimes appealed to by desperate mothers. In Weston-super-Mare in 1944 'the news that we could supply teats for babies' bottles was received with enthusiasm, and few gifts from the American Red Cross could have been more welcome'.[19] 'We have mothers (and grandmothers on behalf of their daughters) almost in tears asking our help,' according to Kendal in August 1944: 'We give them out very sparingly to evacuees but the situation is quite desperate now as *local* mothers are quite naturally begging from us, also for their babies, the local shops having to a great extent been denuded of the very small stock they had by the large number of evacuees who arrived last month.' She feared very bad feelings 'locally if only the evacuee mothers can get teats and not their hostesses'. While many evacuees were certainly hard pressed to meet their basic needs, the women on whom they were billeted were struggling too, particularly those with children. How to distribute benefits fairly was of no small importance.

In these and many other accounts of WVS actions, there is an air of pride and personal satisfaction, of contentment from sometimes hard work well done, and from overcoming obstacles; an awareness that self-interest was overtaken by the solidarities of service; and signs of the pleasure derived from accomplishing things of consequence for the welfare of others, accomplishments that were achieved cooperatively and could be seen as a part of a much larger whole.* The report of

*Appendix B reproduces a detailed report from Westmorland in November 1944 that reinforces these assertions.

Weston-super-Mare's Clothing Officer for 1944 was infused with this sense of satisfaction from lending others a hand:

> The work of fighting moths and checking stock never ends, but to the depot staff the whole interest of our work lies in the people we try to serve – the newly bombed-out, the unaccompanied evacuee schoolchildren, the evacuated mothers meeting heavy expenses, the very old men and women in hostels who have little money for clothes or pleasure, the servicemen's families struggling with amazing courage to make both ends meet in this town of enormous rents on their much reduced weekly income, and people sent by the Public Assistance whose lives often seem even devoid of hope.

She recalled how she and her helpers had 'rejoiced with the bombed-out blonde from London whose chest measured 54 inches when it was found possible to squeeze her into the blouse of her choice'.[20]

Such positive feelings about WVS work are understandable. The following chapter allows us to look more deeply at these aspects of social psychology: the emotions and attitudes and states of mind disclosed through the wartime work of the WVS and the social relationships that this work gave rise to.

CHAPTER 9

MINDS AND EMOTIONS
1939–44

We have seen something of the accomplishments of the WVS on many fronts. However, when we speak of work well done and projects that succeeded, it is worth keeping in mind that few surviving sources said, or were likely to say, much about negligence, inefficiency and failures. In official documents, inadequacies and missteps – and there must have been more than a few – are glided over, as one would expect. WVS documents were biased to be positive, to record encouraging outcomes and to highlight difficulties overcome. There was no mileage in dwelling on defects or incompetence, especially when they were often only temporary and could be corrected. The widely distributed *WVS Bulletin* was meant mainly to raise morale, publicise best practices so that others could learn from them and provide recognition to individuals and localities for work well done.

It should be remembered, too, that in an organisation made

up overwhelmingly of volunteers, blaming other volunteers for their perceived deficiencies would have not only been in poor taste, but counterproductive. Generosity of outlook, praise and encouragement are the essential lubricants of any voluntary organisation, and no one understood this better than Lady Reading. Her weeks were filled with visits to all regions of her far-flung service, where she almost invariably showered volunteers with words of recognition, appreciation and approval, along with messages of solidarity, letters of thanks for work well done and calls for continuing voluntary action. The WVS did not rely much on arm-twisting. Rather, peer pressure and the admirable examples of others did most of the work of promoting solid, reliable performance, which was assiduously sustained by positive reinforcement. And care was always taken to ensure that members would not be pressured to do work for which they were clearly unsuited and would have felt uncomfortable trying to carry out.

We do not hear much about class resentment in writings about the WVS – Lady Reading liked to think that class barriers had been removed[1] – though it would be surprising if some hostility had not cropped up from time to time. One such episode appears in the diary of Dorothy Dixon, who had a full-time job as a shop assistant in Dewsbury. On Monday, 26 October 1942 she attended a big by-invitation-only WVS meeting in the town hall at which the featured speaker was Lady Iris Capell (Dorothy Dixon did not name her, but the *Dewsbury District News and Chronicle* for 31 October did). Miss Dixon wrote in her diary of how she 'looked forward to this very much, thinking we should learn something of the work that is being done in the blitzed areas', but she was disappointed:

The lady (she was a real Lady someone or other), the Vice-Chairman for England and Wales, after insipid speeches from the Mayoress and others, throwing bouquets at one another and occasionally a blossom to we 'groundlings', got up and spoke. She spoke from notes. She said how glad she was to see so many there to listen to her, and said that the WVS was doing such magnificent work and tackling such huge jobs, and nothing was too big for them, and we should be proud of all we were doing to help win the war, and how working for others brought a wider outlook ('vista' she called it), and many of us were realising for the first time that we had duties to others, and we were responding nobly. And that was all!

Dorothy Dixon felt angry. She had wanted to be *informed* about the work being done, 'in some detail'. 'To drag women, mostly middle aged, who have been working all day – and Monday is wash day with many of them – out in the black-out ... to listen to such piffle is no joke.' Her sarcastic conclusion was that 'I suppose we must be thankful we were not charged admittance to gaze on the elite of Dewsbury'. She was not alone in her disdain. A few days later, on 2 November, she attended a meeting of the local WVS. The town hall session was discussed and 'everyone said it was rotten. Those who go netting (working camouflage nets) were bitter about the "platform people" parading in their uniforms but who never go near the "nets". It is hard, dirty, disagreeable work.' (This was true.)* Perhaps

---

*For one, a middle-aged housewife in Bradford, netting was probably her most regular WVS commitment, and she wrote about it on 14 July 1943 in her Mass-Observation diary (she is diarist no. 5423): 'The head of the WVS, in the course of her report on the Service, spoke very highly of our camouflage netting activity, and pointed out that when one of the national organisers visited our workroom she was very much struck with the way our supervisors [of whom the diarist was one] did the horse work. Evidently in other places the supervisors set the scrimmers to work on a net and then retire to the "holy-of-holies" with their knitting and sewing. No wonder our output is enough to supply most of the Northern Command's demands!'

northerners were disinclined to deference when leadership and status were highlighted too unsubtly. The memoir of a teenage evacuee from Middlesbrough recalls that the WVS, most of whom he saw as middle class, 'were vulgarly known in our area as "Widows, Virgins and Spinsters".'[2] Of course, people cast as do-gooders have always got a rough ride in some circles.

How, one might ask, did wartime experiences affect the thinking of WVS members about social class and inequality? Rich women (relatively speaking) and much poorer women certainly rubbed up against each other more frequently than they had before 1939, and this may have altered the thinking of some ladies of means. A speculative suggestion: perhaps the ways in which women of many different backgrounds were thrown together on the wartime home front led some Conservative women to an acceptance of the need for post-war social reform. Certainly the enthusiasm for the Beveridge Report of late 1942, which outlined the prospective workings of a welfare state, was very widespread. Many – perhaps most – Conservative supporters agreed on the need to make the post-war world a better place for most people to live in, and that this would require a degree of state action. There could be no return, almost everyone conceded, to the miseries and injustices of the 1930s. After their wartime exposure to a larger social world with lots of anguish, WVS women were perhaps willing to acquiesce, albeit sometimes grudgingly, to the shocking and unanticipated arrival of a Labour Government in July 1945. Maybe it was not what many of them would have wanted, but most of them did adapt – for a while. Perhaps, then, the shared sacrifices of 1939–45 pushed towards a broader acceptance of egalitarian values. It is noteworthy that Nella Last, a committed Conservative, was initially fairly tolerant of Labour in power and thought that Clement Attlee and his colleagues should be given a fair chance to govern. Lady

Reading herself, certainly no socialist, took pains to foster good relations with Labour and acknowledge the legitimacy of many of its post-war aspirations. Indeed, she and Attlee, in their commitment to late-Victorian values of duty and service, had a lot in common. And, unlike most Victorians, both championed the merits of state planning.[3]

In the main, the WVS was an enormously positive wartime fixture that routinely met the mandates it had been given and eased the lives of countless of their fellow countrymen and women – and lots of homesick, lonely foreigners as well. Pleasure was found in being able to rise to the occasion, whatever the request, and not let others down. The work accomplished was often spoken of with unrestrained pride. The canteen for the Services in the modest-sized port of Dartmouth in Devon grew dramatically after its opening in July 1940, 'when to serve 100 meals a day was considered rather wonderful. During last winter [1941] we rose to an average of between 1200 and 1500 meals a day, and during the last month [August 1942] it has risen to nearly 2000.' It was hard to find the twenty-four helpers needed each day, especially since 'practically every household, large or small, are coping with having men of the Services billeted on them in these servantless days'. But they succeeded, and their task was eased by some of their customers: 'At the moment we have a very large number of real "cockneys" stationed here, and with their constant cheerfulness, their well-known ready wit and humour, and their ever ready willingness to help in any way, they make it a pleasure to look after them and they are so grateful for all that is done for them.' In mid-July 1943 the four-woman mobile canteen from Barton-on-Humber, Lincolnshire was very busy in Grimsby, which had just been raided. 'They did enjoy their work and feel very proud to think theirs was the only canteen without a man driver.' Teamwork that delivered results was something to be proud of. In August 1944 Bebington, Cheshire reported on the reception of evacuees at the ten Rest Centres in the area: 'Our members worked splendidly in the full team spirit, and welcomed this work after the long period of preparation.' Being able to work together for the public good in any circumstances was one of the goals that Lady Reading routinely emphasised.

A long and detailed account of the work of the WVS in the north-west between December 1940 and December 1941, when there was extensive bombing, exuded a sense of pride in what had been accomplished, perhaps well beyond expectations. The Housewives' Service was not fully launched there until after the first raid, but when it was established it was found that 'the simple training given to women who could not offer to leave their homes even for Rest Centre work, and the sense of responsibility for their neighbours accepted by them, exerted a steadying influence on the morale of the public in the worst bombed districts'. At first there were self-doubters:

Some of the recruits, large middle-aged women, breathless after climbing the stairs in the various premises used in districts not well provided with meeting halls, hung back in the doorway and confessed that they felt shy about coming in their shawls to lectures on first aid. But most did not miss an attendance and they finally tucked carefully under their shawls the WVS cards to put in the windows to show neighbours and wardens that there help could be found for the minor casualties, for hysterical or distressed or lonely people; that there was a bucket of water ready. Among the wardens, especially in the poorest parts of Salford, there was an appreciation of the relief these women could give them from hampering odd jobs.

The authors of this report from the north-west thought that in the midst of the wreckage 'the sight of a [WVS] window card in a windowless street has told that an undaunted housewife was still there with herself and her home at the disposal of anyone who might need such local help'. Women of modest standing were now playing larger roles. 'It was curious to hear the shyest of these women, who have probably never had any authority, say calmly, "There would have been a panic in our shelter one night if I hadn't been there."' There was no doubt, the writers concluded, that 'the tenacity and courage of some of these stout women with stout hearts and no breath to spare have played a part in stiffening the resistance to air raids'.[4]

WVS accomplishments were seen as worth celebrating. Late in the war a member in Guildford recalled with pleasure setting up in the spring of 1941 a social club for evacuees. 'We named our club the Friendship Club because we really felt that the members were really so glad just to have somewhere to meet and make friends who had had the same experiences and difficulties to overcome. Blitz experiences formed the main topic of conversation at all the early meetings, and this helped members to get these unpleasant things off their minds in company with others, whose experiences were equally horrid, and this topic of conversation ceased when real friendships were formed.'[5] A report of the work done by the three camouflage-net depots in East Sussex during 1942 noted that one of the women in charge 'invented "bow-tie" garnishing, which has been officially adopted by the Army and is now included in their design charts'.[6] Numerous accounts lauded the cleverness and ingenuity of menders and sewers in converting unpromising material and second-hand clothes into useful and serviceable garments. A member of the working party in Hornchurch, Essex, 'who has herself been "bombed out" twice', was said in September 1941 to be 'a wizard at making little coats, trousers, and frocks from incredibly small pieces of new material, and her sister unravels old knitted goods and makes new garments from the wool'. 'Knickers for a boy out of a lady's scarf is a pretty good effort, I think,' said Ely's Centre Organiser in October 1942. A WVS member in Buxton, Derbyshire who was a language teacher took it upon herself to teach some of the soldiers posted in the area, and her efforts became even more valued when many non-Britons arrived:

> Several of these men could scarcely speak any English when they came and it has been very satisfactory to our member to learn that one man whose English comprised only a few words when he came here could write a perfectly good English letter within three months. Furthermore, on leaving here he matriculated with honours. Our member is, as you may imagine, very proud of her pupils.

In Woking in May/June 1944 dozens of WVS and Women's Institute members, and others, were recruited for part-time work folding and packing uniforms for the Royal Army Ordnance Corps – three women were apparently able to get through work that had previously required the efforts of four men. 'It has given enormous pride and satisfaction to those who have been working on this job to know that some of the garments which they folded for packing on the 17th and 18th May went out with the troops on D-Day.'

Meaningful work well done: this was a key refrain in talk about WVS activities. Perhaps the pleasure came from sewing on hundreds of flashes on servicemen's uniforms in just a few hours, perhaps from a highly successful book drive, or from remarkable turn-out of knitted goods, or from the welcome given to evacuees who suddenly descended on a reception area. The WVS in Carlisle reported that 'during the three years that our camouflage factory was in being our workers garnished approximately 2270 nets and we are proud of the fact that the standard of work was so consistently high that the Ministry of Supply stopped examining the nets; they went straight into action without inspection.'[7] A five-page report from Wallasey in Cheshire detailed all that was done to handle 439 evacuees, mostly women with children from urban areas of Essex, who arrived there on 28 July 1944, and it exudes a sense of pride in how needs had been anticipated – 'stocks of sanitary towels were placed in each Rest Centre' – good food was provided (the menu was enclosed) and transport efficiently organised, babies were accommodated in appropriate cots and blankets 'thoroughly aired', and billeting thoughtfully carried out. 'I am very proud to say that WVS members helped by opening their homes to these families; one of our members took a mother and five children.'[8] To be able to contribute in some tangible way to the war effort was a matter of importance. In July 1944 an account from Worcester described the tasks of a two-woman crew on a canal boat that carried twenty-five tons of flour from Worcester to Tipton, and then went on to Cannock Chase for twenty-two tons of coal, to be delivered to Worcester. 'I thought with something of a thrill just what an excellent war job this was,' one of these women concluded, 'and was glad that I was privileged to share it. In so doing we had provided the cheapest form of carrying, and had perhaps done a little to help keep the roads and railways clear for invasion convoys.'

Being able to make a constructive difference was deeply satisfying. A long account of the work of a WVS canteen that met a hospital train arriving in Langford, Bedfordshire on 18 August 1943 concluded by saying that 'at 1.30 a.m. we went home, tired but delighted to have been given the work to do and feeling that we had really been necessary, and proud that we had served nearly 2000 meals'.[9] The help given from around the country to battered London in the summer of 1944 was a source of pleasure to the women who went there for a week or two. Two members from Cleethorpes had worked at a London canteen in July and returned 'full of the spirit of good humour and understanding that existed amongst the WVS workers and felt that this entirely compensated for the malicious intentions of the flying bombs'. That summer, volunteers from the West Country took pride in stressing how hard they had worked to aid beleaguered Londoners, and referred to themselves as 'Somerset toughs', a self-designation that was repeated in several documents. By the last phase of the war the WVS was well prepared to deal with the consequences of renewed German attacks. Two V2 rockets hit Romford, Essex in November 1944 and the WVS there took pride in being able to lay on a range of services, including a mobile canteen, emergency feeding units, an Incident Inquiry Point, and transport to hospital, and still find time to help the occupants of damaged homes clean up, 'picking up carpets that were covered with soot and beating them' – 'People said they won't forget WVS kindness.'

The WVS was happy to be thanked by those it aided, and some of this gratitude was recorded. Appreciation was frequently expressed by homeless people in desperate need of clothes, for basic decency and self-respect could not be preserved unless a family was adequately clothed (all women could understand this). After a raid, the WVS was the most prominent provider of these and other necessities: a comb of one's own, powder and nappies for the baby, soap, perhaps a torch to mitigate the grimness of the blackout. In February 1943 several copies of letters of thanks from soldiers for the 'Kit Bag Club' in Chesterfield were attached to that month's report sent to London. The report from Woking in June 1944 told of the request of an airman serving in the Mediterranean to send flowers to his wife on her birthday, which coincided with the birth of their baby in a maternity home for evacuees. 'He wrote a most charming letter, enclosing a cheque to cover the cost, and his touching faith in the WVS that they would do what he asked made the carrying out of his request a real pleasure.'

The WVS in Croydon was deeply engaged in the efforts to cope with the damage done by flying bombs during the summer of 1944 and, according to the Housewives' Service there, in its report on a raid on 18 July, 'One noticeable change since these attacks started is that people realise that they can ask for help from women wearing a WVS badge or an armlet, and our members were touched by the expressions of thanks and appreciation which were made to them by all types of people' that day, which had seen extensive property damage and at least nine fatalities.[10] In early August 1944 the WVS in the Maidstone Rural District was asked to feed for some three weeks the civil defence workers and men repairing houses in Staplehurst that had been damaged in the recent raids. 'Hot meals were cooked in the cooking centre and served in the village hall, and a canteen took the tea round to all the workmen twice daily. The praise of these men knew no bounds. Not only were they grateful for the hot midday meal and the tea and buns, but they said the quality of the food was excellent. We feel that this praise from the British Workman more than justified our efforts!'

Members from all walks of life reaped rich personal rewards for the services rendered. Being a volunteer was rarely a one-way street. According to the magazine of the Lewisham WVS in 1941, 'Many a mother, temporarily separated from her children through the so necessary scheme of evacuation, is fighting her heart hunger by doing something under the WVS. It is not only younger women, but many of the older ones who have come out of their quiet corners to do their bit.'[11] Similarly, it was reported from Guildford at the end of 1941 that many WVS members 'who have come through unpleasant times have found relief from their own mental strain in trying to help others'.[12] 'The war years brought me companionship and achievement,' reflected Nella Last in her diary on 19 August 1949, 'and a measure of deep content when I could "help the wheels turning in the right direction", as Churchill once said.' Years before, on 30 April 1940, she had written 'I thank God afresh that I could work at [WVS] Centre and keep back that bogeys that wait to pounce on mothers and wives' (her younger son was in the Army). To feel that one was contributing to work of consequence was important, especially for women who had never worked outside the domestic environment, the majority of whom were too old to enlist in other forms of service even if they could have been spared at home. In performing work of public value, these women were able to feel effective, worthwhile and part of the larger national mission. It was said in December 1943 of the busy clothing exchange in Bedford that, 'Although the floor has holes in it and the roof leaks, there is a great pleasure in finding clothes to fit the children, and hearing them say, "That's nice Mum, ain't it?"' In service to others WVS members found something of an antidote to what might have ailed them psychologically, perhaps passivity or lethargy, perhaps hopelessness or persistent anxiety. Women in the WVS had no need to feel they were nobodies.

Self-confidence soared as women discovered gifts they had not known they had, or they developed skills they previously lacked. One WVS Regional Administrator, speaking in Grantham, Lincolnshire in August 1944, surveyed the last five years and observed that 'it seemed wonderful the way people had grown with their jobs. People who had not confidence in themselves were now finding that they were managing great responsibilities in a most splendid way.'[13] When local organisers reported to headquarters on the success of their members' contributions to fund-raising activities, they sometimes mentioned the financial acumen needed and high level of public trust involved in handling and carefully recording significant sums of money. In Marshland, Norfolk in October 1943 members reported self-improvement as a result of their involvement in the WVS pie scheme that had twenty selling centres in the district open twice weekly. They found that this work fostered 'ready reckoning for the helpers. Four Marshland women will always be grateful to Lord Woolton [Minister of Food] who, through his pies (as they call them), have at last mastered mental arithmetic, starting with groans and ending with smiles.' There must have been thousands of women who improved their organisational and accounting skills as a result of volunteering. The military demanded accurate records of the wool used to knit socks and other comforts for the military; WVS headquarters required detailed counts and itemisation of clothes distributed, funds raised, meals served, purchases made, evacuees assisted and the like. Consequently, many women learned business skills, efficient work practices and how to allocate scarce resources effectively. The statistics they produced also gave Lady Reading and other WVS leaders the evidence they needed to prove to the Home Office and other authorities the value of the work done by a service that in a very short time since its founding had become a prominent presence throughout the country.

Signs and symbols are an important means to foster solidarity and pride in an organisation. For the WVS distinctive badges and armbands, the window card displayed by members of the Housewives' Service, and especially the full uniform served this purpose admirably. They linked members together and also communicated capability to outsiders.[14] From Bishopton, Renfrewshire in Scotland came the opinion in April 1941 that the 'WVS uniform is now a "pass" to take one anywhere!' According to Lady Reading a year later, 'The little badge of the WVS was respected everywhere and was a symbol of service.'[15] 'Felt rather noble at putting on my WVS frock on Sunday', said Helen Lloyd on 25 June 1944 as she set off to check on a nearby Rest Centre that had received refugees from bombing ('the evacuees were charming,' she found, 'all the refugees were grateful – I have never felt so proud of the WVS'). Designations of WVS membership gave their wearers an air of authority – and of course that was part of their purpose. 'A uniform always carried more authority than ordinary clothes', recalled Mrs Spencer of Gorleston-on-Sea, Norfolk. 'I was always very proud of mine. I believe I was the first in Gorleston to have one.'[16] Nella Last recounted her excitement in first putting on her WVS uniform on 6 March 1942. 'I put my WVS coat on and I felt as proud as a queen in it and chuckled at my childish pride, for dark green is *not* my colour. It's decidedly on the big side' – but she was good at alterations – 'and altogether I know I look about my worst in it. Nevertheless I was a very proud soldier. I pray I may never disgrace my uniform and can act as good as I feel always, whatever test or trial comes.'

A uniform conferred benefits to the wearer in the course of her work. In Taunton, Somerset the WVS Welfare Visitor represented her organisation at the local Billeting Office, and had found 'by experience the value of WVS uniform. When I make my first visit to new evacuees it gives me a good introduction.' She had taken in two evacuees herself and 'I am sometimes able to influence other households to do the same, and incidentally sympathise with them in their many difficulties'. In May 1941 WVS members in Swansea assembled, military style, to be inspected by the Earl of Plymouth upon officially receiving two mobile canteens donated by the Lord Mayor of London's National Air Raid Distress Fund. 'The day was brilliantly fine and it was a goodly sight. Many appeared in full uniform and many appeared in the "special" overall with regulation hat. The latter, all grouped together, looked extremely nice, the bright green of the overall blending very well with the surroundings.' Uniforms meant that the WVS could participate in processions and ceremonies with other services. It could show itself and be judged by the public to be a movement of importance to the nation. Following the 'gruelling experience' of dealing with evacuees in the Isle of Ely in the summer of 1944, the Organiser reported in September that 'Tribute was often paid to the WVS by the trust the evacuees put in anyone in our uniform'. On a distinctly practical level, Helen Lloyd discovered the advantages of her uniform when, on 5 September 1941, she was driving a legless man to Roehampton for medical care when her car broke down. Repairs were done promptly in Wandsworth, 'thanks', she said, 'to the magic of my WVS uniform'. WVS uniforms did sometimes open doors to urgently needed assistance, helped elicit cooperation from local authorities, weakened the reluctance of householders to billet evacuees, injected a degree of balance into power relationships when dealing with military authorities and conferred an air of gravitas to fellow citizens facing loss and grief. Although a report of heavy bombing on 19 October 1943 in the London suburb of Sudbury does not explicitly say so, wearing a uniform must have helped the women counselling the victims: 'It is a harrowing job and although kindliness is essential, those interviewing must be of a pretty "tough" fibre to stand all the tragedies.'[17]

Much of the work done by the WVS during the second half of the war was routine and usually (except for the summer of 1944) unrelated to the sorts of emergencies that had been prominent in 1940–1. These jobs involved few, if any, encounters with danger and no risks beyond those that anyone in wartime Britain was obliged to confront. We get a sense of the week-to-week activities at the local level from two minute books that have survived: one from Thatcham, Berkshire for the period from January 1944 until the end of the war, the other from the Housewives' Service in Lower Stratton, near Swindon in Wiltshire, for 1942–5.[18] In Thatcham, the most prominent issue for fortnightly discussion concerned fund-raising and decisions with regard to granting money to war-related causes deemed worthy. Members actually raised a lot of money – hundreds of pounds – and met regularly to agree on how to disburse it. Some went to organisations (Aid to China Fund, Polish Relief Fund, the Red Cross, Mariners' Friends Society, Friendless Sailors' and Soldiers' Parcels Depot), some to individuals such as POWs or their families, and selected members of the Forces. Particular assistance was directed to badly bombed Lewisham in south-east London at the end of the war. The concerns in Lower Stratton seem to have been similar, though the members there were certainly less well off and spent a lot of time darning socks, sewing and making blackout curtains, as well as attending lectures, demonstrations and other special events. In both places, collecting salvage was a regular assignment, as was gathering rosehips in the autumn. None of these activities was glamorous, and whatever excitement may have been part of the regular meetings was well concealed in the minutes.

There was, though, a great deal of camaraderie. These and other WVS records suggest that the WVS at the local level often served as a kind of social club, focused on unspectacular, everyday concerns. And why not? One of the positive dimensions of wartime Britain was that people joined together for worthwhile purposes, and these shared tasks came to provide a platform for conversation and companionship. On 21 February 1944 Dorothy Dixon in Dewsbury wrote of 'the WVS tea party at L's Café. Eighteen of us sat down to fish and bread and *butter* and scones, and cake and pineapple and cherries. Then we went to the pictures.' The demands of wartime, whether actual or anticipated, fostered new social exchanges and solidarities. Women in the WVS, most of them middle-aged or older, were drawn out of their homes and connected with other women about whom they would otherwise have known little. It was almost inevitable that everyday pleasantries and a certain licence to be merry would become part of meetings and work parties. Normal life, with its customary chit-chat and gestures of courtesy, routinely entered into the endeavours of what was in fact a national service, since, understandably, the currency of small talk and modest treats helped to pass the time agreeably. On 4 January 1944 Lower Stratton's WVS held a 'social' and 'All members gave the tea and each brought a friend. There were many prizes given and won by members and their children. We all went away feeling refreshed and ready for anything 1944 might bring.'

Such clubbish, companionable get-togethers were not uncommon, especially in places where the leadership was vigorous or at least steady and residential geography conducive to social gatherings. Indeed, good-natured parties were seen as morale-boosters, a means of fostering positive feelings and confidence among local members. These social and psychological payoffs were explicitly recognised in early 1941 in

Leighton Buzzard, Bedfordshire; here, as elsewhere, whist drives were popular, as was the party dance held at the end of the year. 'These activities', thought the Centre Organiser in December 1941, 'do a lot of good in keeping the members together'. A 'very successful social evening' was held in October 1941 for the WVS of Spalding, Lincolnshire; it was thought to have been 'a most popular event and although no mention of our work was made, it has greatly added to enthusiasm generally'. In January 1944 in Clay Cross, Derbyshire 'Everything this month is overshadowed by the party' thrown for members; 'I thought we needed a change', wrote the Organiser, and this may well have been a moment in the war, in the winter and after four and a half years of strife, when many women were feeling stale or depressed and could do with something uplifting. The WVS acknowledged the merit of doing whatever might help to keep spirits up, and was aware, no doubt, that many members were coping with their own worries, fatigue and sorrows. As one observer said of WVS work parties in 1944, 'The sociability of them breaks the tension of the strain they are under most of the time'.[19]

The Head Housewife for the WVS in Chelmsford and the adjacent districts, writing in 1943, was keen to stress how her Service helped to connect women with one another, and soften the harshness of wartime drudgery (or worse). She concluded her thorough account of the work of that year with the claim that

The real value of the Service is shown in the spirit of comradeship that is apparent throughout the area. Neighbourliness is helping to relieve the stress of present day life; shopping for each other, helping in sickness, minding others' children, pooling methods of using wartime foods to the best advantage are some of its manifestations. Friendships are being formed, sick people being visited and lonely ones becoming less isolated. It is to be hoped that the essence of the Service will help to sweeten our communal life long after the reason for its being has ceased to exist.[20]

Shared laughter provided a welcome release and helped create a sense of commonality; perhaps it even enhanced commitment. Meetings were not expected to be devoid of humour. Some training sessions were deliberately arranged to include light-hearted elements, such as quizzes and playlets. In the autumn of 1943 in Birmingham a 'play, "When the Rattles Sound", was acted by Housewives from a working-class district' before an audience of some seven hundred WVS. 'They did not act at all but were just themselves with a little comic relief, which comes naturally to them, thrown in.' A Canadian woman who visited Britain in early 1944 and wrote an account of the WVS's work thought that its leaders 'have learned by experience that a meeting should have some fun attached to it, for women are tired and need relaxation, and laughter seems to clear the mind'.[21] 'We laugh a lot at [WVS] Centre', wrote Nella Last on 14 March 1940, 'and I know I laugh and clown more than I've done since I was a girl.' She tried to act gaily and appear light-hearted and amusing, whatever her actual feelings, and this gaiety with others, she thought, was one of her principal contributions to wartime morale. On 3 July 1943, after attending a WVS gala at the cathedral in Manchester – attended by around 1200 'women of all types and sizes and class' and 'an experience to be remembered' – she prayed once again 'that I would have strength and courage to go on to the end of the road, that I might be given patience and kindness and [be able] to keep that humour which sees laughter and fun in sometimes dreary, tiresome things'.

An anecdote recounted at Barrow's WVS Centre on 14 July 1942 and reported by Nella Last gives a flavour of such solidarity through levity. A doctor had spread a tale that a 'Polish flyer who had been in a hospital took a turn for the better and rapidly began to "sit up and take notice". The doctor said "I'm delighted with your recovery. You can have anything at all you fancy – or would you like anyone to come in?" The Pole said "I think I'd like a woman now, doctor. You may send one in tonight. I like plump ones." The doctor said in a shocked way "Hush – you are in England now and not on the Continent. English ways are different altogether and they would be very shocked if they heard a remark like that" and got the reply "Then why the Women's Voluntary Services?"'

This story was much enjoyed by the WVS members present and, according to Mrs Last, further witty remarks were spoken in the same vein and 'set a few of the more ribald ones off into a louder fit of laughter than the joke did'. At the canteen later that week, when she was briefly out of the building, two Canadian Sergeant Pilots invited her and another married woman to the cinema. Mrs Howson 'had tactfully refused and I felt sorry for the lonely soldiers and if I'd have seen them would have suggested they come to 9 Ilkley [her home], for they were a homely type and I knew they only asked us because of that, but it was no good talking to that giddy bunch for they insisted I'd "made eyes".'

One could not be expected always to be serious. At a WVS meeting in Dewsbury on 2 November 1942 alarm was expressed about the depletion of WVS ranks because of the 'pell-mell conscription' of women – hundreds of thousands had been called up during the previous year or so for national service of various kinds (e.g., the Land Army, munitions and the uniformed military auxiliaries). According to Dorothy Dixon, this gave rise to 'some ribald talk when someone suggested that the best solution

would be for all we younger ones to have babies [thus exempt-
ing them from conscription]. I pleaded it wasn't necessary in my
case as I was already working full time. Everyone laughed as I
was the only "spinner"* there.' Some months later her words
about the ending of a WVS meeting on 1 March 1943 (the
members seems to have met in a room at the Baptist chapel) testify to a sort of mood that must have been familiar: 'we drifted
off WVS business on to stories of old chapel-going days and the
meeting broke up in laughter'. There must, too, have been a few
occasions when contacts with the needy provoked a little
humour. In mid-August 1944 the WVS in St Pancras, London
played its part in finding clothes for 'six French volunteers,
refugees or evacuees from Cherbourg. They were very pleased
with most of their clothing, particularly the overcoats, but our
knickers were greeted with hoots of mirth and very politely
refused. They were all young girls, so one can hardly blame
them.'

Everyday gestures of bonhomie or jest, sympathy and concern, along with shared, concrete achievements, injected an air
of normalcy into a war-dominated society, while small treats
and entertainments helped to pass the time agreeably and keep
people motivated. (Wartime austerity meant that most pleasures had to be modest.) Attempts were made to enliven the
endless fund-raising for the war effort with jocular auctioning
of small items, whist drives, bring-and-buy sales and raffles of
goods, some of them scarce and desirable such as a bottle of
whisky or a lemon. These events brought women together.
They also served as distractions from other cares. For some
women they were occasions to get and stay warm for a while,
for others they were opportunities to escape a tiresome husband. At the very least a woman who left her house for WVS

*Presumably a colloquial version of 'spinster'.

work would rarely have to be alone. In September 1944 the Centre Organiser in Cleethorpes remarked on the continuing presence at the British Restaurant of 'an elderly lady who lives alone and is so deaf that she meets very few people in her private life. Every day she comes to the restaurant and washes up and, in addition to being of great help to us, she says that she has not been so happy for years.' A report of 8 December 1941 from the Centre Organiser in Margate, Kent also stressed the WVS as a vehicle for hope and optimism. Margate was an evacuation area; it had lost as much as 80 per cent of its pre-war population and most of its tourist trade. The combination of depopulation, economic decline, the blackout and vulnerability to air raids 'all tended to create a loneliness which was bad for us,' she observed, 'and therefore WVS with its multifarious activities has proved a boon for us women.' She proceeded to give details of these diverse activities, acknowledging the happy fact that her husband was the mayor – which ensured a cooperative local authority – and concluded with the words, 'All our members take pride in doing anything that is asked of them and I am proud to be associated with such a cheerful, capable and loyal band of workers.'[22]

The Housewives' Service was especially well suited to bringing women together for it was rooted in the positive aspects of neighbourliness, of women looking out for each other and each other's children, and the fact of people living close together. Here was an accessible, practical way for women to become involved in useful war work. A report from Chelmsford on the activities of the Housewives' Service in Central Essex during 1943 concluded with high praise for its social virtues:

The real value of the Service is shown in the spirit of comradeship that is apparent throughout the area. Neighbourliness is helping to relieve the stress of present-day life. Shopping for each other, helping in sickness, minding others' children, pooling methods of using wartime foods to the best advantage are some of the manifestations. Friendships are being formed, sick people being visited and lonely ones becoming less isolated. It is to be hoped that the essence of the service will help to sweeten our communal life long after the reason for its being has ceased to exist.

Much the same point about constructive comradeship and the combating of loneliness through group meetings of the Housewives' Service had been made in a 1941 pamphlet from Liverpool.[23] Aiding the victims of raids was almost bound to oblige members to pull together, and these experiences were not likely to be soon forgotten. Feltham in Middlesex suffered doodlebugs in the summer of 1944 and in September it was reported that 'there is a wonderful cooperation amongst the Housewives in helping the bombed-out. In one district a member has returned to her home, which was very badly blasted, and each member contributed something towards setting up her kitchen utensils. In another district we are helping a member who has completely lost her house, and was in hospital for a long period, to get what remains of her carpets removed from Council storage and cleaned.'

Social solidarities occasionally cut across class barriers, notably at times of crisis. Death tended to be a social solvent – and it certainly was at the end of April 1942 when the WVS, aided by six bus drivers, was actively involved with the Queen's Messenger Convoy in feeding thousands of distressed people in just-blitzed Norwich. This was a tense day. An emergency mortuary was at work; children were seen searching for their dead mothers. At the end of a packed day the Convoy withdrew to a quiet location and, in the words of this heartfelt account,

Here the Cambridge WVS team, the Eastern Counties bus drivers and the Ministry of Food official all settled down to one perfect level. All were one happy band of grimy, tired workers in full accord, with no social distinctions whatever. Bus drivers and ladies were squeezed together on chairs and settees, arms lightly thrown across shoulders to make more room, jokes and laughter in full measure – this after 18 hours of intense work under very harrowing circumstances. It was a truly remarkable scene.

They rose the next morning at five, prepared for duty at their canteens, and provided relief for most of the day. Then they drove back to Cambridge, 'bus drivers co-driving with the lady drivers. We reached our base at Trumpington about 7.45 p.m. tired, grimy, after 40 hours of almost continued work, a happy united band, feeling that the job had been worth every effort, and very well done ... To the six Eastern Counties bus drivers we cannot give enough praise. They were always on the spot for all the heavy work and without them the ladies of the Convoy could not have carried on – the work was far too strenuous.'[24]

War brought strong feelings to the surface of everyday life, and women often found occasion – more so than previously – to speak of these feelings. After a bomb fell on Weston Woods in Albury, Surrey on 21 July 1944, Helen Lloyd went out to survey the damage, which, fortunately, was modest. 'Albury being my own village,' she wrote, 'I undertook part of the visiting myself, and it gave me the opportunity to judge the great value of this form of welfare work. I had also not appreciated before the length of time it takes. The visitor's duty is not accomplished until she has seen every bit of damage, and has heard every detail of where each member of the family was and what they were doing when the bomb fell. But undoubtedly the effect of a sympathetic audience has a very stimulating moral effect.' She had earlier remarked on the value of 'sympathetic visitors to whom householders could tell the story of their adventures' after Ripley had been bombed exactly a month earlier.[25]

Consolation, reassurance, understanding, validation of individual need – these were important things to be able to offer. Lady Reading, who was noticeably psychologically minded, stressed the importance of empathy for those being served. 'Always have food for bombed-out people that is easy to eat,' she advised in 1941. 'The first thing people lose is their spectacles, and the second their teeth. Be compassionate and understanding.'[26] As for the givers, whether helping face to face, in work parties or in some other way, they got a lot in return for serving. With the end of the European war, Nella Last summed up her sense of gratitude on 10 May 1945: 'It's been a long and often trying road but I found comradeship and bought peace of mind when otherwise I'd have broken. The knowledge that I was "keeping things moving in the right direction" in however small a degree steadied me, helped my tired head to rest peacefully at night, with strength to begin again when morning came.' These were sentiments that had emerged intermittently in her diary throughout the war. 'I always feel a thankfulness for opportunity of service', she wrote on 19 May 1940. 'I think my reason would go if I had to be unable to do anything for at times the black wave of depression that sweeps over me and makes me feel as if my efforts are like sweeping back the Atlantic with a broom is terrible. My weapons, though, are at hand and I get my sewing machine out and sew or else sort magazines and papers for Sailors' Home if I have them, or failing that go out in the sun and look for people to beg from.'

These were times when there were good grounds for fear, and surely almost all women were afraid at some time or other, for themselves, and for those they loved. On 20 June 1940 Nella Last was, as usual on a Thursday, at the WVS Centre, and as usual she and others got into conversation – this was a critical moment, with France about to fall and Britain in great peril. 'We talked of bombing raids at lunch and our reactions. Mrs Woods is big and brave. She says she will keep calm and not be frightened but Mrs Bowman and Miss Ledgerwood and I are all small and dread it so much. It's the noise that will frighten me for a bad thunder storm turns "my bones to water" and makes me really ill, although I'm not really a coward on the whole ... Mrs Waite says "Don't worry. We will *all* be terrified together" and says we will forget our terror in trying to comfort and help others.' Here, surely, was one of the psychological pillars of the WVS's success.

CHAPTER 10

ENDINGS – AND CARRYING ON: 1945 AND BEYOND

By the end of 1944 almost everyone expected that the war in Europe would soon be over. This ending, when it came, was bound to have a major impact on the WVS, which had been created specifically to deal with the challenges of war at home. Our concern in this chapter is to show what its members were doing during the last months of war and the first months of peace, and to disclose some of the thinking then about the future – *if any* – that the WVS might be imagined to have in the post-war world.

It was business as usual for the WVS at the end of 1944 and into 1945 – helping out in hospitals, hosting servicemen, distributing orange juice and vitamins, conducting book drives, routinely monitoring the welfare of evacuees, whose numbers, though declining, remained substantial in the summer of 1945, and much more. There were also some changes. For example, the WVS still knitted tens of thousands of garments, many of which were now intended for deprived peoples in newly liberated countries. Some of the clothing stock that remained in WVS hands was sent to formerly occupied Europe, and some was given to various groups of refugees and displaced people (there were lots of them in 1945), as well as to a wide range of Britons in distressed post-war circumstances.

The war was ending in 1945 but not yet over, so in the short term there was still much work to do, and in a few places the WVS was busier than ever as welfare workers. Occasionally a new initiative was reported. In Long Eaton, Derbyshire an after-school play centre was set up for the children of war workers and was staffed daily by the WVS and women from other organisations in the town. It was said in January that the children 'seem to be of the most unruly type and it has been a really hard job ... The game that seems the most popular (if allowed) is Postman's Knock – in fact any kissing game that they can think of!' Some jobs involved the replaying of assignments carried out in previous months. During, mainly, the second quarter of the year, evacuated children were returned to their city homes, and the WVS helped by serving as escorts as they had done in earlier mass movements of evacuees. 'We shall miss them,' according to the Centre Organiser in Axminster, Devon; 'it was a happy ending that two members of the Housewives' Service, who had both been foster parents, were able to accompany the children back to Waterloo on June 25th.' A very detailed account from Worcester that month of the evacuees' journey home concluded by recording 'a very real feeling of respect for the courage of the "Cockney" who had stood up to bombing, evacuation, re-evacuation, giving help and taking help as only a Britisher can'.

Attending to the welfare of troops only gradually diminished, and in some places remained a priority even after

273

hostilities had ceased. The process of demobilisation continued through 1945 and 1946; many men had to wait for months before they were out of uniform. In the meantime, there was little to engage them militarily (notably after Japan capitulated in August 1945), 'the boys' had to be 'looked after'. In June there was thought to be 'a slowing down amongst the WVS members' in the Fylde Rural District of Lancashire, but still more to do, for 'we have in our district a great number of troops and they look to the WVS for help in different ways'. It was said in September that the WVS in the Windsor Rural District was still giving a lot of help to the three hundred RAF personnel at Sunninghill Park:

> They ask us about almost everything pertaining to domes-
> tic life and comfort, and, as they are constantly changing
> their numbers, those coming in start us off afresh. It was
> extremely pleasing to find a number of our Housewives
> who, on learning that so many of the men wanted hospi-
> tality at weekends for their wives and children, offered to
> form a roster of WVS who would have them for a day or
> two ... It was their own idea, and many of the RAF have
> told their hostesses it was the happiest three days of their
> War experience. They were staggered when told that there
> was nothing to pay for their rooms, only their food.

Not all tasks were a continuation of the work of previous years. Allied victories presented opportunities, directly or indirectly, for new services and relationships, aside from expanding the prospective recipients of knitted goods. In May 1945, Walton and Weybridge in Surrey appealed for blackout material 'to be converted into pinafores for French children'. In that spring and summer, a few places hosted groups of Dutch children, putting them up for a few weeks, finding them clothes and footwear, and helping to restore their health and vitality. A gift-giving in reverse occurred in early 1945 in the form of toys received from Belgium: children there had been asked to give up some of their best toys, which were then sent across the Channel and distributed by the WVS to British youngsters, with priority accorded to those whose fathers had been killed in the war.

From time to time WVS records shed light on the dark side of British life, as manifested in accounts of experiences that may not have concerned the organisation directly. It was reported in July that two evacuees had just returned to their West Country billets:

> The woman with whom they had been billeted for several years had the occasion to go to London shortly after the return home of her evacuees, and took the opportunity to go and look up these two children, for whom she had great affection. She found them living in the most distressing circumstances ... Nine or ten adults and children living in two rooms. Both the boys were white and miserable, and told her that they were expected to spend all day at the cinema. Their mother was out at work all day. The grandfather (a bookie) frankly said that they did not wish to be bothered with children. All they wished was to enjoy themselves without the worry of the kids.

This 'good lady' brought the children back with her to her country parish, where she hoped to be able to 'keep them at her own expense, provided that the parents will send down the necessary clothing'. Stories of this sort do, of course, need to be treated with caution,[1] but one thing is clear: these were frequently difficult, even dangerous, times for children, many of whom were at the mercy of harsh or indifferent or depressed adults, whether in their own family or the household of strangers.

There were, as well, unavoidable ruptures in family life, mainly as a result of evacuation but also in some cases in connection with children returning home after years of living happily with foster families. Being tossed about in this way must have been painful, perhaps even traumatic for some children. In December 1944 it was reported from the Basford Rural District in Nottinghamshire that the 'children evacuated from some areas returned home on official instructions before Xmas and there has been a tragic side to this return as both foster-parents and children have become greatly attached to each other and the children's own parents have become strange to them in these years of absence.' This problem – the problem of excellent foster-parenting – had been around for some time. In November 1941 Harpenden, Hertfordshire, noted in its account of evacuees that 'a few parents who have been separated from their children for more than two years seem to feel that they are losing them. The better the billet the more they feel this, and in some cases it seems that children are taken home because they are too happy here.' On 11 July 1945, Nella Last wrote a detailed account in her diary of the unhappiness of an evacuee obliged to return to his parents.[2] Then there were the sad stories of children who had no home to return to. The Basford Organiser went on to say that, 'We still have a few children with us whose home situation makes it impossible for them to return at present, such as a small boy whose father is serving overseas and whose mother has gone to live with another man.'

Undoubtedly the most widespread and important new initiative from late 1944 was the re-homing scheme. This was designed to get basic household furnishings from parts of

276

Britain that had not been recently destroyed to people in the south-east who had been bombed out of their homes, either permanently or temporarily. These people were in need of many of the basics of life, most of which were by now unobtainable in shops: cutlery, crockery, chairs, tables, washstands, curtains, towels, bedding, blankets, pots and pans, glassware, teapots, kitchen utensils, brushes, perhaps cleaning materials and a bucket. During the few months from the end of 1944 through the first half of 1945 around fifty war-damaged boroughs in the south-east were 'adopted' by cities and counties to the north and west, and sent gifts to rebuild households. To take some examples, Lambeth received items collected and sent from Somerset; Lewisham from Berkshire; Woolwich from Bournemouth; Streatham from Bath; Wimbledon from Leicestershire; Croydon from Carlisle; Stoke Newington and Fulham from Derbyshire; Greenwich from Buckinghamshire; Beckenham from Staffordshire; West Ham from Cleethorpes; Hornchurch from Bedfordshire, the Isle of Wight, the Isle of Ely, and Norfolk; Ilford from Lancashire; Willesden from Rutland; Wandsworth from Devon; Carshalton from Huddersfield; Coulsdon and Purley in Surrey from Bradford; Woolwich from Dorset; and Bexley from Dudley. In many places this gift-giving was promoted as the 'Good Neighbour Scheme', an apt designation that was intended in part to counteract any feeling among the recipients that were the targets of charity. Overall some eight thousand tons of goods were collected by the WVS nationwide and distributed to a hundred thousand families in need.[3]

The WVS, in cooperation with local authorities, was very active in publicising and organising these re-homing collections, and it had a lot of success. Gifts were actively solicited. Sometimes photos from the adopted borough were put on public display in the donor region to arouse people's better feelings. Posters were put up, leaflets and handbills distributed, advertisements placed in newspapers and announcements made in cinemas. Then systematic collections were carried out and, in due course, trucked to the recipients. Hundreds of loaded vehicles were despatched from donor districts to the south-east. Solihull in Warwickshire reckoned in March 1945 that it had sent sixteen-and-a-half tons of goods in four van loads to Shoreditch – 'some 7500 articles, large and small'. Hackney received fifty-four van loads from Shropshire, each of about five-and-a-half tons, which were distributed among around six hundred families. It was understood that in some parts of Shropshire 'a gift or gifts has been received from every house',[4] and, according to the Atcham Rural District, they had been both numerous and varied, ranging from a vacuum cleaner to an egg cup. At the request of Hackney's WVS, a large assortment of brushes had also been despatched. 'Our appeal for Battersea met with a wonderful response,' according to Westbury, Wiltshire in January, 'considering this is a working-class district. One thing struck us forcibly – that the poorer the house, the greater the wish to give.' Small house-holders in Eccles, Lancashire were also reported to have been 'exceedingly generous' (April). Collecting gifts in Minehead, Somerset for Lambeth in February was 'the sensation of the month', and in the Abingdon Rural District, then in Berkshire, the 'scheme eventually proved so wildly successful that it has involved endless work!' (March). Cleethorpes started its campaign just before Christmas 1944, with the local council firmly on side and 178 WVS members helping with the collection.

While the re-homing campaign usually met with success, there were some variations. In February it was reported from Barnstaple that most of the gifts came from the rural districts; 'the response in the Borough was negligible and any appeal made fell on deaf ears'. By contrast, in Dawlish, also in Devon, the previous month, 'We had very few refusals and these were due to illness etc. and not to lack of interest'. Several villages near Gainsborough had already contributed items in December 1944, intended for Leytonstone, including 'a couch, two upholstered chairs, three bedroom chairs, a rocking chair, china, curtains, ornaments, household linen, mop heads, dusters, [and] tea cloths ... We have a small nucleus for another collection and have been offered eight sacks of very soft feathers for pillows and cushions and we are hoping to be able to obtain material to make full use of this useful gift.' Lincolnshire's Brigg Rural District Council supplied a lorry to fetch donated goods (also for Leytonstone) from the scattered villages in April, one of which 'gave us an organ which the two old men with the lorry would play and entertain the villagers [with] on the route. We had many funny episodes on our journey round the villages with the lorry. One old couple gave up their treasured 1887 Jubilee glass cake basket and hoped another old couple would get it. We found that most people were anxious to give of their best if possible.' This was a standard verdict from the regions that donated. Such generosity, according to Ashburton in Devon, which had collected for Wandsworth, was thought to 'show the spirit of thankfulness which emanates from most individuals in these quiet spots'. A few of these gifts may have represented a real sacrifice, as was the case in the Langport Rural District of Somerset, where one woman in March gave 'a perambulator in very good condition which she could have sold for £8, but which she wishes to go to some young wife or widow of a serviceman [in Lambeth] who needs it and cannot afford to buy one'.

Burton-on-Trent in Staffordshire helped to refurbish the homes of people in Bermondsey, and (like most donor areas) set about their work systematically in the early spring of 1945. After a collection depot had been secured, leaders of the Housewives' Service canvassed just about every house 'to gain the interest of the householder and arrange to collect the gifts. The loudspeaker van was loaned to us, and we toured one district each evening asking for everyone's help ... The Centre was opened each afternoon with a staff of Housewives to receive and sort out gifts and to note any large goods to be collected by the rescue van and lent us by the ARP.' The results were heartening: 'The response to our appeal was marvellous and the gifts were varied and in splendid condition, only very few needing small repairs, which were done by kind friends.' (In Wantage, Berkshire in February a member's husband did many small furniture repairs.) Goods were sorted and packed, then on 14 March 'we despatched the first two van loads consisting of over 4000 articles, among which were 50 beds, 59 blankets, 59 mattresses, pillows, linen, crockery, kitchen goods and furniture. As soon as this load had gone we began packing the next one. Meanwhile gifts kept coming in. We had several people in to encourage us who came from Bermondsey, either as evacuees or old residents there.' Another load was sent off on 21 March, and it included about a hundred chairs of various kinds, washstands, tables, fenders and crockery – and 'two aspidistras with a little bit of Burton soil'.

In Burton, as in most other places, this re-homing campaign was highly satisfying, and probably brought out the best in people. It was a very busy time, 'but we all felt it was really worth while, and the appreciative letters we have received have been ample reward for our labours. Our helpers report how very willingly the people of the town have contributed, and this has made the collections a greater pleasure.' The campaign was pretty much finished by April; nearly nine thousand items totalling some twenty-four tons were donated – 'we think this is quite a good result for a town of this size'. Then a little follow-up work was done:

> We went to Bermondsey to see the distribution in progress, and found it a very difficult task, but one which was being dealt with very efficiently. We met some of the people and they were most grateful for our help. Seeing them and the battered district made us realise just how worth while our efforts had been. We have also received some most touching letters from some of the recipients which we shall always value.

Newspapers in the south-east sometimes published photographs of vans being unloaded or the donations being distributed, along with suitable words of appreciation.

Visits by outsiders to London in early 1945 tended to prompt reactions similar to those from Burton. In February the Centre Organiser from the Cookham Rural District in Berkshire visited Lewisham, 'and she now realises how desperately everything that can be sent is needed, and also under what dreadful conditions the bombed out are living'. Likewise, the Centre Organiser from Wantage, who accompanied a delivery of goods in March, was 'most impressed with the working of the scheme and the cheery atmosphere of the WVS Centre [in Lewisham]. Considering the hard work and havoc around it rather made me feel that our side of the job was a very small one.' In February a sailor on leave showed up at the depot in Broughton, Lancashire where gifts were being received for Ilford, asking to help: 'he had been billeted at Ilford, and knew what the people there had suffered, and if we could find him a handcart, he would go around' collecting donations (he then spent three days of his leave doing this). A visit in April to Leytonstone by a WVS member from Louth in Lincolnshire was considered a 'privilege'; she observed the distribution of goods and 'the delight of these plucky people made one feel that the whole scheme had been worth while'. Similar admiration for afflicted fellow citizens was conveyed from Caterham, Surrey in March: 'We are struck by the pluck of the women who, after being bombed out, have been put in requisitioned houses badly patched up and often bare of comforts, and hardly a grumble from any of them.'

The way in which the re-homing scheme actually worked in Caterham was the subject of a detailed account by Helen Lloyd in June 1945. Seven three-ton lorries supplied by the Canadian Army collected goods from the various villages, which were then delivered to Caterham, where they were unpacked and put on display. 'For two days a stream of bombed-out families arrived at the showrooms for their presents, while lorries manned by the National Fire Service were in waiting to take the furniture and bulky packages to their homes.' A wide range of items was available, including 'enough linen and bedding for every householder to have a pair of sheets and a couple of blankets. Some had not slept in sheets since their homes were bombed.' The organisation of the distribution was in the hands of Caterham's WVS: 'The recipients were allowed into the showrooms four at a time and each was given a WVS escort to help them spend their points to the best advantage. These had been allotted according to the degree of damage to their house and to the size of the family, and there was such an abundance of goods that everything was pointed as low as was consistent with the official rules of the scheme.' (In Hackney, the allotment of points was to be: fifty for a house demolished, to be demolished, or beyond repair; twenty for a house that was temporarily unfit to live in; and thirty for each member of the household.)[5]

Helen Lloyd went on to describe the emotions evident at

the site: 'It was a moving experience for those who helped the recipients to choose their presents. Some were almost dazed by the display, others were nearly in tears.' While some wants were shared by most people, others were more specialised:

Some had set their hearts on an easy chair or a really good piece of furniture. To others an eiderdown or a frilly silk cushion were treasures beyond price. A lace tea table cloth made the day for an elderly woman who explained that she knew good things when she saw them as she had been a parlourmaid most of her life. A hospital nurse who had lost the treasured contents of a china cabinet through bombing felt she had made good her losses by finding some good cut-glass bowls and a set of chased wine glasses. A man 'shopping' for an invalid wife asked for useful things only and was speechless with pleasure when he found he could have everything necessary for the kitchen besides crockery and knives, forks and spoons. A young woman confessed rather shyly to her wish for 'something really pretty' and happily spent her last remaining points on a blue Wedgewood powder bowl and a pair of vases for her dressing table.

Gardening tools received particular notice. 'Two maiden ladies were overcome with emotion when they received a complete set of new garden tools', and there were tears of joy – their bungalow garden had been wiped out by a flying bomb.[6] Miss Lloyd concluded by observing that in the course of the distribution 'it was made plain that it was not only the material gifts that brought pleasure to these bombed families but it was [also] the fact that they had not been forgotten. "How is it that people so far away have thought of us?" was a remark that was heard again and again. Could the donors have been present they must have felt that any sacrifices they had made were more than amply repaid.'

Another new initiative involved sending WVS members to work abroad, almost always to support men in the Forces. The request for WVS participation came from the Chair of the Navy, Army and Air Force Institutes (NAAFI) to assist with the running of clubs and canteens overseas, and Lady Reading agreed on the condition that accommodation and expenses, including travel, be funded by NAAFI. By the end of 1944, fit, experienced volunteers, usually unmarried and aged between twenty-five and forty-five, were busy dispensing 'tea and sympathy' and creating homelike surroundings in various theatres of war, including Belgium, Italy, France and the Netherlands; similar services were made available to merchant seamen in Rouen and Cherbourg. The volunteers were active in trying to make the spartan premises they were given as cheerful as possible – walls were painted, curtains and pictures hung – and to furnish them with whatever amenities could be obtained: books and magazines, writing paper, board games, music – in early 1945 several places in Leicestershire were collecting gramophone records to send to Burma. Along with these reminders of home, WVS members lent friendly ears to these commonly worried, homesick men – their worries sometimes centred on the loyalty of wives and sweethearts at home – and offered, they hoped, helpful advice and sometimes practical assistance, such as facilitating communications with loved ones.[7]

While work overseas tended to be well publicised, it was in fact always very small in scale. In order to consider an overseas assignment a woman would have to have no home of her own to manage and she would have to be in good health, adaptable, mature and willing to be away from the British Isles for a long time (at least six months). These constraints made for a limited pool of candidates, and one rarely reads in an urban Narrative Report of more than one volunteer for work out of the country. Overseas service never occupied more than a few hundred volunteers, and numbers probably peaked shortly after the war. In later 1946 around 730 WVS members were reported to be working overseas.[8] So while some of the scattered British Forces were beneficiaries of this outreach, overseas service was a drop in the bucket of WVS welfare provisions.

With peace came the return home of men in uniform, including POWs, whom the WVS sometimes assisted on their journeys – Westbury, Wiltshire wrote in April of a 'Get you Home' scheme – and often helped to receive in suitable style. In April 1945 Ramsgate's WVS was asked to go with their mobile canteen to Manston Aerodrome to help receive POWs from Germany. 'After having the great privilege of helping at Dunkirk at the beginning of the war, the thrill of being able to do another little bit at the end was wonderful.' Nine planes landed, with just over two hundred men.

> Preparations had been made to make the big hangar cheerful. Big bunches of flowers were placed on the tables, an orange on each plate, sandwiches, cakes, chocolate and ten cigarettes, and a daily paper on each chair. When the planes landed they were met by the WAAF, who brought them to have their tea, and then we looked after them and had the chance of talking to them ... and they seemed genuinely pleased to be able to talk freely.

In the late spring in Droylsden, Lancashire the POWs were visited individually by a WVS member and 'a gift box containing cigarettes, handkerchiefs, shaving soap, money and a "Welcome Home Letter" has been presented to each one ... Many were helped with a gift of pyjamas, and light vests were asked for. Men with sore feet received a gift of carpet slippers. Advice was given regarding coupon credits.' These men, it was said, 'were unanimous in their praise' of the Red Cross parcels they had received while in captivity, courtesy the WVS. When liberated but ill POWs had arrived in Huyton, Lancashire in April, the WVS mobile canteen was called out twice 'to supply tea and sandwiches to the stretcher-bearers and ambulance drivers meeting hospital trains' and the members felt it a special privilege to greet them [the POWs] and to give them cigarettes.' In August the WVS in Smethwick, Staffordshire went to Cosford RAF Camp and 'helped to entertain 750 men, many of whom had just returned from prison camps in Germany.' They bore with them around a hundred small gifts and 'three large birthday cakes'.

Soldiers, though, did not always arrive home to warm welcomes, or to find their families intact, and in these circumstances WVS members sometimes functioned as social workers. It was reported from Kendal in February 1945 that

We have a spate of welfare cases to deal with – broken homes owing to unfaithful wives chiefly. In one case Mrs Pennington was able to patch up a peace and husband and wife are together again, but in another case there the returning soldier found his wife with an Italian prisoner, the home has been broken up and the children are in an institution. In yet another case we were able to arrange for an illegitimate child to be looked after by another relative when the husband came home from the Far East.

Cases of family welfare were mentioned again two months later, most of them concerning 'marital unfaithfulness or differences. Several cases have been straightened out and the homes saved; others have been reported on and are being followed up and helped. Many prisoners of war have returned, causing much rejoicing, but alas in some cases to find the wives have gone with other men.' It was reported from Twickenham in November that one soldier returned home 'to find his home destroyed, his wife gone away with someone else and his son still evacuated to the country. He has been given a temporary bungalow and we helped him with gifts.' He was said to be 'courageous and hopeful' and grateful for the help he had received.

The post-war challenges to family welfare were widely acknowledged, in particular the desperate need for housing. Wartime bombing had left much of the nation's housing run down, damaged or completely destroyed; it was certainly entirely inadequate to the nation's needs. While there was little that the WVS could do about this problem directly, it did publish an interesting appeal in October 1945 in a special issue of the *WVS Bulletin* that was concerned with housing:

Some of us, perhaps, have houses in which there are several rooms we do not use. If we fill their emptiness by giving accommodation to a homeless young couple or family we shall be doing as good a job for our country as any which were done here during the war in Europe. So many young married couples are now leaving the Services, and it is vitally important for the future of the country that they are enabled, as soon as possible, to set up homes of their own; even if such homes consist only of two rooms in someone else's house as a temporary place until their own home is ready for them. Unhappy marriages are not going to do the nation any good, and nothing contributes to unhappiness as greatly as a feeling of not being wanted in someone else's house, or family interference.

Here, according to this front-page editorial, was another way in which the WVS could be of assistance to state policy – indeed, a virtual helpmate. 'Young couples should have a place of their own and we must do our best to see that they get it. If we can help we shall not only be gaining friends but we shall be helping the housing programme in a very practical and vital way.' These thoughts are among many from post-war WVS sources that show its acceptance of planning as a vital path, though perhaps not the only path, to national well-being. A degree of socialism found favour almost everywhere.

There is much evidence from 1945 and early 1946 of the WVS concerning itself with individual hardships, troubled families and 'small matters' of personal well-being, including helping to mark such happy occasions as evacuees' golden wedding anniversaries. The instances of the support given, both to civilians and those still in uniform, were certainly diverse: talking to a mother who, it was said, frequented cinemas and pubs at night and neglected her children; attending to the needs of a girl arriving 'in great distress' in St Annes-on-Sea, Lancashire from a blitzed hotel in London, with only the clothes she was wearing; counselling confused people on rationing and how to make good use of their points; taking turns to 'sit up at nights with an ill child who had to have oxygen and whose parents were worn out with the nursing of that child and two others, less dangerously ill'; and assisting 'a GI bride in difficulties' and putting her in touch with a lawyer – it was said to be hard to help such women 'falling between the US and UK authorities'.[9]

Other interventions were suitably heart-warming, such as making enquiries and successfully locating the intended recipient of a cable from a repatriated Far East POW that the Post Office had been unable to deliver; finding a suitable dress for a member of the ATS to wear as bridesmaid at her sister's

wedding; and helping an aged woman write letters to her relatives in Australia – 'she knew what she wanted to say, but
could not write herself'.[10] (Helping with letter-writing,
whether at canteens or hostels or elsewhere, was a longstanding WVS service.)[11] The rendering of personal assistance to
struggling families was almost always written about enthusiastically. 'It is gratifying that sooner or later these sorts of
difficult cases are referred to the WVS', thought the Centre
Organiser of the Abingdon Rural District in March 1945. In
September 1945 the WVS in Bebington, Cheshire had
second-hand furniture from one of its hostels to dispose of
and was pleased to be able to give it 'to ex-servicemen and
other families setting up a house for the first time'. Practical,
hands-on support was a WVS speciality, and it was of particular importance at a time when other welfare services were,
in some places, virtually non-existent and persons in need had
nowhere else to turn.

In such a frayed society, riddled with damaged people and
broken relationships, help and healing were in high demand.
But they were provided unreliably and inconsistently, and volunteers often had to step in to fill – or at least try to fill – the
many gaps. Without the WVS many people in distress, especially women, would have been even worse off. What was on
their minds is usually impossible to say, though occasionally we
get a sense of their feelings from a letter of thanks, which,
though probably written at someone else's request, might disclose personal circumstances that must have been painful. One
such letter, almost pathetic in its humility, was written on 30
January 1945 by a Miss M. Williams from the maternity ward
in the county hospital in Louth, Lincolnshire. She thanked the
WVS in Mablethorpe for a parcel of baby clothes that had
been sent to her: 'I shall never be able to thank you enough.
Besides, words fail me to describe my feelings when I heard of

your kindness. Please accept my greatest thanks, and also my humble apologies for any trouble it may [have taken] you to collect the beautiful garments.' Under her name she wrote, 'ATS girl. Husband-to-be killed at Arnheim.'[12]

WVS documents from 1945 and early 1946 disclose much about activities ending, facilities being shut down and jobs that no longer needed to be done or women who were less interested in doing them turning their attention to other matters. Rest Centres, which had aided the victims of air raids, were closed and their goods dispersed, and virtually all other operations connected with civil defence were terminated. The needs of both evacuees and the Forces at military camps had been prominent priorities for many WVS Centres – but no longer, as evacuees went home and most members of the Forces were demobbed. The raison d'être for the WVS seemed to be vanishing. And there were other changes. Finding staff for the ever-declining number of canteens that did continue to operate was often becoming more difficult. Women were resigning from offices that they may have held for some time, while others were moving out of the community in which they had been living and volunteering, perhaps to return to their pre-war homes. Others still were rejoining their husbands. Some jobs were now being done by paid workers. And many volunteers were burnt out and felt they needed to rest and recuperate – few were young, and ill health and exhaustion were often mentioned. Most of these developments were both understandable and predictable.

The Narrative Reports reveal a wide range of attitudes to the prospect of carrying on into peacetime. In Cleethorpes, to take an example of continuing commitment, a meeting in June of some seventy members (around 10 per cent of the Centre's total membership) 'was almost amazingly unanimous in its desire to go on with work wherever it was necessary, although there were rather vocal murmurings with regard to the British Restaurant demands on their labours. This was the only type of work which they seemed to want to lose.' (Future restaurant service in Cleethorpes was expected to centre on summer visitors to the seaside town.) A meeting in later 1945 in Dawley, Shropshire revealed a similar disposition to continue their membership. It is no doubt the case that shared achievements and the friendships forged in wartime in some places fuelled a desire to preserve the WVS – or at least its spirit.

Other places witnessed much less keenness. By May 1945, Housewives' meetings were no longer being held in Great Yarmouth: 'Some members are doing knitting, and hope to finish up by the end of June. The members are asking if they can be disbanded, as there are so many jobs to do in their own houses now. Most Housewives have taken the WVS blue cards down from their windows, also the gas cleansing cards as there is no further use for them.' Broughton, Lancashire reported in November that 'our members are sadly depleted'. Weston-super-Mare, which had produced lengthy annual reports on its work during the war, had little to say in early 1946, and the woman in charge of the clothing exchange said she 'would like to be given a definite date for closing the exchange as her helpers have either resigned or will be away during the summer. She feels she will not be able to carry on for long.' By September 1945 members in Oakengates, Shropshire had less time for WVS activities. 'Their men-folk are coming out of the Forces and need looking after. The social activities of Church and Chapel are starting again. And it should not be assumed that we are now "ladies of leisure" whose only ambition is to take part in Kleen-ezi-like pilgrimages from door to door for any and every deserving cause.' By November there were so many resignations in Boston, Lincolnshire that the

County Organiser decided to arrange a ceremonial farewell meeting, which three hundred people attended.

In Cumberland, where opinion on the future of the WVS was thoroughly canvassed in mid-1945, there was agreement that the WVS's days were and should be numbered.[13] 'The general feeling was that we should definitely finish as an organisation,' according to a summary of the proceedings of a conference of Centre Organisers at the end of May. Offices were closing or planning to close, welfare work was being wound down or transferred to other organisations. 'It would be difficult to convince members of the WVS that there is now any one job which the WVS alone can tackle, after our present activities are completed,' observed the County Organiser on 5 June. She wondered, too, 'if our Headquarters quite realise that in districts that have suffered very little enemy action the rank and file of the WVS have been merely standing by'. She recommended a general stand-down, but that the leadership should remain as 'liaison officers' for a while. 'If the need should arise for our civil defence work to be revived within a reasonable length of time, I am sure Lady Reading could count upon a rapid build-up of the organisation.'

Overall, the level of commitment was eroding. 'Since VE day we have found it extremely difficult to get volunteers to do such work as has come along,' according to Birmingham in June. 'A few volunteers still continue to help at the hospital, but several are not intending to carry on over next winter as they find the long journey, often involving three different buses, is too much strain during the winter months.' A meeting in June of the WVS staff of the Gainsborough Rural District concluded that 'members were gradually drifting away and could not be held by the work already suggested by WVS ... We all feel that in our area our members would immediately rally if an emergency arose, but to stop a further drift away it would be helpful to have a "standing down" order.' It was reported in June that in Westbury, Wiltshire members 'are quite glad to take life a little easier and to have the opportunity of giving a little attention to home affairs'. In Kendal in July, 'more work parties are winding up and it is getting harder and harder to find knitters to finish the wool for Liberated Europe'. The mending party for the Forces in Taunton was wound up in June 'as many members were evacuees. No work is coming in at the moment, but St Mary's Work Party have undertaken to do anything that does come in, so we are sending them our patches and darning wool.' The July report from the Louth Rural District (North) in Lincolnshire noted a meeting in Somercotes where the Organiser and her deputy were present. 'The eleven members present all resigned, and did not wish to be put on the reserve list [for emergencies]. These people have done excellent war work and are now feeling they must attend to domestic affairs.'

In other localities, too, the WVS was on the verge of shutting up shop, probably for good; indeed, by September some centres had completely ceased to operate. Enthusiasm for volunteering was waning as women around the country felt that they had worked hard enough for long enough and deserved a respite. 'I find the general attitude towards WVS is apathetic', according to the Centre Organiser in the Long Ashton Rural District in Somerset in December 1946. This sentiment was undoubtedly widespread during later 1945 and 1946.

There was, then, lots of uncertainty within the WVS as to how much more work to do, and what women's priorities should be in a time of peace. The report for April–June 1945 from the Fylde Rural District in Lancashire ended with the comment that, 'Although there seems to be a slowing down amongst the WVS members, we feel that there is still more to be done before we can conscientiously "stand down".' ('Standing down' events were in fact widely observed in mid to late 1945. Congleton in Cheshire held one on 7 November, 'but we are carrying on with the knitting as long as garments are needed'.) 'We have here in our District a great number of troops', the Fylde report continued, 'and they look to the WVS for help in different ways. The Centre Organiser is writing a special letter to all members telling them of these facts and trusting to their patriotism to carry out this splendid voluntary work to the end.' With peace came other distractions. In July, many members in Ashton-under-Lyne, Lancashire were 'enjoying well-earned holidays; other members have been occupied, in a private capacity, with the Parliamentary elections, and work has slackened off in consequence, but we hope to start activities afresh at the beginning of September.' (This did in fact happen.)

From Surrey's Godstone Rural District in June one reads of 'a strong feeling in the villages that WVS wartime work is over, and that social work and general helpfulness can be carried on now by the Women's Institutes and individuals. A fine service like the WVS should not degenerate into mere "getters-up of flag days".' Similar views were reported that month from Grantham, Lincolnshire and Pershore, Worcestershire, and from the Axminster Rural District in August – and also from Chippenham, although there 'others are very anxious to carry on and do everything possible to help'. In September the report from the Biggleswade Rural District strove to sum up the conflicted feelings at the end of the war: 'There was at first almost a complete "down tools!" and great rejoicing that we had, under many difficulties, been able to do our job to the end, and members were certainly very disappointed to hear that we were still needed but were extremely loyal to the organisation, and all village representatives are willing to continue and we think most of the members.' However, there was also a general wish 'to combine with the Women's Institute movement as they feel that there will not be sufficient work for the two independent organisations to work separately'. (In country districts there had commonly been an overlap between WVS and WI wartime activities, and some women belonged to both organisations – though the WVS preferred to see itself as a service rather than an organisation.)[14]

The words of the Centre Organiser in Clay Cross, Derbyshire, written in April/May, testify to the sense of closure that many members were expressing. She was planning to resign soon:

> I have so very much to do besides, and I do not think the WVS work I should be called upon to do [in peacetime] necessary enough for me to continue to try and fit it in. As for helping the Local Authority, when Local Authorities needed a link between themselves and the Ministries I think WVS served a very useful purpose, but now that Local Authorities will be working on their own again, I do not see the need for this organisation ready to take on anything.

Should volunteers be required for certain tasks, she thought they could be readily obtained in other ways and through more focused organisations. Her opinion was 'that WVS has been a marvellous inspiration, very ably organised, and has served a very useful purpose, but that the need for such purpose in Clay Cross is over'. A little later, in July, she raised the idea that too much volunteer work might undermine the work ethic of – as she put it – 'the so-called working classes', whose 'idea of work is that by doing any they are conferring a favour on someone, not earning the right to live. Mr [Herbert] Morrison [Leader of the House of Commons in the new government] wants telling so very loudly and clearly.' (Labour's election victory that month did not sit well with many WVS members.) She went on to say that 'I have quite enjoyed representing WVS here and think the organisation has done a great work but that its work should be terminated. No one is going to work for their living if someone else is going to do everything for them.' While her hostility to future voluntary work was unusually aggressive and her reasons perhaps not typical, the act of pulling back from commitments and finding meaning elsewhere was evident in the lives of tens of thousands of women.

By 1947 WVS membership had certainly declined, though it is not clear by how much. Perhaps the decline was around 50 per cent, perhaps more. There are no reliable statistics for these years, and anyway it would probably be impossible to establish how many continuing members were active and how many considered themselves to be only 'on reserve'. Whatever the numbers, three points should be kept in mind.

First, the WVS was certain to shrink dramatically in numbers with the return of peace. Just as most men in the Forces expected to be demobbed, so, too, many if not most women in the WVS wished to stand down from their duties. This was to be expected. Service 'for the duration' was a common wartime expression, and for a lot of people it meant only until victory was won. 'So, we come to the end of our journey,' as Whitstable, Kent put it in August, 'in which so many members have taken their share of duty, to make it a splendid effort.' In the spring of 1945 the members in Dawley, Shropshire had been hoping – as were many other centres – for a definite date 'on which WVS as first organised could be "stood down"', given that the wartime crisis was over.

Second, those women who did remain in the WVS after 1945 were probably its keenest and most diligent wartime workers. Those who resigned were (we suspect) disproportionately those who had been less committed and less active.

With even a much reduced membership, there was still an impressive core of WVS activists willing to continue whatever work wanted doing.

Third, while tens of thousands of members disassociated themselves from regular WVS work, many of them did agree to be available to help with any emergency that might arise. They thus maintained from 1945 a limited connection with voluntary service, and this willingness to be on call bolstered the WVS's claims to be in a position to respond quickly and effectively to urgent demands, an assertion that no other civilian body could make as persuasively. Perhaps the WVS would find a role for itself in winning the peace? But perhaps it would not. No forecast could be confidently made.

Puzzlement and wavering and scattering in different directions were understandable. The incentives for constructive commonality and shared strivings were bound to be weaker in peace than in war. War created the sort of social glue that was improbable in peace. On the one hand, a significant minority of women did continue to be attracted to some form of public service and hoped that suitable opportunities to be useful beyond the home would not disappear. It was important, these stalwarts felt, to be able to help others in some capacity and within a structured framework, as long as this work did not undermine opportunities for paid employment – the WVS accepted the principle that work should be remunerated wherever possible. But voluntary service, when it clearly did have a role to play, often by filling a void that paid labour could not, could be performed in all kinds of ways and by various means, many of which pre-dated Lady Reading's organisation and a few of them new. The WVS in Bexhill, East Sussex reported in August 1945 on the departure of some of its members and added that many 'are being absorbed into other local organisations, notably the newly-formed Association of Bexhill Citizens which offers a wide scope to those who wish to carry on with some form of social service for the good of the town'. Whether the WVS would remain a vital vehicle for service to the nation was, for some people in the later 1940s, a moot point.

Since the raison d'être for the WVS had been to aid and support war-related activities, why should it be expected to survive into the post-war world? Even if important welfare needs persisted, why couldn't they be handled by other voluntary organisations? Perhaps, according to another perspective at the time, most of these social needs should be looked after primarily by a properly welfare-oriented government committed to the principles of the 1942 Beveridge Report, which had been so widely praised. What possible role could the WVS have in this new world? Most Labour women had no particular attachment to the WVS, and some Conservative women who did were not thrilled with the prospect of working voluntarily in support of the new Labour government whose election they had opposed.* In later 1945 many people felt that the service's days were numbered.[15] For example, the voices heard at a meeting in Buckinghamshire in (apparently) the third quarter of 1945 suggested that many Centre Organisers thought that the WVS should fade out after the war and 'their work should be taken over by paid labour in the end'.[16]

These questions received different answers within the higher echelons of the WVS itself. Some prominent members favoured winding things down and moving on; others wanted the

*The Centre Organiser for Blackpool, in her letter of resignation of 16 June 1947 to Lady Reading, explicitly raised this political consideration: 'I know that you are anxious for Blackpool to be reorganised but as I am actively interested in politics as a Conservative, and as the WVS works directly with a socialist government, I feel I am not the one to do it.' (WRVS Archive, Box 436, file R.10/2/BL.)

organisation to continue its good work in some way or other. There is no doubt as to where Lady Reading stood: she saw the WVS as a vital contributor to post-war reconstruction – or, as she put it on one occasion, to post-war 'convalescence'.[17] The process of recovery after such a crippling war would be arduous; it would need all the support that women could give it. In 1945 Lady Reading likened the nation to a person who had been ill and was now in the process of being nursed back to health:

> We, as a nation, are not yet completely through the nursing period, and we have to visualize that ahead of us lies that convalescent period, and that if we ignore the calls there are on us, we shall be doing grievous harm to the patient we have nursed so carefully, and, in so doing we shall be impairing its health, and its strength to do good for all time.[18]

The call to serve, she declared, remained compelling. Women should continue to be useful to others beyond their families and find meaning through work of social value. Voluntary service was an expression of generosity of spirit, sustained in part by compassion and empathy. This, of course, might be said of many organisations devoted to good works. What was unique about the WVS, according to Lady Reading, was that it had become 'the hyphen between officialdom and ordinary human beings. It is, in a way, the interpretation of official help to the ordinary man and woman in an ordinary compassionate way.'[19]

It was by helping to link, though practical service, state policy to human needs, by working to foster common ground between hard power and soft power (or lack of power), that the WVS could justify its future existence. Or, to put the matter differently, the WVS was distinctive in functioning as a large, effective, care-giving arm of the state. It saw itself as an institutional service to the nation, akin in some respects to the women's auxiliary services in the Forces or the Women's Land Army, though unlike them it was rooted in locality. On 24 October 1947, when Lady Reading spoke at a meeting in Lewes, East Sussex, she stressed the various ways in which the WVS in peacetime could put itself 'at the disposal of local authorities', which were assuming greater responsibilities and yet lacking the resources to fully carry them out.[20] The WVS could help fill the gap between needs and official means. It could do this cheaply and efficiently. And it could allow the best of British values to continue to be constructively expressed in peacetime. As the conclusion to its 1948 report on a decade's work put it, 'WVS has no monopoly of virtue in the matter of voluntary effort', but it did see itself as possessing a 'curiously strong *esprit de corps* by which the whole vast organisation is bound together, an *esprit de corps* which, after all, must come naturally to women who so proudly wear the emblem of the Crown upon their badge as a sign that they serve King and Country'.[21]

Lady Reading's outlook was explicitly rejected by some prominent WVS members. On 29 August Lady Gregory, the Centre Organiser for Chichester Rural District (East) made a speech in connection with the closing down of the WVS in the county. She made a key point:

Our Chairman, Lady Reading, has asked us to carry on in the post-war but we in West Sussex feel that there is nothing left for us to do that cannot be done by a permanent organisation such as the Women's Institute, SSAFA [Soldiers', Sailors', and Airmen's Families Association] and other societies, so we are closing down after the victory over Germany and Japan. We were an organisation formed for a national emergency and for civil defence and we feel that is over.[22]

Perhaps the crucial issue here was that, for her and others, the WVS was intended to be *impermanent*, in contrast to other organisations concerned with social welfare. Lady Gregory's was an opinion that gave priority to reinvigorating the efforts of better established and more long-standing providers of welfare, usually charities. It also rejected the claims of pre-eminence, implicit or explicit, by the WVS. Her opinions enjoyed the support of most Centre Organisers and other WVS leaders in West Sussex at this time.[23] In Surrey, the WVS leadership was also doubtful about carrying on, and at a meeting in Reigate in May 1946 was regretting that there had been no official stand down: 'The WVS is now petering out in many places, instead of going out on a Wave of Glory, such as it undeniably deserved.' Most of the ladies present wished 'to be able to return to their pre-war activities in their various spheres'.[24]

The head of the WVS in Kendal and Westmorland held similar views, and on 7 June 1945 she wrote a letter that directly challenged Lady Reading's recent call to carry on. Mrs Hornyold-Strickland had already been told by some Organisers that they wanted to resign, and 'some of our best workers have been evacuees who are now leaving Westmorland for good . . . Most of us who are permanently here do feel that after five years our own neglected homes and husbands and families need us' – some women undoubtedly noted that Lady Reading had neither – 'and very few will be willing to sign on for more than to be called back in a *real* emergency. Most of the WVS jobs that we have undertaken in this county and worked up can now be carried on quite efficiently by existing permanent societies.' Traditional modes of charity, she thought, could and would be revived; and she went on to give details as to how almost all of the work then and recently being done by the WVS could in fact be carried out effectively by others. '*Most of us feel very strongly*', she concluded, 'that by September we shall be considered by many to have become redundant, and we should far prefer to wind up then as an officially run office, and do any odd jobs from our homes, signing on simply for recall in a *grave emergency only*.'[25] Much the same sort of thinking was found in Scotland, where many doubted that the WVS should or could continue to play a major role in peacetime, and its head, Lady Ruth Balfour, was explicitly at odds with Lady Reading.[26] During the war the relations among the various providers of welfare (WVS, WI, Red Cross, Girl Guides et al) had generally been mutually supportive; afterwards they became, at least for a while, more competitive, and the high profile of the (upstart) WVS did not sit well with some other services, which were not shy to make their views known, notably the Women's Institute.

Quite a few people assumed that the government would, in due course, endorse the idea that the WVS be disbanded. In September 1945 the government did agree to extend the WVS's funding – and thus its life – for another two years, mainly to help with the difficult transition from war to peace: many people recalled the struggles and disappointments of 1919–20 and did not wish to see them repeated. While this political support was important, it left open the question of what would happen in the longer term. Would these two years simply become a final chapter? While the WVS was widely admired for all that it had done during the war, this admiration alone would not be enough to keep it afloat during the hoped-for years of peace. The WVS did not have deep roots in British society. It was the offspring of a serious but short-term crisis, and as an organisation it was closely linked to government, whose priorities might change. After attending a WVS meeting in Preston on 5 November 1947, Nella Last did some reading between the lines: 'Lady Reading spoke well as usual,' she wrote, 'but even she could not hide the fact she thought the future prospects a bit dim.'

EPILOGUE

What accounts for the survival of the WVS? How did it sustain its relevance to post-war society?

In answering these questions it is vital to appreciate that the respect felt for Lady Reading was extraordinary. There is no doubt that this respect was deserved. During the war praise seemed to follow her wherever she went. She had a commanding presence, but she was also unstuffy, vivacious, approachable, often made jokes and was as egalitarian in dealing with others as the culture at that time would permit. She was also an adept administrator, highly efficient and had no use for casual practices.[1] Lady Reading was also an excellent public speaker. When Helen Lloyd, who was not easily impressed, heard her speak at Redhill on 30 May 1941, she found her 'magnificent. She made the best speech I have ever heard by a woman. She was really funny and genuinely inspiring and I came away proud of the WVS, so much so that I feel it a disgrace that the office is closing on Whit Monday.' After hearing Lady Reading, women apparently often felt spurred to put out even more effort, and to commit even of more of their time to national service. It was said in September 1942 that the memory of her five-day visit to the Isle of Wight 'will long remain an inspiration'. This was how almost all members who met her on her travels reacted to her. Given that neither money nor coercion played any role at all in attracting and keeping members, visionary leadership was crucial.

Lady Reading's visits to localities (and she made hundreds of them) were triumphant successes. She consistently gave voice to a compelling blend of noble ideals and down-to-earth practicality. It was common for women to write of feeling 'privileged' to have met her or heard her talk. Virtually everyone warmed to her personality, almost immediately. Her charm; her natural authority; her selfless dedication to duty (which members observed for themselves: she never boasted of this); her sensitivity to others; her knack for knowing about the work that had been done (much of it unglamorous) and openly showing her appreciation for this work; her awareness that the efforts of volunteers should never be taken for granted or undervalued; her can-do optimism and generous vision of service – all these qualities earned her a degree of loyalty that was truly remarkable, and which was enthusiastically and almost universally sustained up until at least early 1945. It is probable that tens of thousands of women met Lady Reading or heard her speak during the war, and almost none of them had a critical word to say of her. We, as authors, became alert to these repeated expressions of admiration and were thus on the lookout for evidence on the other side, for disapproval or at least reservations, for remarks that were even mildly negative. We found almost nothing – aside from a couple of opinions that she was inclined to over-praise others.

This respect for Lady Reading is undoubtedly the major reason why she was able to function as a virtual autocrat. The WVS was in no way democratically structured. It had no committees; it had no constitution; it was run from the top down, though what was done at the grassroots and reported to head-quarters might and frequently did influence later directives from senior administrators. But since the WVS was run flexibly and with due regard for the realities of women's lives – their household responsibilities, their health, perhaps their limited mobility, the variations in members' temperaments – women were usually asked to do only what they would feel comfortable with. They were not shoved around. Value was assigned to whatever jobs they felt able to perform. There was room for almost everyone to take satisfaction from doing her bit, and helping out in her own way. The organisation of the WVS and its ethos and chain of command (to the extent that it existed) were very different from those of the military. Lady Reading, in short, led a benevolent despotism that took care to be encouraging and not to push its members too hard. Hers was a leadership that worked.

The immediate post-war role of the WVS was bound to be more modest than its wartime one. After all, the WVS had been designed mainly to deal with emergencies that either were no longer probable or ceased to exist as a possibility, though it did continue to demonstrate its value when natural disasters occurred, such as during episodes of serious flooding.[2] Whatever the needs of peacetime Britain, they were – with rare exceptions – regarded as less urgent than the needs of a Britain fighting the most demanding war in her history, sometimes with her back to the wall. Peace meant the winding down of all kinds of activities, and one of the organisations that might well have dwindled or even gone under was the WVS.

A major reason for its survival was that the government valued what it did and thought that some of this work would still have to be done after the war, at least for a while. The WVS not only had an impressive track record, but its services had been provided and continued to be provided inexpensively. A lot got done at relatively little cost – and this was sure to weigh on the minds of a government presiding over an almost bankrupt nation. In short, the WVS was a bargain. This was, in part, why the new Labour government granted it a two-year extension in September 1945. At a time of austerity, the economical functioning of the WVS was a significant factor in its favour. Since public funds were insufficient to begin to meet all the pressing needs of post-war welfare, the services of volunteers, if efficiently and competently delivered, were not likely to be passed up. Proven efficiency, along with size – perhaps some fifteen hundred Centres and still large numbers of active members – was a decided asset of the WVS. It routinely claimed to be able to get the job done and had shown it could do so time and time again. Since there were still many jobs to be done in the field of domestic welfare – and the post-war WVS was diligent in publicising all that it was doing[3] – allowing it to continue to work in the interest of the state was (in the eyes of those in power) prudent and responsible public policy. The WVS was, almost inarguably, a useful and effective service in support of the state that had enabled its creation.

From the government's point of view, one of the weightiest considerations in favour of the WVS – not initially, but as the Cold War intensified – was its potential value for civil defence. This was the original rationale for the service, and though it greatly weakened in the period from 1945 to 1947, it started to regain currency from the late 1940s. As the Home Secretary, James Chuter Ede, put it in a letter of 9 February 1951, money invested in the WVS was 'a cheap insurance premium for the services which we expect to receive from them in an emergency'. From the state's perspective, by the early 1950s the other work of the WVS may actually have

been of secondary importance. 'It is true that in peacetime the
WVS are largely engaged in supplementing the social services,' wrote Ede, 'but they are taking an increasingly active
interest in civil defence work, and they have played a considerable part in obtaining volunteers for part-time work in an
emergency.'[4] This became a major justification for the funding that the WVS received from government: £150,000 to
£170,000 annually in the immediate post-war years, which
was mainly for overhead expenses, including paid staff. Had
this public funding been withdrawn – and there were argu-
ments circulating that it should be – the WVS would either
have had to fold or to redefine itself in a fundamental way,
probably by significantly limiting its ambitions and the scope
of its activities.

If one key reason for the survival of the WVS was government support, the other was Lady Reading. She was relentless
in her quest to ensure it a future. The WVS was her life and
she was determined not to lose it. All those qualities of dedication and drive that she had poured into wartime leadership
continued to be robustly evident after war was over. She pulled
strings; she made good use of her many valuable connections;
she fought back criticisms of the WVS's privileged position
from the leaders of other voluntary services, including the
Women's Institute and National Council of Social Services; she
cultivated constructive relations with the Labour government;
and she never wavered in her commitment to the ongoing
value of the WVS in helping to meet the needs of British
social welfare. She promoted, usually with success, the WVS
as a crucial agent of peacetime reconstruction, an agent that
was better equipped to accomplish these goals than traditional
philanthropic bodies.* Lady Reading constantly championed

*The WRVS did not become a registered charity until 1992.

the spirit of public service, almost in a religious sense, and a
significant number of WVS members continued to be inspired
by her elevating vision. Incontestably, hers was a powerful
voice, set against a background of widely acknowledged
wartime successes. Absent her tireless, unyielding, steely leadership in the years after 1945, it is unlikely that the WVS
would have survived.

After 1945 the WVS continued to have a hand in a great
variety of everyday welfare activities. One is struck by this
impressive diversity of activities in the report given on 25 July
1946 by the Centre Organiser in Brighton to a regional meeting in Tunbridge Wells. She said that

> they were always terribly busy, but she did not know if theirs
> would be considered entirely WVS work. They still gave
> out a great deal of clothing to old people, British Legion,
> SSAFA and Assistance Board cases. In fact, every organisa-
> tion in Brighton came to them for clothing. The hospital
> car service averaged 4000 to 5000 miles a month, driving
> for the hospital, the Ministry of Pensions and the Education
> Authorities. They helped the blind at St Dunstans. 40,000
> to 45,000 lbs. of chocolate milk powder had been distrib-
> uted to schools, YWCA, Youth Clubs, etc. They helped
> with between 15 and 20 National Savings Groups. They
> acted as Country Agents for the Children's Country
> Holidays Fund, distributed welfare foods and took gift foods
> to hospitals, homes and old people. They also helped with
> the Marriage Guidance Council, and lately had been able to
> assist in three cases. About 75 per cent of people eligible for
> the Lord Mayor's Distress Fund had been interviewed at that
> office, and amongst other things they had bought second-
> hand furniture for people and had paid out about £600
> during the last few months. People came to them with all

sorts of queries, and she thought this was because the WVS office was always open.[5]

In addition to this list, *The WVS Guide*, a 110-page booklet published in 1948, documents the very wide range of services that it was delivering to post-war society.

Two conclusions can be drawn from this material. First, much of what the WVS was doing in Brighton, and in most other places where it remained active, related to the immediate post-war dislocations and distress. This was a damaged society that needed all the help that it could get: cries for help were everywhere and insistent, and wartime experience had well equipped the WVS to respond to these cries. Second, most WVS services were still offered at the request of and in support of other groups and established institutions. The WVS did very little independently. When other bodies needed help, whether hospitals or child-welfare organisations or prisons or housing authorities, they often appealed to the WVS, and it did what it could to lend a hand.

These two characteristics of post-war service do suggest, however, that in the longer term the WVS might be in trouble. The most pressing needs stemming from wartime ruptures and hardships were likely to diminish – despite austerity, the later 1940s proved to be years of full employment and expanded state welfare – and most of the organisations and institutions that received assistance from the WVS in 1946 might soon rebuild and renew themselves to the point where they would have no further need for its help. These developments could well have left the WVS with not much to do, or at least not enough to keep it afloat as a major actor in the field of social welfare.

Almost everyone agreed that the WVS had a useful role to play at times of emergency. Occasionally the nation was reminded of this utility, perhaps most dramatically during the crippling floods of 1953 (see Appendix C). This capacity to respond to domestic crises enhanced its attractiveness to Westminster, and the WVS also drew new life from the revived official concern with civil defence at the end of the 1940s and during the early 1950s, when the tensions of the Cold War were especially acute. Nella Last's diary shows how the tensions surrounding the outbreak of war in Korea brought back to life the civil defence activities of the WVS in Barrow-in-Furness, where the WVS had greatly receded in importance during the later 1940s. Helping to cope with emergencies, whether natural disasters, or the sudden arrival of groups of refugees or a possible nuclear attack (there was a brief period around 1950 when such an event was thought to be survivable), was a proven sphere of competence for the WVS. However, as intermittent emergencies would probably not be enough to sustain a committed service of volunteers, it would also have to be capable of effective action in other more routine respects. Any successful service needed to have regular, everyday tasks to perform, which could give its members operational experience, personal satisfaction and social standing. And whatever priorities the WVS might decide on – it is hard to see that it could have continued to uphold indefinitely its very broad agenda of the immediate post-war years* – it was going to have to sustain itself at a time when those interested in voluntary service had a growing array of possibilities to choose from. Indeed, worthy causes have proliferated in modern times, many of them appealing to values and ideals much like those espoused by the WVS.

---

*The range of these services is detailed in Virginia Graham, *The Story of WVS* (London: HMSO, 1959); *Report on 25 Years' Work 1938–1963* (WVS, 1963); Katharine Bentley Beauman, *Green Sleeves: The Story of the WVS-WRVS* (London: Seeley, Service & Co., 1977), Parts II–IV; and some of the Narrative Reports that we have sampled from the 1950s.

It is not the purpose of this book to unravel the rich history
of the WVS (and later WRVS) since the mid-twentieth century, or to recall the many useful and important functions that
it continued to perform. That story is still to be written. What
we might suggest here is a tentative perspective seen from the
vantage point of the second decade of the twenty-first century.
Our suggestion is that, in the longer term, after various twists
and turns and periods of self-examination in the later twenti-
eth century and first years of the twenty-first, the WVS did
find a clear focus, one that was less concerned with public
crises and more related to one specific matter of growing concern in the modern world – getting old, infirm and often
more socially isolated.[6] Helping the aged had been a concern
of the WVS during the war years: by the mid-1940s it was
running social clubs for old people, Darby and Joan Clubs,
which started before war's end, along with Meals on Wheels
and versions of Home Help, and these and other measures ori-
ented to the elderly subsequently grew in prominence. Much
of the social work that the WVS had once done and probably
wanted to continue to do would eventually be taken over by
public authorities and salaried professionals, or occasionally by
other volunteers – one thinks here of salvage, nurseries and
other facilities for childcare, hospital auxiliaries, housing, food
education, extra-curricular schooling, youth welfare and aiding
refugees. The needs of the elderly, though, were both expanding and (most people thought) inadequately served; there was
undeniably a hole to fill, notably outside the regulated social
sector.

It was evident that longer life expectancy would ensure sen-
iors a greater prominence in society at large. Here, then, was
a large and expanding challenge to social service that was both
certain to persist and crying out for immediate attention. The
state provided pensions and medical care, but there was a lot

that it could not or would not do. So, an enlarging opportunity for useful voluntary service could be clearly discerned. By the early twenty-first century the WRVS had found ways to identify the elderly as not just very important, but in fact central to its mission.

Lady Reading, though modern in many of her methods, held to traditional values. She advocated something of an anti-consumerist perspective, framed in crusading language. In March 1950 she spoke of how 'through voluntary service a tremendous amount can be done, because the war has left us physically poor, shabby from a clothing point of view, short from a housing point of view. We may be poor in appearance,' she went on, 'but we are richer than we have ever been before, in the experience we have had, and in the character of our men and women. We have to fight life anew.'[7] This was something of an extension of wartime zeal and self-sacrifice, transposed onto the world of post-war constraints. Such ascetic values could not last. But the practical commitments to useful service could and would be sustained, and they would persist into more recent decades when, despite their much greater prosperity, many human needs were still left unaddressed. These needs were thus candidates for the disciplined attention of those willing to give of themselves on behalf of the welfare of strangers. The WVS changed a lot over the years; it had to in order to survive. Being able to reinvent oneself or one's movement is almost always an asset, and this is a key reason that the WRVS still flourishes, seventy-five years after its birth.

APPENDIX A

A LETTER OF THANKS, 1941

While members of the WVS often mentioned the gratitude they received from those who benefited from their services, the actual voices of these people are rarely heard (aside from formal letters of thanks from, say, a military officer on behalf of his troops). The following letter, dated 11 August 1941, from a Mrs Rowles, an evacuee from Mitcham, Surrey, then living in Dorchester, was handwritten (probably) and sent by the WVS to Chicago. Before posting, a typed copy was made of it, which is held in the Dorset History Centre and inserted in the WVS Dorchester Day Book for June 1944–May 1945.

Reproduced by permission of the Dorset History Centre, reference D.444/4.

To the Ladyships of the American Red Cross,
    I Mrs Rowles wish to thank everyone that has been so kind to me and my children for such lovely clothes that have been given to me by the Women's Voluntary Service in Dorchester. I am sure I could not be treated

any better by these ladies in fitting my children up with warm clothing for the winter. Each one of my children have been fitted up separately with most lovely knitted jumpers and other warm clothing. I happen to be one of those unfortunate mothers to lose everything in the world I possess. My home was completely destroyed by a landmine. Me and my seven children were in an Anderson shelter and thanks to that shelter for it saved our lives. After our shock we went to Dorchester having no home or clothes to wear. These ladies at Dorchester Women's Voluntary Service have put an end to my awful worry of clothing for this winter for all my children through the kindness of you ladys and others of the American Red Cross. I cannot tell you by letter our [sic] hundreds of others must feel as I do at this moment for all your kindness. If only one day I could do something for America I would be one of those mothers to be the first. Still for all we have lost, all we have suffered, our hearts are still the same and I am sure our spirit will never be broken. We are just waiting for that great day when the lights of London shine again. Our houses are gone, our lovely buildings, but the Capital of good old London will always be there so I close my letter with my deepest thanks to you American ladys, also to the Dorchester Voluntary Service, for I am sure if you could only see these ladys how hard they are working with your help. They look very tired but still they carry on.

So thanks to one and all of you.

From a mother of a family that has lost everything through enemy action.

On the back of this copy an unnamed WVS member wrote: 'Isn't it nice to find such gratitude? It makes up for so much of the other kind of thing. I did all the work in this case.'

APPENDIX B

WVS REPORTS ON ITS WORK

The following three documents show the commitment to detailed recording that is found in many WVS-generated sources. Each can be read as a sort of self-portrait of group action.

THE NARRATIVE REPORT FROM THE NEWBURY RURAL DISTRICT, BERKSHIRE, AUGUST 1943

Since the testimony from monthly Narratives Reports is so prominent in this book, it is worth reproducing in full one of these documents, thus giving a sense of the varied issues that might be covered. No Narrative Report can be said to be typical. Many, probably most, are brief and minimally informative; only a minority are detailed and wide-ranging. So much depended on the mood, assiduousness, personal circumstances and literary skills of the writer, usually though not always a Centre Organiser, along with the nature of the work that had been done in the preceding month (some jobs seemed more worth writing about than others). A Narrative Report was supposed to be arranged according to categories set out by headquarters. In the case below, the Report, which is held in the WRVS Archive, was written by the Secretary of the WVS Centre in the Newbury Rural District.

1. **EVACUATION**. There is a slight decrease in the numbers of evacuees this month, possibly owing to the holidays. Several children have gone home and six are not returning. The figures therefore are mothers 76, Children 159, Adults 85, Unaccompanied children 85, Teachers 4. Making a total of 411 evacuees, counting the two children still in the Newbury Rural District Hostel.

2. **CLOTHING**. The Clothing Depot have received as free gifts three handkerchiefs and one undervest this month, and give out one boy's shirt to the SSAFA [Soldiers', Sailors' and Airmen's Families Association]. Otherwise there is nothing to report.

3. **ARP & HOUSEWIVES**. The Basic Training Lectures are arranged to take place next month prior to forming a Housewives section at Brimpton. It has been impossible to do anything this month owing to the Harvest and the children's holidays. Plans are however being made for further lectures to be held in various Parishes, where it is hoped to form a Housewives Section.

4. **REST CENTRES**. There was an unofficial rehearsal of the Mobile Rest Centre which went off well. It took approximately 45 minutes to load the Van and 15 minutes to unload. This Exercise was arranged so that the crew should know what to do and how to pack the Van should they be called out unexpectedly.

5. **CANTEENS**. A great many troops have left Newbury and the District. Mrs Hawker, who is head of the Soldiers' Club WVS Canteen in Newbury, received the following letter from a Sergeant in a Pioneer Corps: 'On behalf of

myself and the boys of the company which I belong [to], I wish to express our appreciation of the great work you and your Lady Assistants at the Soldiers' Club were doing during our stay in Newbury to make life in the Forces enjoyable. We were all very sorry indeed to leave Newbury, and it was not until we had left that we fully realized what a great part the Soldiers' Club had played in our lives there. A good cup of tea and a piece of "Home Made" put us in mind of home. Long may the Soldiers' Club continue. Who knows? Perhaps we may one day be again stationed in the vicinity.' When the RASC [Royal Army Signals Corps] left Newbury they presented to the Soldiers' Club a large photograph of the Company together with a list of names to go underneath the photograph, which is being framed and hung in the Club.

6. **COMMUNITY FEEDING**. All schools are having holidays. Therefore there are for the moment no school lunches.

7. **WELFARE WORK FOR THE FORCES**. The Make and Mend class at Donnington Castle House has finished, the troops having left the neighbourhood, but can be resumed should it be required at any time.

9. 10. 11. 12. & 13. Nothing to report.*

14. **NATIONAL SAVINGS**. There is a National Savings Group in each parish and in most cases the Group is run by a member of the WVS. A plaque has been received from the Air Ministry for the Wings for Victory Week. Each Group obtaining the target qualified for a Certificate of Merit.

15. **SALVAGE**. Eight tons of waste paper has been collected in Chieveley. The Salvage Officer in each parish is constantly visiting the householders and keeping them up to

---

*She omitted no. 8. The topics about which she wrote nothing were Working Parties, Hospital Service and Supplies, Transport, Refugees, Queen's Messengers, and Information Bureau.

the mark. There is little heavy metal left. It has been collected and sold in most of the parishes.

16. **COOPERATION WITH THE MINISTRY OF LABOUR.** A few more war workers and their families have been billeted in the Newbury Rural District. It has become increasingly difficult to find accommodation in the Rural District – every part of it has been carefully combed.

17. [*Meetings and Lectures.*] Nothing to report.

18. **OTHER ACTIVITIES.** The WVS were asked if they could provide and run a tea tent at a local horse show, given in aid of the Newbury Hospital. This they did and had a most successful afternoon in spite of a wet day. Profits from the tea turned over to Horse Show Committee – £29 19s 6d. A very charming if somewhat unusual letter was received at the Newbury RD WVS from a soldier who had lost his wife. He wrote saying he had heard what excellent work the WVS did, and how kind and helpful they were, so he ventured to write and ask if the WVS could introduce him to someone who would eventually become his wife and a mother to his two children. He was terribly lonely and felt he could not exist without 'female companionship'. The letter is having careful attention.

REPORT OF THE WVS COUNTY ORGANISER FOR WESTMORLAND, 1 NOVEMBER 1944

Annual reports were also presented in some places, though most have apparently been lost. We reproduce here one that survives in a county record office.* At a conference at County

*Cumbria Archives, Kendal, WDSO 92/1–2

Hall, Kendal on 1 November 1944, Mrs Mary Hornyold-Strickland, the County Organiser, welcomed members of her audience, which included officials from local government and regional WVS headquarters; Centre Organisers; village representatives; heads of Rest Centres, kitchens, work parties, canteens, and mothers' clubs; and members of the Women's Institute and Women's Cooperative Guilds. She then proceeded to give a very thorough report of the county's work that year, from which the following are extracts.

Reproduced with the permission of the Cumbria Archives, Kendal and Mrs Angela Hornyold-Strickland.

The membership for Westmorland County and Kendal Borough is 2,875. The WVS County Headquarters moved to new offices early in the year. More space and light and air were thus obtained, and more room left at Lowther Street for the Clothing Depot. Grateful thanks were due to Mr Greenwood and his Department for arranging the move.

The first work since the last report was of course the distribution of such welcome Christmas gifts from Canada, Australia and USA as jam, sweets and apples for all evacuee children in hostels, and many local children in hospitals and orphanages.

More lectures in First Aid and Nursing were given to WVS members by St John Ambulance members, for which we were very grateful, and our own Training Officer, Miss Una Smith, gave many classes in anti-gas, fire-fighting and ARP, and also in cobbling and household repairs. Excellent lectures in the latter subjects were kindly arranged for us by the Education Authorities, who also supplied us with Make Do and Mend teachers. Miss Smith will make use of her skill in the near future giving classes to Girl Guides and Rangers. She organised some excellent playlets last spring and summer with young Kirkby Lonsdale actors and actresses on 'How to (and How not to) Run Rest Shelters'. These proved popular and useful.

In January last, in conjunction with the Ministry of Health and the Red Cross and Federation of Women's Institutes, we tried to organise a system of Home Helps throughout the County during the bad 'flu epidemic. Lowther area produced an excellent example of this service. Other work for the Ministry of Health's Department has included help with the Blood Transfusion Service. WVS provided transport, and a special tribute is due to Miss Kathlyn Rhodes, who has hardly missed a Sunday going out with the Mobile Unit and keeping the records. The WVS van also distributes cod-liver oil and orange juice from the Food Office in Centres in South Westmorland and the Lakes. The Volunteer Car Pool is endlessly used for the transport of cases to hospital, and has had many urgent calls recently on behalf of expectant mothers. Miss Urquhart will give a report on the work of the VCP generally. One of the most useful services we have been able to give to mothers and babies since August has been the free supply in urgent case of rubber teats for bottles, which have been quite unobtainable in shops. We have also lent prams, some local gifts, others supplied to us by WVS headquarters. Once more Meathop Sanatorium begged for help when they were short-staffed, and Witherslack WVS nobly filled the breach – luckily it was only necessary for a short time. Although we were unable to provide a WVS cook at Dr Dow's request for Trerose Maternity Home, I was able to tell him where he could get an evacuee for the whole-time post. Windermere WVS, at his urgent call, did really hard work getting Ibbotsholme ready as a nursery. Ambleside and Arnside Centres have kept up their valued help with two war nurseries, and we also do what we can for Abbot's Hall, Quarry Garth and other nursery units with the provision of food gifts, making up of clothing, toys, etc. WVS also helped in a staff crisis at Enyeat Hostel, and all the hostels and other children's homes have shared in gifts available. A great debt of gratitude is due to the USA for many of these gifts, especially clothing, Wellington boots, teats, hot water bottles, oil stoves for use in shelters, urns, and much of the food. The Canadian Red Cross also deserve our thanks for clothing and jam.

Mrs Hornyold–Strickland then went on to give detailed accounts of the clothes and shoes that had been supplied that year, the garments mended and knitted, and the efforts of the clothing and footwear exchanges. There were lots of accounting challenges: 'Over 6700 coupons [for clothes and shoes] have passed through the coupon banking account, another fresh nightmare with which the office is now faced monthly.' She also lauded the work of the Forces canteen. 'Without mentioning figures it can be said that for more than four years WVS have staffed it efficiently for seven days a week, fourteen hours a day, and often for much longer. The Canteen has a reputation for good, cheap food and comfort of which it is very proud, and is known, as they say, from Land's End to John O'Groats.' She remarked as well on the distribution of monthly food letters,* the staffing of British Restaurants, the success of the pie schemes, salvage work by cogs, savings campaigns, escorting children, and collecting herbs and rose hips and jam jars – over six thousand of the latter were 'taken to the Forces Canteen at Carnforth,

---

*Food education was a recurrent theme in WVS communications, which included the distribution of leaflets, and its *Bulletin* routinely printed advice on nutrition, appealing recipes, economical cooking and avoiding waste.

where they cannot have too many as these jars are the only mugs they have for the troops' tea'. Then there was the hospitality offered to troops (many of them foreigners) by the WVS in Windermere, and from July to large numbers of evacuees.

Evacuation was of course the biggest job this year, and is still present in a very modified form. July and August brought many hundreds of mothers and children from buzz-bomb areas to safety here, and Kendal, Windermere, Patterdale, Ambleside and Kirkby Stephen WVS all had to put their Rest Shelter training into practice, everywhere, apparently, with successful results and to the satisfaction of the Local Authorities. Appleby did not have to sleep people, but gave dinners. Shelters in Kendal were kept open for as many as four consecutive nights and on several occasions for more than one night, and there were nine shelters in the Borough. There was complete cooperation between WVS and other helpers, both men and women, belonging to the different churches and chapels whose premises were used, and with the Red Cross, St. John's, the Guides and Scouts and Civil Defence messengers and the Wardens and Fire Guards, who all lent a hand.

The vast majority of the evacuees were most grateful for the comforts provided. Some were disappointed at not finding themselves at Blackpool. Others thought they must have got as far as Scotland, but had never heard of Westmorland. One woman went back from the Lakes because she could not stand the 'hush' of the countryside. Another could not stand the noise of the cocks and hens. One said her fourteen-months baby missed its father so much she had to take it home. Another said she supposed she'd have to choose between looking at the b____ bombs in London or looking at the b____ nothing in a South Westmorland valley. However, she chose the valley for a number of weeks, and her friends from London joined her there. One of the nicest stories was of the very expectant mother who longed for a bath in a small and crowded Kendal Shelter where there was no privacy until a bright helper bethought herself of putting the large tin bath in the pulpit – a quite successful effort. Then there was the mother in Windermere who let her pile of nappies grow and grow until the somewhat anxious hostess suggested it was high time to wash them. 'And what are the WVS for, then?' was the indignant reply.

Ambleside organised a club premises where the mothers could go to wash and iron and cook, and the evacuees themselves were made responsible. Windermere organised a weekly afternoon social, but Kendal has run a Club every afternoon including Sundays ... Classes in Make Do and Mend and cobbling were arranged, and games and toys provided. A sadder side of the evacuation has been the old women sent up to Windermere, some over 90, and feeling the cold and damp rather a lot. We have clothed 147 of them, found walking sticks, a bath chair, shawls, etc., and helped to arrange Church services for them in the hostel. Some are now in hospital, and these are being visited by WVS.

Here should be mentioned the splendid service given by a number of the Westmorland WVS in London during the buzz bomb blitz. The Region urgently begged for their services, and it was stated by Lady Reading that no Region had answered the call better than this one, Region 10. Miss Gwen Smith, our Windermere Organiser, and Mrs Connell did very hard work for a fortnight on end, and Mrs Connell did it twice in a London hostel for repair gangs. No light job, from 5.30 a.m. to 11 p.m., feeding hungry men and doing an immense amount to keep up their morale. The workmen just could not believe that the WVS were unpaid volunteers ministering to their needs, and told Lady Reading and officials of the Ministry of Labour that they just could not show funk on their job when these ladies were so plucky. Mrs Bagot drove a mobile canteen for a fortnight in South London, the Misses Glasson and Mrs Astrid Wilson did varied work in different parts of London, as well as escorting train loads of evacuees, as did Mrs Blagden, Welfare and County Salvage Officer, whom we are soon to lose from Westmorland where she will be sadly missed.

A word now about school canteens. These have increased considerably in the past year, and there are now 22 in the County. The WVS has not often failed to answer Mr Trevelyan's call for helpers, having been told by Headquarters that there is no finer form of war work than this. But the Education authorities know that it is getting increasingly difficult to provide rotas for the work. Members are tired after five years of war work, with fewer people to do it. Illness has claimed many of the best (due probably to overwork and strain) and the time is not far distant when we shall have to tell the LEA [Local Education Authority] reluctantly that it is impossible to keep up the rotas of voluntary helpers.

It should be stressed here that WVS is of course only an Emergency organisation. For as long as we are called on by the Government to continue under the various Local Authorities and Government Departments for whom we work we shall of course try our best to fulfill all requirements, but as soon as demobilisation releases women who will be available for and need paid jobs our usefulness will cease. Miss Foster Jeffery [from Regional Headquarters] will bear out that I discussed this point with Lady Reading at a conference, having a horror lest WVS should ever come to be considered 'tiresome women making jobs for themselves', but was told very firmly by our Chairman that no one, not even the Prime Minister himself, knows yet when the emergency is likely to be over, and that he will be the one to give the word when our services can be dispensed with. Until then we must struggle on, and certainly for a good many months to come there is work to be done. So where possible we will not fail the Education Department as to school canteen helpers. A questionnaire on this subject is to be filled in.

A SHORT HISTORY OF THE WVS IN THE AXBRIDGE RURAL DISTRICT, SOMERSET

The following account was attached to the March 1945 Narrative Report from Axbridge Rural District and is held in the WRVS Archive. It offers a perspective that encompasses six years.

The WVS for Civil Defence started in the Axbridge RD in February 1939 with a Centre Organiser and twelve group Representatives. By 1944 the membership had risen to 1,134 of whom 563 were Housewives trained to deal with minor casualties and home gas-cleansing and with a Village Representative, a Senior Housewife and their deputies in each of the 33 villages. Two Divisional Housewives had been appointed for North and South Mendip respectively.

Closest contact has been maintained with the Local Authority throughout. Lord Beaverbrook's appeal for aluminium during the Battle of Britain made WVS known in every village and hamlet and necessitated a central depot to deal with the collection. From this sprang the Central Office in Axbridge, which together with a Clothing Depot and Welfare Centre grew from make-shift to fully equipped and adequate premises.

The first important duty was helping the Local Authority with billeting and welfare including collecting ration books etc. of the 10,000 odd evacuees from bombed areas in London, Bristol and the South Coast. Other strictly Civil Defence duties have been the providing of about 40 Queen's Messengers and helpers, many of whom went to Bath during the blitz; staffing two mobile canteens used during the Weston blitz, as well as for Home Guard and Civil Defence exercises; the organisation of first-aid dressing stations in all villages where there was no Red Cross; sending members as relief to London during flying-bomb attacks in 1944; also providing Volunteer Car Pool drivers and assisting with re-clothing after local sporadic raids and during the Weston blitz in 1940 and 1942.

Regular activities include the servicing of the British Restaurant in Axbridge and a canteen for the Forces in Cheddar; driving vans for school-feeding (about 40 members); Volunteer Car Pool drivers (about 50 members); mending for troops; knitting for Forces, Merchant Navy and children in liberated Europe; staffing rural pie-rounds in North and South Mendip; assisting the Food Office annually with the distribution of ration books etc. Camouflage nets have been made, hospitality freely offered to tired workers from London – and the latest activity in 1945 has been the collection of household goods for Lambeth re-housing scheme.

APPENDIX C

THE WVS AND THE FLOODS OF 1953

On the night of 31 January–1 February 1953, there were monster storms in parts of the British Isles (and elsewhere, especially the Netherlands). A car ferry went down off the coast of Northern Ireland and 128 people lost their lives; there were over three hundred other deaths as a result of the massive floods that night, almost all of them in settlements in, on, or near the Thames Estuary and in coastal regions of East Anglia (Essex and Norfolk were hit very hard). 'Thousands were rendered homeless,' according to the *Illustrated London News* of 7 February, 'and from every quarter of the flooded districts poignant stories were recorded. Some were drowned in cars on the roads, dead were found on roofs or caught in trees, and families were marooned in flooded houses, crouching in lofts and upper storeys in their night attire. Public services were disrupted and fears of epidemics were an added anxiety.' Over thirty-two thousand people had to be evacuated from their homes; there was widespread damage to farmland; and twenty-four thousand houses were flooded, some of them wrecked beyond repair.[1]

This was a major disaster – much larger than the floods of

1946 and 1947 – and it summoned the sort of relief efforts that the WVS and others had put out during the first half of the 1940s. 'It is "like the war all over again",' wrote Tom Driberg in the *New Statesman*, 'not only because of the troops, but because of the spirit of comradeship and hospitality among the thousands of voluntary workers who have "mucked in" – the hotel-keepers and yachtsmen at Burnham-on-Crouch who have looked after evacuees from Foulness and cooked meals day and night, the boat-builders who have crossed to the islands dozens of times every twenty-four hours bringing off boat-loads of the homeless, the ladies who have made the Royal Corinthian Yacht Club a model rest-centre.'[2] Rest Centres suddenly sprung up along the East Anglian coast, many of them staffed by WVS members.

It was the WVS's capacity to respond to a crisis and initiate rapid action that made it one of the first services that the authorities turned to as waters rose and flooded the landscape. Well-honed skills, flexibility and a nation-wide organisation put the WVS at the centre of crisis response, working alongside many of the same local authorities and other emergency personnel that had been wartime partners.

The storm that was to devastate the east coast started in the north-east. At seven o'clock on the evening of Saturday 31 January the Centre Organiser for Billingham in County Durham was called by the police: the River Tees had burst its banks and poured into three hundred houses in the Port Clarence area. As the night wore on and destruction surged southward, WVS Centres in flooded areas were summoned into action.[3] In Harwich, at three o'clock in the morning, the newly appointed Centre Organiser was rung up by the town clerk and asked to open the local Rest Centre. The Organiser in Cleethorpes, finding it 'quite impossible to call a meeting of our members to make organised plans for our flood campaigning', improvised instead. She divided members into groups of thirty, arbitrarily assigned them to be available at specific times and dispatched letters, delivered by the Scouts and Guides, giving women their orders. She doubted that these 'somewhat dictatorial plans' would succeed, but was overjoyed when the members 'accepted the days allotted to them without grumbling or fuss'. Some of her workers had not yet completed their civil defence training and were thus 'uninitiated in the innermost orgies of a WVS emergency', but the good work they did in February 'have cemented them, we hope, for ever'. In Lowestoft members worked by candlelight in the police station, and did their best to comfort dazed, shocked, and rain-drenched residents as they fled from low-lying areas.

The WVS in eastern counties threw themselves into the work, usually in tandem with local authorities and private charities, reviving the skills and working relationships that had been evident in wartime. Hot sweet tea, warm clothing and food were provided in the early hours of the crisis. From three o'clock on the Sunday morning the Herne Bay centre cooked food by the light of two candles and began to serve needy people an hour after they had been called out. In the following fortnight they dispensed some 1100 emergency meals. Elsewhere the WVS went – often by boat – to feed men working on the sea walls and civilians marooned in, or unwilling to leave, their homes. Some WVS members arrived by tractors or on lorries, and mobile canteens again proved their worth. At Sandilands in Cleethorpes members waded out to a hotel where emergency crews were billeted; they found the workers sleeping in damp blankets, with no means of getting warm. So they collected wood for fires, started drying the blankets, made hot tea and did their best to provide some sort of comfort for men striving to protect others.

332

As in wartime, some women acquitted themselves impressively. A Norfolk member who lost both her parents in the floods ensured that work was carried on by her deputy who, with her colleagues, served hot drinks for four days to 150 emergency workers. A Centre Organiser on Canvey Island, marooned all night in her flooded home, donned her WVS uniform and, when rescued, went to the Rest Centre in Benfleet where she worked steadily for fourteen days until she could return home. In Mablethorpe, Lincolnshire the clothing exchange on the seafront caught the 'full force of the rushing breakthrough', while the WVS headquarters had 'four feet of water in and lots of mud and sand'; most of the goods – clothes, first aid equipment, stretchers and blankets – were a total loss. Many members' own houses were inundated. But the Organiser, aided by three Girl Guides, quickly set about cleaning the buildings; the Red Cross and others replaced emergency equipment; and the WVS got back to work.

In more fortunate regions the WVS continued with its usual work as well as contending with challenges posed by the disaster. In Chesterfield the WVS helped at the hospital, supported national savings, assisted old people's welfare, served a canteen, billeted people, oversaw changes in the blood transfusion service, contributed to organising a children's concert, participated in a house to house canvassing for civil defence and transported invalids to classes and appointments – as well as helping with flood relief. The latter included receiving 468 parcels of clothing that individuals had dropped at the office, as well as loads of donations delivered by car and lorry. Most had to be carried up two flights of stairs, and then sorted and labelled. It was tiring work, even with the help of 'two boys from a garage'. When the office was full, more space had to be sought, which again meant much climbing and strenuous hauling of goods.

One of the biggest tasks facing the WVS was handling the enormous volume of enquiries about displaced people. This proved to be difficult since many homeless people were taken in by friends or relatives, or had been taken by car or train to London without any record being made of who they were or where they had gone – the sort of record-keeping that had been routine in wartime. In the meantime, Food Flying Squads, supplied by the Ministry of Food and mostly staffed by the WVS, fanned out across the damaged areas to meet urgent nutritional needs. These were large-scale enterprises and had been first tested in bombed cities in 1940–1. Most squads consisted of canteens, one food store van, camp stores, a water tanker, a motorcycle and a utility van; they were staffed by thirty to forty people. Leicestershire operated its new convoy for the first time during the floods, though training had not yet been completed. When the convoy was in Mablethorpe it was supplying over six thousand meals a day to contractors' men, lorry drivers, police and firemen. An enormous effort was sustained for three weeks.

Help also came from distant places, as volunteers threw themselves into work reminiscent of wartime, especially the provision of clothing for those who had lost their homes. Appeals were made across the nation for garments, footwear, bedding and other essentials, and citizens dug deep to donate. The WVS was a critical organiser of this appeal. Members gathered together to sort and pack the tens of thousands of items that were donated, with many who had drifted away from active service after 1945 proving eager to lend a hand. Nella Last recorded in her diary for February 1953 an exceedingly busy week for the WVS in Barrow-in-Furness: cleaning, mending, packing and sending off the mountains of clothes donated. 'The thought of all the homeless cold people in the flooded areas haunted me,' she wrote on 3 February. 'I packed a pair of shoes I can do without, some shirts Cliff [her son] once sent, two old but well mended vests of my own and two of my husband's.' Her thoughts and actions echoed across the country, and even her generally uncooperative husband offered to clean and polish all the donated shoes and replace worn laces.

Dealing with masses of household good was no easy task. It strained even the WVS's well-established skill at operating clothing depots and re-housing the homeless. There was actually such a surplus of donations that the WVS was able to dispatch large quantities of clothing to needier parts of the world. By July 1953 a million garments had been sent to Korea, two million to the Middle East and half a million to other parts of Europe, and it was committed WVS volunteers who kept at this work long after public concern had subsided. All these efforts showed the WVS still very much at the ready and keen to respond to whatever needs the nation had to confront.

NOTES

INTRODUCTION: A CALL TO ARMS

1 Imperial War Museum, Photograph Library, MH 93 and 95; see also *The Times*, 17 June 1938, pp. 13 and 17. A detailed account of the formation of the WVS has been written by Matthew McMurray (March 2008), the archivist for the WRVS, and is available on its website. There are several files in the National Archives at Kew that include documents on the early history of the WVS, notably HO186/105 and 314, and (especially) HO186/569 and HO356/2, along with a helpful file in the East Sussex Record Office, CD9/133/1 and another in the Staffordshire Record Office, D421/2/11. In the WRVS Archive, Box 229 holds a volume of statistics on enrolments and Box 235 press cuttings on Lady Reading's speeches in 1938–41. A two-page summary of her life, listed under Stella Isaacs, is in the most recent edition of the *Oxford Dictionary of National Biography*. A useful discussion of the founding of the WVS is provided in James Hinton, *Women, Social Leadership, and the Second World War: Continuities of Class* (Oxford: OUP, 2002), pp. 19–21.

1: EVACUEES 1939–40

1 This paragraph and the following three paragraphs depend heavily on two sources, WRVS Archive, Box 345, Report on Huntingdonshire, 1 February to 10 October 1939, and a later document, the 'County Organiser's Report' of 15 January 1942; and a valuable unpaginated file concerning the WVS in 1939–41 in the Huntingdonshire Library and Archives (HALS), HINCH/11/94. The first and last two quotations in these paragraphs are from the former.

2 Caroline Clifford and Alan Akeroyd, *Huntingdonshire in the Second World War* (Stroud: Tempus, 2007), pp. 10 and 37.

NOTES

3 WRVS Archive, Box 348, Region 4, County of Huntingdon Organiser's Report, 15 January 1942.

4 *Hunts Post*, 14 September 1939, p. 5, and *Ely Weekly Guardian*, 6 October 1939, p. 10.

5 HALS, HINCH/11/94, 'Child Guidance Officer', undated and unsigned typescript. Further details regarding Miss Alcock and her work are in the WRVS Archive, 'Care and Treatment of Difficult Children', Box 31, packet 1 (Xmas 1939).

6 Mrs St Loe Strachey, *Borrowed Children: A Popular Account of Some Evacuation Problems and Their Remedies* (London: John Murray, 1940), pp. 80–2.

7 Susan Isaacs (ed.), *The Cambridge Education Survey: A Wartime Study in Social Welfare and Education* (London: Methuen, 1941), p. 32.

8 HALS, HINCH/11/94, 'Report of East Lodge, Leighton, Hunts', January 1941, unsigned typescript.

9 *Ely Weekly Guardian*, 6 October 1939, p. 10.

10 'Report of East Lodge, Leighton, Hunts', op. cit.

11 Mass Observation Archive (MOA), TC66/21/F, report from Worcester, 31 July 1940.

12 WRVS Archive, Box 33, packet 9 [soon to be HQ/CR/E18]. This eleven-page document presents a good summary of the county's evacuation plans.

13 Surrey History Centre (SHC), 5380/2/1, 'The Evacuation: Dorking Received London Guests', p. 5. This scrapbook of press clippings, correspondence, photos, and other sources relating to Dorking is invaluable in documenting the early months of the war for the WVS.

14 SHC, 1532/1/51; this is part of a thorough five-page report, undated but clearly written around November 1939.

15 Richard Titmuss, *Problems of Social Policy* (London: HMSO, 1950), Appendix 9.

16 SHC, 1532/1/53-55; WRVS Archive, Box 345, documents on Rickmansworth in later 1939.

17 SHC, 1532/1/51 and 5380/2/1, p. 8.

18 *Leighton Buzzard Observer*, 26 September 1939, p. 5; *North Beds Courier*, 10 October 1939, p. 3; *Dunstable Borough Gazette*, 3 November 1939, p. 1; and *Bedfordshire Times*, 1 December 1939, p. 10.

19 *WVS Bulletin*, no. 2, December 1939, p. 4.

20 SHC, 5380/2/1, p. 8.

21 SHC, 1532/1/52.

22 SHC, 1532/1/55.

23 WRVS Archive, Box 31, packet 1 (Xmas 1939).

24 WRVS Archive, Box 345, reports of 30 November 1939, p. 1, and December 1939, p. 2.

25 WRVS Archive, Box 345, Huntingdonshire meeting, 25 July 1939.

26 WRVS Archive, Box 734, 'WVS in Region VII: How We Started!', p. 1.

27 'War Strain in Children', *British Medical Journal*, 25 January 1941, p. 124; and Samuel E. Gill, 'Nocturnal Enuresis: Experiences with Evacuated Children', *British Medical Journal*, 10 August 1940, pp. 199–200. A perceptive view of this wartime problem is presented in Titmuss, op. cit., pp. 120–5 and 349.

28 Jon Newman and Nilu York, *What to do when the Air Raid Siren Sounds: Life in Lambeth during World War Two* (London: Lambeth Archives, 2005), pp. 4–5.

29 SHC, 8261/9/6/9, unpaginated (but pp. 3ff).

30 WRVS Archive, Box 345, report of the Centre Organiser.

31 Strachey, op. cit., pp. 83–4 and 128.

32 WRVS, Box 31, packet 1 (Xmas 1939), p. 2.

33 Some of the stresses and ill feelings stemming from evacuation are summarised in Titmuss, op. cit., especially Chapter 8. Juliet Gardiner offers an excellent survey of the subject in her *Wartime: Britain 1939–1945* (London: Headline, 2004), Chapter 2.

34 WRVS Archive, Box 33, packet 9 [soon to be HQ/CR/E18], 'Report of evacuation plans for Surrey'.

35 Strachey, op. cit., p. 82.

36 WRVS Archive, Box 346, Reports from the Cromer Urban District and Erpingham Rural District, March/April 1940, p. 1, May 1940, p. 1, and June 1940, p. 1; and *The Times*, 12 June 1940.

37 WRVS Archive, Box 31, packet 1, 'Christmas in Caernarvonshire'.

38 SHC, 5380/2/1, p. 4.

39 *Isle of Ely and Wisbech Advertiser*, 25 October 1939, p. 7; *Wisbech Standard*, 6 October 1939, p. 7.

40 Staffordshire Record Office, D421/2/6, p. 1; Kendal Archive Centre, WDSO 92/1-2, Westmorland Report for April 1941.

41 Norman Watson, *WRVS in Scotland: Seventy Years of Service* (Edinburgh: Black & White Publishing, 2008), p. 22.

42 Statistics on evacuation are conveniently found in Titmuss, op. cit., Appendix 2.

43 HALS, HINCH/11/94, letter dated 31 May 1940.

2: MOMENTUM BUILDS 1939–40

1 WRVS Archive, Box 345.

2 Staffordshire Record Office, D421/2/8.

3 Berkshire Record Office, D/Ex 856/4.

4 *Isle of Ely and Wisbech Advertiser*, 2 October 1940, p. 5.

5 *WVS Bulletin*, no. 3, January 1940, p. 8.

6 Charles Graves, *Women in Green (The Story of the WVS)* (London: Heinemann, 1948), p. 47.

7 *Isle of Ely and Wisbech Advertiser*, 11 September 1940, p. 5.

8 *WVS Bulletin*, no. 7, May 1940, p. 11.

9 Staffordshire Record Office, D421/2/6, p. 4 (report of discussions at a conference of Staffordshire Centre Leaders, 2 March 1940).

10 *WVS Bulletin*, no. 7, May 1940, p. 10.

11 Staffordshire Record Office, D421/2/12, p. 2.

12 Staffordshire Record Office, D421/2/6, pp. 3–4 (report of discussions at a conference of Staffordshire Centre Leaders, 2 March 1940).

13 Staffordshire Record Office, D421/2/11, p. 4.

14 *WVS Bulletin*, no. 8, June 1940, p. 2.

15 WRVS Archive, Box 833, Coventry Report R76/38.

16 Staffordshire Record Office, D421/2/6, p. 1.

17 WRVS Archive, Box 734, 'WVS in Region VII', typescript, p. 2.

18 *WVS Bulletin*, no. 8, June 1940, p. 2.

19 MOA, Diarist no. 5331.

20 Files concerning WVS escorts of enemy aliens are found in the WRVS Archive, Boxes 200 and 741.

21 WRVS Archive, Box 368.

22 J. D. Lewis, *W.V.S. in Kent* (Maidstone: *Kent Messenger*, 1945), pp. 63–4.

23 Surrey History Centre, 1532/1/48-53.

24 WRVS Archive, Guildford NR, June 1940.

25 WRVS Archive, Box 367, file R5, Surrey 1940–1947.

26 WRVS Archive, Box 759, Salvage file, 'Salvage Memorandum, 14 June 1940'.

27 WRVS Archive, HQ/NR/R2/1940-CB/KuH.

28 *Hunts Post*, 18 July 1940, p. 5.

29 MOA, TC32/41; Graves, op. cit., p. 19.

30 WRVS Archive, Box 736, Housewives Service file, 'Story of the WVS Housewives Service', p. 5.

31 *Midland Counties Express and Wolverhampton Chronicle*, 2 August 1941, p. 8.

32 WRVS Archive, 'Bedfordshire: Heads of Departments Meeting Held in WVS Office on Tuesday, March 11th, 1941', Mrs White's Report, attached to the Narrative Report from Bedford for that month.

3: 'A SUPREME BATTLE FOR THE WORLD'S FREEDOM' 1940–1

1 The subject is well covered in Juliet Gardiner, *The Blitz: The British under Attack* (London: Harper Press, 2010). An authoritative reference source is Winston G. Ramsey (ed.), *The Blitz, Then and Now* (3 vols.; London: Battle of Britain Prints International, 1987–90). Volume II deals with 1940–1, volume III with 1941–5.

2 WRVS Archive, Box 734, 'Impressions of the London Blitz from September to December 1940'. Unless otherwise indicated, this typed five-page document is the basis for the rest of this section.

3 WRVS Archive, Region 5, Quarterly Report for June–September 1940, pp. 1–2.

4 WRVS Archive, Box 734, 'Post-Raid Welfare in a London Borough', p. 3.

5 WRVS Archive, Region 5, Quarterly Report for June–September 1940, p. 2.

6 MOA, FR529, 'Report on Aftermath of Towns Blitzes', 19 December 1940, p. 4

7 *WVS Bulletin*, no. 84, October 1946, p. 2.

8 Norman Longmate, *Air Raid: The Bombing of Coventry* (London: Hutchinson, 1976), pp. 238 and 199.

9 Surrey History Centre, 5380/2/3, letter of 5 February 1941.

10 WRVS Archive, Box 734, 'Report on WVS call to Glanford Brigg to help at Coventry', 29 November 1940.

11 WRVS Archive, Box 734, 'Extracts from Confidential Reports from Region IX, 1941'.

12 WRVS Archive, Box 847, Region 7, Bristol NR, May 1941; and a second Narrative Report from Bristol for December 1940/January 1941, which was titled 'Unofficial Report' to distinguish it from the explicitly 'Official Report'.

13 IWM, #92/8/1, Private papers of A. Lee Michell.

14 Doreen Wright's diary, which has recently deposited in the Warwickshire Record Office, still lacks an accession number.

15 WRVS Archive, Box 734, Report from Region 5, Group 6, April–December 1941.

16 Graves, *Women in Green*, pp. 129–31. The origins and character of these convoys are explained in R. J. Hammond, *Food, vol. II: Studies in Administration and Control* (London: HMSO, 1956), pp. 364–7 and 380.

17 WRVS Archive, Box 734, 'An Account of the Convoy's Visit to Bootle'.

18 Norman Longmate, *How We Lived Then: A History of Everyday Life during the Second World War* (1971; London: Pimlico, 2002), p. 366. This book is based mainly on oral recollections.

19 WRVS Archive, Box 734 (file on post-raid work), 'Women's Voluntary Services for Civil Defence' (undated typescript, clearly 1941).

20 WRVS Archive, Box 734, 'Impressions of the London Blitz', p. 3.

21 WRVS Archive, Box 734, 'Post-Raid Welfare in a London Borough', p. 4.

22 *Lewisham Log: Magazine of the Lewisham WVS* [1941], British Library, P.P.1941.7001.acl.

23 WRVS Archive, Box 734, 'Extracts from Confidential Reports from Region IX, 1941'.

24 WRVS Archive, Box 736, Housewives Service file, 'WVS in the North West, December 1940–December 1941', pp. 5–6.

25 *WVS Bulletin*, no. 70, August 1943, p. 3.

26 Gardiner, op. cit., pp. 211–12.

27 WRVS Archive, Box 847, Region 7, Bristol NR, December 1940–January 1941.

28 Bristol Record Office, 11757/n, WVS Report of 27 December 1940.

29 WRVS Archive, Box 847, Region 7, Bristol NRs, March-May 1941.

30 WRVS Archive, Box 734, 'WVS in the North West, December 1940–December 1941', p. 1.

31 *WVS Bulletin*, no. 22, August 1941, p. 2.

32 Bristol Record Office, 11757/n, WVS Report of 27 December 1940.

33 Imperial War Museum, C. A. Newbery, 'St Pancras at War 1939–1945' (#97/28/1), typescript, p. 105, an account of the work of the WVS by Mrs Dorothy Agnew.

34 WRVS Archive, Box 734, p. 5.

4: RECOVERY 1940-1

1 Shropshire Archives, 6683/3/398/16, p. 4.

2 Hampshire Record Office, 38M49/E6/1.

3 *Bath Weekly Chronicle and Herald,* 16 October 1940, p. 7.

4 *Bath Weekly Chronicle and Herald,* 16 November 1940, p. 4.

5 *Bath Weekly Chronicle and Herald,* 13 July 1940, p. 5, and 26 October 1940, p. 7.

6 WRVS Archive, Box 347, Cambridge Report on Evacuation, September 1941.

7 WRVS Archive, 'Emergency Rest Centres', typescript filed with Leicestershire Narrative Reports, 1940.

8 WRVS Archive, 'Heads of Departments Meeting Held in WVS Office on Tuesday, March 11th, 1941', filed with the Narrative Report from Bedford.

9 *WVS Bulletin,* no. 13, November 1940, p. 3.

10 Bristol Record Office, 11757/11, Report of WVS Housewives, December 1941, p. 4.

11 WRVS Archive, Bristol's 'Unofficial Report' for December 1940/January 1941.

12 Mary Cox, *British Women at War* (London: John Murray, 1941), p. 54.

13 Cumbria Archives, Kendal, WDSO 92/1–2, Report for 1940.

14 Bristol Record Office, 11757/11, December 1941 Report, op. cit., p. 5.

15 WRVS Archive, Box 347, Watford Report for 1940.

16 WRVS Archive, Printed Quarterly Reports, Region 11 (Scotland), 30 November 1940, on refugees from bombed areas.

17 *West Sussex County Times,* 6 December 1940, p. 5.

18 *Bath and Wilts Chronicle and Herald,* 1 February 1941, p. 3; similar concerns about youth activities were reported by a WVS leader in Staffordshire in March 1940 (Staffordshire Record Office, D421/2/6, p. 3).

19 Lynne Olson, *Citizens of London: How Britain was Rescued in its Darkest Hour* (New York: Random House, 2010), p. 82.

20 Essex Record Office, D/DBg 80/30, letter from James F. Hough, 25 November 1940/2 January 1941.

21 Norman Longmate (ed.), *The Home Front: An Anthology of Personal Experience 1938–1945* (London: Chatto & Windus, 1981), pp. 75–6.

22 MO Archive, Diarist no. 5433, 21 June 1942.

23 Cumbria Archive Centre (Kendal), WDSO 92/1-2, Report of 17 June 1940 by Miss Foster Jeffery and Narrative Report for October 1940.

24 The diversity of needs that the WVS addressed is nicely portrayed in Norman Longmate's *How We Lived Then: A History of Everyday Life during the Second World War* (1971; London: Pimlico, 2002), pp. 281–7 and 363–8. This book draws heavily on oral recollections, which, of course, are now rarely available.

25 *WVS Bulletin,* no. 19, May 1941, p. 5, and no. 20, June 1941, p. 3.

26 T. Geraghty, *A North-East Coast Town, Ordeal and Triumph: The Story of Kingston-upon-Hull in the 1939–1945 Great War* (1951), appendix.

5: LIFE'S NECESSITIES 1941–4

1 One of the most thorough wartime surveys of the work of the WVS, including much of what is discussed in this and the following chapter, was written
by a Canadian visitor from Winnipeg: Margaret Konantz in *Women's Voluntary
Services for Civil Defence, Great Britain* (Ottawa: Department of National War
Services, 1944). A copy is held in the WRVS Archive. Charles Graves, *Women
in Green (The Story of the WVS)* (London: Heinemann, 1948) is still useful.

2 *WVS Bulletin*, no. 36, October 1942, p. 5 and Barbara Drake, *Community
Feeding in Wartime* (Fabian Society, May 1942), p. 17. Konantz was told in
1944 that 1145 canteens were being run by the WVS, employing some forty-
eight thousand volunteers (op. cit., pp. 21 and 13).

3 Cumbria Archives, Kendal, WDSO 92/3, Canteen Report of 6 November
1945.

4 Imperial War Museum, no. 85/6/1, Hilda Appleby, 'My Work in the WVS
from 1939 onwards' (typescript), pp. 1–2.

5 WRVS Archive, no. 2011-0027.

6 R. J. Hammond, *Food, vol. II: Studies in Administration and Control* (London:
HMSO, 1956), p. 384n.

7 Ibid., p. 394, 398–9 and 411; and Konantz, op. cit., p. 12. Much useful infor-
mation is found in a work written in 1945, *British Restaurants: An Inquiry
Made by the National Council of Social Services* (London: Oxford University
Press, 1946).

8 *Dewsbury Reporter*, 7 November 1942, p. 1, and *Surrey Times*, 29 October
1943, p. 4.

9 This account of Bexhill's British Restaurant is based on a substantial file in the
East Sussex Record Office, DR/B61/10.

10 Konantz, op. cit., p. 13.

11 WRVS Archive, Report for the year in the 1944 Kesteven file.

12 Richard Titmuss, *Problems of Social Policy* (London: HMSO, 1950), p. 426n.

13 Imperial War Museum, #88/50/1, 'The Journal of Mrs. Rose Uttin', p. 34.

14 WRVS Archive, Kesteven, Lincolnshire Report for 1 June 1943–31 May 1944
(in 1944 file for Kesteven), p. 5.

15 *Grimsby Evening Telegraph*, 6 December 1943, p. 3; *Gainsborough Evening News*,
8 June 1943, p. 3.

6: COMFORTS, COLLECTIONS AND CONVIVIALITY 1941–4

1 WRVS Archive, Ref. 2011-058, Glasgow Station Guide Diary of Roberta
Young; and *WVS Bulletin*, no. 46, August 1943, p. 3.

2 WRVS Archive, file SAL 8; and reports in the *WVS Bulletin* for July 1941 (no.
21), October 1941(no. 24), March 1942 (no. 29), and April 1943 (no. 42).

3 *WVS Bulletin*, October 1941, p. 5.

4 WRVS Archive, Narrative Report for Minehead, Somerset, April 1944, and Narrative Report for the Llandeilo Rural District, Carmarthenshire, May 1941; Imperial War Museum, Photo HU 63821, 8 March 1941; and *WVS Bulletin*, no. 31, May 1942, p. 5.

5 East Sussex Record Office, CD9/133/1, WVS report on work in 1942.

6 WRVS Archive & HC, Narrative Reports for Daventry and Kettering, December 1943 and Northampton, April 1944.

7 Imperial War Museum, #97/28/1, C. A. Newbery, 'St. Pancras at War 1939–1945', p. 112.

8 WRVS Archive, Frome Rural District, Somerset, October 1943–January 1944.

9 WRVS Archive, letter attached to the October 1941 Narrative Report by the Centre Organiser from Spalding, Lincolnshire and addressed to her.

10 Norman Watson, *WRVS in Scotland: Seventy Years of Service* (Edinburgh: Black & White Publishing, 2008), pp. 80–1.

11 WRVS Archive, Narrative Report from the Totnes Rural District, June 1944, p. 2.

12 *West Sussex County Times*, 8 November 1940, p. 4.

13 The account in these three paragraphs is based on several reports from Gainsborough in the WRVS Archive, most by its Centre Organiser, during the last three months of 1942.

14 *Grimsby Evening Telegraph*, 1 December 1943, p. 3.

7: CASUALTIES – ANTICIPATED AND ACTUAL 1941–3

1 Some of the efforts to recruit women into the Housewives' Service in the Borough of Lambeth in London in 1942 are documented in file MBL/TC/CD/1/84 in the Lambeth Archives.

2 East Sussex Record Office, CD9/132/2.

3 Sutton Local Studies & Archives Centre, Acc.93 (a typed document, undated but almost certainly from later in the war, in a file folder of various WVS sources).

4 WRVS Archive, Box 436, file no. RIO/2/BRY.

5 The sources we have used from Mablethorpe, Lincolnshire, almost all of which were written by the Centre Organiser, Evelyn Shallcross, are held in the Second World War Experience Centre, Wetherby, West Yorkshire and are arranged chronologically. This document is catalogued as Shallcross, E, LEEWW:2001.1842.1.4, correspondence 1942. We are indebted to Anne Wickes for her advice on this collection.

6 WRVS Archive, HQ/NR/R4/1943-ESX.

7 WRVS Archive, Narratives Reports, July 1942, from Cleethorpes and Louth Rural Area South.

8 *WVS Bulletin*, no. 32, June 1942, p. 1.

9 WRVS Archive, Notes attached to the Narrative Report from Norwich for June 1942.

10 WRVS Archive, Box 734, letter to 3 May 1942 to Miss A. Wade.

11 WRVS Archive, Box 734, 'Report on Norwich Raid, April 30th to May 1st, 1942: Work of the Queen's Messenger Convoy in Norwich', p. 3.

12 Ibid., p. 1; WRVS Archive, Box 734, 'Friendly Cargoes – Bath'; and Niall Rothnie, *The Bombing of Bath: The German Air Raids of April 1942* (Bath: Ashgrove Press, 1983), p. 131.

13 Bristol Record Office, 11757/11.

14 WRVS Archive, Box 734, 'Wembley (Sudbury) Incident, October 19th, 1943', p. 1.

15 Second World War Experience Centre, Shallcross, E, LEEWW:2001.1842.1.4, correspondence 1942.

16 WRVS Archive, 'Annual Report on the Work of the Mobile Canteen, 1944', attached to the Weston-super-Mare Narrative Report for January 1945.

8: EMERGENCIES IN 1944

1 Surrey History Centre, 1532/4/85 & 87.

2 Imperial War Museum, no. 1661 92/8/1, Private papers of Anne Lee Michell, diary for 4 September 1941.

3 Surrey History Centre, 1532/4/86.

4 Surrey History Centre, 1532/5/1-23.

5 National Archives, HO 186/1805, letter of 20 January 1944 from E. B. Davies; *WVS Bulletin*, no. 55, May 1944, pp. 2–3; WRVS Archive, Chertsey, Surrey Narrative Reports for February–April and October 1944, and Box 734, 'Region V: Report of the Work of the WVS at Flying Bomb Incidents during the Period 15th June to 22nd July, 1944', p. 1.

6 Sutton Local Studies & Archives Centre, Acc.93 (in a file folder of various WVS sources). While this typed three-page document is untitled and undated, it almost certainly dates from 1944. See also Juliet Gardiner, *Wartime: Britain 1939–1945* (2004), pp. 650–1.

7 Croydon Local Studies Library and Archives Service, AR491/1/1, part of the Evelyn May Sandison Collection. This file comprises some 31 single-spaced typewritten pages, and includes two late raids, on 20 October and 15 November 1944, the former a V2 rocket.

8 WRVS Archive, Narrative Reports from Woodhall Spa, Lincolnshire (July 1944), Cleethorpes, Lincolnshire (July and August), Walton and Weybridge, Surrey (July), Leicester (July, p. 6), and Downham Market, Norfolk (August). Numerous other places noted but did not describe members' trips to aid the London area that summer. Anne Lee Michell visited London from Wellington, Somerset to help with cope with the doodlebugs' damage (diary, 15–17 July 1944, in the IWM, no. 1661 92/8/1).

9 WRVS Archive, Box 734, 'Report on Reinforcements' (1944), p. 1.

10 Richard Titmuss, *Problems of Social Policy* (London: HMSO, 1950), pp. 426–8.

11 *Supplement to the Isle of Ely and Wisbech Advertiser*, 12 July 1944, p. 11.

12 Second World War Experience Centre, Mablethorpe/Shallcross Collection, Shallcross, E, LEEWW:2001.1842.1.6, correspondence 1944.

13 Titmuss, op. cit, pp. 429–30.
14 Cumbria Archives, Kendal WDSO 92/1-2, Interim Report on Evacuation by Miss Woodall, Social Worker, 21 July 1944.
15 WRVS Archive, Box 736, Housewives Service file, 'Extract from Monthly Narrative Report, York, October 1943'.
16 Dorset History Centre, D.552/10, Shaftesbury WVS Bulletin, June 1945.
17 WRVS Archive, Box 734, 'Invasion Beach Canteen'.
18 Wiltshire and Swindon Archives, G24/225/28, letter of 4 October 1942.
19 WRVS Archive, 'Clothing Depot Report for 1944', attached to the Weston-super-Mare Narrative Report for January 1945.
20 Ibid.

9. MINDS AND EMOTIONS 1939–44

1 For example, *Hunts Post*, 17 May 1945, p. 6.
2 John T. Wright, *An Evacuee's Story: A North Yorkshire Family in Wartime* (Harbury: privately printed, 2007), p. 30.
3 In composing this paragraph, we have been indebted to some of the ideas in the Conclusion to James Hinton's *Women, Social Leadership, and the Second World War* (Oxford: OUP, 2002).
4 WRVS Archive, Box 736, Housewives Service file, 'WVS in the North West, December 1940–December 1941', pp. 7–8.
5 WRVS Archive, 'Club for Evacuated Mothers, February 1941 to February 1945', attached to the March 1945 Narrative Report from Guildford.
6 East Sussex Record Office, CD9/133/1.
7 WRVS Archive, Box 437, 'WVS Carlisle County Borough Report' (undated, but apparently just after the end of the war), p. 2.
8 WRVS Archive, Box 437, 'Report of Reception of Evacuees from the South', Wallasey, Cheshire, 28 July 1944.
9 WRVS Archive, Box 348, Region 4, Biggleswade Rural Centre, 'Report of Work Done by the WVS when an Overseas Convoy of Wounded Troops Arrived'.
10 Croydon Local Studies Library and Archives Service, AR491/1/1.
11 *Lewisham Log: Magazine of the Lewisham WVS* (1941), p. 13.
12 WRVS Archive, Box 734, 'The Work of WVS Centre, Guildford Borough' (December 1941).
13 *Grantham Journal*, 25 August 1944, p. 7.
14 Details on what members of the WVS wore may be found in two useful sources: Jon Mills, *Within the Island Fortress: The Uniforms, Insignia & Ephemera of the Home Front in Britain 1939–1945, No. 1, The Women's Voluntary Services (WVS)* (Orpington: Wardens Publishing, 2005); and Matthew McMurray, 'WVS Uniform 1939–1945: The Introduction and Development of the Uniform of the Women's Voluntary Services for Civil Defence' (WRVS, 2009), which is available online on the WRVS website.
15 *Evening Standard* (Swindon), 8 April 1942, p. 4.

16 Imperial War Museum, Ref. 01/40/1, Mrs Spencer's memoir of war in Gorleston-on-Sea, Norfolk.

17 WRVS Archive, Box 734, 'Wembley (Sudbury) Incident, October 19th, 1943'.

18 Second World War Experience Centre, 'Women's Voluntary Services, Thatcham Branch, Minutes Book', LEEWW.2000.266.3.5; and Imperial War Museum, 'Housewives' Services WVS, Lower Stratton, Wiltshire', Misc 167 (2567).

19 Margaret Konantz, *Women's Voluntary Services for Civil Defence, Great Britain* (Ottawa: Department of National War Services, 1944), p. 23.

20 WRVS Archive, HQ/NR/R4/1943-ESX.

21 Ibid., p. 10.

22 WRVS Archive, Box 734, 'Organisation, Activities and Work of the Margate Centre WVS' (8 December 1941).

23 WRVS Archive, Box 822, file for 1941.

24 WRVS Archive, Box 341, file no. R4/7, 'Report on Q. M. Convoy's Visit to Norwich, April 29th, 1942' [the visit actually seems to have been 30 April–1 May].

25 Surrey History Centre, 1532/5/14 and 5.

26 Lady Reading, *It's the Job that Counts: A Selection from the Speeches and Writings of the Dowager Marchioness of Reading, Chairman of Women's Voluntary Service for Civil Defence* (privately printed, 1954), p. 17.

10: ENDINGS – AND CARRYING ON: 1945 AND BEYOND

1 Identifying details have been removed from this case; full information is available in the WRVS Archive.

2 Patricia and Robert Malcolmson (eds), *The Diaries of Nella Last: Writing in War and Peace* (London: Profile Books, 2012), pp. 218–19.

3 Women's Voluntary Services, *Report of Ten Years' Work for the Nation 1938–1948* (1948), p. 40; Norman Watson, *The WRVS in Scotland: Seventy Years of Service* (Edinburgh: Black & White Publishing, 2008), pp. 84–5.

4 Hackney Archives, H/CC/2/20, letters of 13 and 26 April 1945.

5 Ibid., Report of the Controller and Rehousing Officer, 18 January 1945.

6 WRVS Archive, Narrative Report, Caterham, Surrey, June 1945.

7 Some details on overseas service are found in the Unsworth MS in the WRVS Archive, Box 735.

8 The National Archives, CAB124/914, memo of 11 October 1946.

9 The first two specific cases are from the Abingdon Rural District and St Annes-on-Sea, both in January 1945; the latter two from the Abingdon Rural District in February 1945 and the Axbridge Rural District, Somerset in January/February 1946.

10 These three 1945 cases are from Crewe in October/November, Louth in February and Accrington in July.

11 *WVS Bulletin*, no. 18, April 1941.

12 Second World War Experience Centre, LEEWW: 2001.1842.1.7.13.

13 This material, from the late spring and summer of 1945, is in the WRVS Archive, Box 437.

14 Jane Robinson, *A Force to be Reckoned With: A History of the Women's Institute* (London: Virago, 2011), Chapter 7.

15 Some of the debates at this time on the future of the WVS are recounted in James Hinton, *Women, Social Leadership, and the Second World War: Continuities of Class* (Oxford: OUP, 2002), Chapters 8 and 11.

16 WRVS Archive, Box 403, R.6/2.

17 *Hunts Post*, 17 May 1945, p. 1.

18 Lady Reading, *It's the Job that Counts: A Selection from the Speeches and Writings of the Dowager Marchioness of Reading, Chairman of Women's Voluntary Service for Civil Defence* (privately printed, 1954), p. 57.

19 Ibid., pp. 57–8.

20 East Sussex Record Office, C/C 71/88; and CD 9/133/1.

21 *Report of Ten Years' Work for the Nation 1938-1948* (WVS, 1948), p. 53 (dated December 1948).

22 WRVS Archive, Box 1056, packet 6.

23 WRVS Archive, Box 366, file R12/3, a three-page report on a WVS meeting held in Chichester on 25 May 1945.

24 WRVS Archive, Box 367, Surrey file 1940–47, 'Report of Meeting of Surrey Centre Organisers and Centre Staffs'.

25 Cumbria Archives, Kendal, WDSO 92/1-2.

26 Watson, *WRVS in Scotland*, pp. 90–1 and 96–100.

EPILOGUE

1 Chapter 5 of James Hinton's *Women, Social Leadership, and the Second World War: Continuities of Class* (Oxford: OUP, 2002) documents this emphasis on efficiency and organisational discipline.

2 National Archives, HO 356/2.

3 A thorough summary of its activities was presented in its *Ten Years Work* (1948).

4 National Archives, CAB 124/914, memo of 11 December 1948 and letters of 9 and 14 February 1951. These documents are among various useful sources in a file that deals with the future of the WVS, 1945–51. HO 356/3 is also of value. In the WRVS Archive, the most pertinent files are HQ/CR/A1-38/4 and especially 5.

5 WRVS Archive, Box 62/2.

6 Some of these changes are charted in Norman Watson, *WRVS in Scotland: Seventy Years of Service* (Edinburgh: Black & White Publishing, 2008), Chapters 9–11.

7 Lady Reading, *It's the Job that Counts: A Selection from the Speeches and Writings of the Dowager Marchioness of Reading, Chairman of Women's Voluntary Service for Civil Defence* (privately printed, 1954), p. 109.

APPENDIX C

1 A succinct account of these floods may be found in David Kynaston, *Family Britain 1951–57* (London: Bloomsbury, 2009), pp. 257–9.
2 *New Statesman*, 7 February 1953, p. 141.
3 The evidence for the account in this Appendix drawn from various Narrative Reports and the *Report on WVS Work in the East Coast Flood Disaster 1953* (WVS, 1953), held in the WRVS Archive.

ACKNOWLEDGEMENTS

Our major debt, by far, is to Matthew McMurray, the Archivist at the WRVS Archives and Heritage Collection. He played a big role in getting our project launched. He did all sorts of things to aid our research, both when we were in Devizes and when we were working at home. He answered numerous questions and advised on matters of interpretation. In the second half of 2012 he twice read drafts of our text and offered many suggestions as to how we could make our presentation clearer and avoid misleading statements. He also saved us from some factual errors. Matthew's involvement in this project has been crucial and always constructive, and we are very happy to be able to recognise all that he has done in support of *Women at the Ready*.

Several other people have helped us in various ways, notably Gordon Wise at Curtis Brown; Jennifer Hunt, Hannah Tinkler and Pete Franks at the WRVS Archive; Owen Emmerson; Kate Holliday at the Cumbria Archives in Kendal; Robert Bell at the Wisbech Museum; Chris Bennett at the Croydon Local Studies Library and Archives; Jessica Scantlebury and her colleagues at the Mass Observation Archive, University of Sussex; Mike Page and his colleagues at the Surrey History Centre in Woking; Esther Bellamy at the

Huntingdonshire Library and Archives; Heather Dulson at the Shropshire Archives; Kath Shawcross at the Sutton Local Studies and Archive Centre; Anne Weekes at the Second World War Experience Centre in Wetherby, West Yorkshire; Rosanna Wilkinson and Simon Offord at the Imperial War Museum; and the staffs at the Bristol, East Sussex, Staffordshire, West Sussex and Wiltshire Record Offices and the Dorset History Centre. Archives in Britain are a national treasure, and we are much indebted to those who run them so efficiently.

We have benefitted as well from the work of our editors at Little, Brown. In the late summer of 2012 Claudia Dyer read an early version of our text and offered many perceptive and helpful suggestions for improvement; and at the end of the year her colleague, Zoe Gullen, copy-edited our revised text with admirable care and encouraged us to make numerous changes for the better. We are grateful to both for their criticisms and thoughtful advice, and to Linda Silverman for her help with illustrations. Sarah Ereira was responsible for the excellent index.

Finally, we wish to acknowledge wise counsel we received decades ago. In the later 1960s we were young research students, Canadians living for a while in England and learning the ropes of serious historical enquiry. Our thesis supervisors were Jim Dyos at the University of Leicester (for Patricia) and Edward Thompson at the University of Warwick (for Robert), and from them we learned a great deal about our craft. In particular, we saw them as examples of historians committed to deep archival research, and to the importance of immersing oneself in the wide range of primary sources that was almost always a vital foundation for the writing of good social history. Social history, too, should embrace the whole population, poor and affluent, the powerful and the (relatively) powerless, and those in between.

ACKNOWLEDGEMENTS

The influences of these two historians are, we feel, with us still in this work on the WVS. It did not take long (mainly in 2010) for us to recognise the richness of the WRVS Archive and Heritage Collection, and to see the opportunities it offered for a fuller understanding of the wartime lives of hundreds of thousands British women, men and children. Had we not in our youth enjoyed the advice of two historians who had a great love of and respect for original documents, allied to vibrant imaginations, perhaps the fruitful possibilities of work in the WRVS Archive might have passed us by. If we have been alert to these possibilities, this is partly a matter of luck, partly a matter of timely support from the current WRVS and partly a matter of once observing Jim Dyos and Edward Thompson creatively engaged in the work of writing history.

Nelson, British Columbia
February 2013

351

Patricia and Robert Malcolmson are social historians with a particular interest in Mass Observation, diaries and British society around the time of the Second World War. Together they have edited several Mass Observation wartime diaries for record societies (London, Bedfordshire, Dorset and Surrey), as well as three volumes of diaries produced by Nella Last of Barrow-in-Furness between 1939 and the 1950s. Their other publications include (by Robert) *Popular Recreations in English Society 1700–1850* (1973), *Life and Labour in England 1700–1780* (1981) and, with Stephanos Mastoris, *The English Pig: A History* (1998); and (by Patricia) *English Laundresses: A Social History 1850–1930* (1986) and *Me and My Hair: A Social History* (2012). They live in Nelson, British Columbia.

INDEX

children: accommodation for, 19,
116, 227; air raid planning for,
196; bed-wetting, 31–4, 109,
188; bombed out, 67, 75, 100,
103; care of evacuees, 2, 26–7,
113, 233; clothing, 63, 130,
157–8, 163–4, 228, 257,
315–16; crèches, 19; 'difficult
boys', 30–1; Dutch, 274–5;
employment, 137; evacuation
scheme, 12, 61; evacuees
welcomed, 14–15, 226;
footwear, 7, 22, 63, 126,
160–2; health issues, 21–2,
62–3; noisy, 151; numbers
evacuated, 21; orphaned, 106,
268; play facilities, 23, 26,
273; potato picking, 239–40;
psychological support, 15–16,
134; relationships with foster
parents, 35–6, 61–2, 135–6,
167, 275–6; residential
nurseries, 165–7; returning
home, 38–40; salvage
collection, 5, 169–70; toys for,
172–3; travel to school, 25,
161, 162; visits by parents, 30,
38; WVS escorts, 51, 103,
124, 134, 273
Christmas: canteens, 146; dinners,
113; evacuee problems, 29,
181–2; parties, 2, 17, 26, 113,
171, 184, 235; presents, 17, 26,
27, 171, 322; US soldiers, 179
Church Army, 143, 201
Churchill, Winston, 41, 122n,
149, 257
Citizens' Advice Bureau, 52, 117,
212
civil defence: ARP role, 195–6;
canteens, 94, 240, 256;
exercises, 197–201, 329;
Housewives' Service, 195–6;
regions, 2; Rest Centres,

196–7; services, 199; training,
195, 197, 202, 332; WVS
helpers, 74, 329, 333; WVS
role, 3, 12, 43–4, 49, 218–19,
290, 307–8, 311, 328–9
class relations, 70, 105, 237–8,
247–50, 268–9
Clay Cross: social activities, 263;
WVS future, 295
Cleethorpes: bombing, 212;
British Restaurant, 267, 291;
exercises, 200; help for flood
victims (1953), 331–2; re-
homing scheme, 277, 278;
training, 202; WVS activities,
179, 186, 290–1; WVS
volunteers in London, 222, 255
clothing: Army uniforms, 253;
baby clothes, 289; boots, see
boots; coupons, 157–60, 161,
206, 207, 324; decontamination
195; depots, 98–100, 102,
111, 118, 121, 126, 130, 157,
159–60, 164, 188, 203, 207,
220, 238, 243, 245;
distribution, 206–7, 258, 309,
335; donations, 28, 70, 113,
118, 126, 129, 206, 315–16;
324; exchanges, 7, 163–4,
257, 291, 324; for ATS, 160;
for Dutch children, 274–5; for
evacuees, 13, 23, 27–8, 34, 63,
103, 111, 117–18, 228, 238;
for flood victims, 332, 333,
334; for homeless, 70, 76, 77,
98–9, 133, 255; for refugees,
56, 57, 110–11, 266, 273; for
seamen, 45, 50; for soldiers,
59, 177; knitting, 6, 12, 45,
139, 273; laundry, 237;
mending, 129, 139, 158, 163,
176–7, 252–3; rationing,
157–8, 206; Rest Centre
stores, 123, 196, 198, 212;

Lower Stratton, Housewives'
Service activities, 261, 262
Luton: billeting officers, 174;
bombing, 70; Canadian gifts,
125; evacuees, 120; Rest
Centres, 77–8; WVS social
work, 185

Mablethorpe, *1*; baby clothes,
289; bombing, 211; evacuees,
227, 228; exercises, 198;
flooding (1953), 333, 334
Maidstone Rural District, 256
Manchester: bombing, 77;
canteens, 87; cathedral gala,
264; evacuees, 39–40
Margate, evacuees, 267
Marshland: evacuees, 126, 127;
pie scheme, 258
Mere and Tilbury Rural District,
230
Michell, Anne Lee, 88, 215
Midsomer Norton: evacuees, 226;
WVS members in London, 223
Minehead: book-binding, 171; re-
homing scheme, 278
Ministry of Agriculture, 239
Ministry of Aircraft Production,
65
Ministry of Education, 235
Ministry of Food, 93, 95, 133,
152, 153, 269, 334
Ministry of Health, 16, 49, 61,
186, 232, 235, 322–3
Ministry of Information, 68, 146
Ministry of Labour, 50, 173, 174,
182, 183, 321, 326
Ministry of Pensions, 216, 309
Ministry of Supply, 254
Morrison, Herbert, 295
munitions workers, 165, 182–5,
265

NAAFI (Navy, Army and Air

Force Institutes), 284
Narrative Reports, 6–7
National Council of Social
Services, 308
National Union of Girls' Clubs,
117
Newbury Rural District, 131,
318–21
Newcastle, children evacuated
from, 39
Newhaven, Housewives' Service,
196
Norfolk, evacuees, 26
Norwich, bombing, 195, 203,
205, 206–8, 238, 268
Nottingham: convoy sent to, 93;
evacuees, 116–17
nurseries: billeting arrangements,
22; residential, 165–7; social
centres, 23, 115; started, 123;
supplies for, 103, 157, 166,
172, 323; WVS helpers, 113,
312
nursery schools, 21, 52, 102, 103

Oakengates, WVS activities, 291
Oakham: boots for children, 161;
canteen, 148; clothing
exchange, 163–4
Ockham, bombing, 216
Okehampton Rural District, 229
Oldbury, canteen from, 83, 87
overseas service, WVS, 284–5
Oxford: evacuees, 112–13; WVS
Centre, 48

Penarth, bombing, 78–9, 97, 99
Pennington, Mrs, 239, 286
Penrith, Rest Centre exercises,
198
pie scheme, 153–4, 258
pig-keeping, 63–4
play centres, 23, 26, 62, 273
Plymouth: blitz practice, 198;

Soke of Peterborough, driving training, 52–3

soldiers: air raid work, 76, 88; American, 178–9; baths for, 51; billeted, 182; books and magazines for, 48; Canadian, 265; canteens for, 53, 58–9, 125, 144–6, 240, 319–20; language teaching for, 253; marriages, 286–7; uniforms, 253; wives, 123–4, 159; wounded and sick, 50, 61, 173, 242; WVS relations, 139, 175–6, 255–6

Soldiers', Sailors', and Airmen's Families Association (SSAFA), 300, 319

South Shields: children evacuated from, 39; WVS activities, 51

Southampton: bombing, 77, 83; evacuees from, 130

Southend: evacuees from, 62; mobile canteens, 146

Southern Louth Rural District, 202

Spalding: evacuees, 225; social activities, 263

Stafford: clothes from, 99; evacuees, 62

Staffordshire: evacuees, 38, 40; re-homing scheme, 277; WVS organisation, 55

Stamford: unexploded bomb, 212; WAAF convalescent home, 174; WVS activities, 187

Surrey, evacuations, 12, 18–25, 34, 35

Sutton, Surrey: Housewives' Services, 196; WVS activities, 8, 218

Sutton Coldfield, 99

Swansea: bombing, 71, 77, 80, 99;

mobile canteens, 260; WVS activities, 55, 124, 133–4

Swindon: clothing depot, 243; overseas servicemen, 179

Taunton, WVS activities, 259, 293

Thatcham, WVS activities, 49, 261

Thingoe, fish and chips, 126

Tiverton, 'Welcome Club', 178

Toc H, 24, 188, 235

toys: collecting, 102; for Christmas, 26, 27, 235; for East Lodge, 16; for nurseries, 323; for play centres, 26; for social centres, 23, 234, 326; from Belgium, 275; fund-raising sale of, 49; making, 166, 172–3

Turpin, Clare, 150–2

V1 flying bombs (buzz-bombs, doodlebugs): attacks, 193, 214; Croydon records, 220–1; defences against, 217, 240; effects, 217, 219–20, 283; evacuees from, 229; first launched, 217; WVS relief work, 217–18, 222–4, 255, 256, 326, 329

V2 rockets, 193, 214, 255

WAAF (Women's Auxiliary Air Force): canteens for, 148; clothing for, 187; convalescent home, 174; hospitality for, 51; welcome for POWs, 285

Wakefield, refugees, 57

Wallasey, evacuees, 254

Walsingham, evacuees, 227

Walther, Phyllis, 9, 130, 140, 159